Scripture References and Permissions

- KJV: Scripture quotations marked KJV are from the Holy Bible, King James Version (Authorized Version), first published in 1611. Quoted from the KJV Classic Reference Bible, © 1983 by The Zondervan Corporation.

- NKJV: Scripture quotations marked NKJV are from the New King James Version, © 1982 by Thomas Nelson, Inc. Used by permission. All rights reserved.

- Scripture from the Amplified Bible, © 1954, 1958, 1962, 1964, 1965, 1987 by The Lockman Foundation. Used by permission.

- NIV: Scripture marked NIV is from the Holy Bible, New International Version® (NIV®), © 1973, 1978, 1984 by the International Bible Society. Used by permission of Zondervan. All rights reserved. [Biblica]

- HCSB: Scripture quotations marked HCSB are from the Holman Christian Standard Bible®, © 1999–2003 by Holman Bible Publishers. Used by permission. Holman Christian Standard Bible®, Holman CSB®, and HCSB® are federally registered trademarks of Holman Bible Publishers.

- Unless otherwise noted, all scripture is from The Holy Bible, English Standard Version® (ESV®), © 2001 by Crossway Bibles, a division of Good News Publishers. Used by permission. All rights reserved.

- MSG: Scripture marked MSG is from The Message, © 1993–2003 by Eugene H. Peterson. Used by permission of NavPress Publishing Group.

- Blue Red and Gold Letter Edition™, © 2012 BRG Bible Ministries. Used by permission. All rights reserved. BRG Bible is a registered trademark (U.S. Patent and Trademark Office #4145648).

Introduction

Therefore, laying aside all malice, all deceit, hypocrisy, envy, and all evil speaking, as new born babes, desire the pure milk of the Word, that you may grow thereby, if indeed you have tasted that the Lord is gracious.
—1 Peter 2 NKJV

At the end of every seven years you shall grant a release of debts, and this is the form of the release: Every creditor who has lent anything to his or her neighbor shall release it; he shall not require it of his neighbor or his brother, because it is called the Lord's release. Of a foreigner you may require it; but you shall give up your claim to what is owed by your brother . . .
—Deuteronomy 15 NKJV

(Things that make you go *hhhhmmmmm*)

A stone is heavy, and sand is weighty, but a fool's wrath is heavier than both of them.
A satisfied soul loathes the honeycomb, but to a hungry soul, every bitter thing is sweet.
Ointment and perfume delight the heart, and the sweetness of a person's friend gives delight by hearty counsel.
—Proverbs 27

Hatred stirs up strife, but love covers all sins.
—Proverbs 10

Like an apple tree among the trees of the woods, so is my beloved among the daughters.
Like an apple tree among the trees of the woods, so is my beloved among the sons. I sat down in his shade with great delight, and his fruit was sweet to my taste. He brought me to the banqueting house, and his banner over me was love. Sustain me with cakes of raisins,

refresh me with apples, for I am lovesick.
His left hand is under my head, and his right hand embraces me.
—Song of Solomon 2 NKJV

To everything there is a season, a time for every purpose under
heaven: A time to plant, and a time to pluck what is planted; a time
to break down, and a time to build up, a time to weep and a time to
laugh, a time to mourn and a time to . . .
—Ecclesiastes 3 KJV

When I feel as though I am losing hope, I think of things like the words in Psalm 147:1–8. What can't a God that calls each star by its name and a God whose understanding is infinite not do? I know He knows all my needs, so I will wait. I will regain hope and wait. Lord, thank You for a word that encourages us and helps us to be patient and wait on You, in Jesus's name. Amen. cms

* * *

Wisdom and Understanding
January 1

Behold, I will do a new thing; now it shall spring forth;
shall ye not know it? I will even make a way in the wilderness,
and rivers in the desert.
The beast of the field shall honor me, the dragons and the owls:
because I give waters in the wilderness and rivers in the desert,
to give drink to my people, my chosen.
This people have I formed for myself;
they shall show forth my praise.
—Isaiah 43:19–21 KJV

I am ready for all the great things God will bring into my life. Some new things and some changes, some may be uncomfortable, but all will be for my spiritual promotion.

Life is constantly changing; new and old, life and death, stop and start, laugh and cry, good day, bad day. When life becomes just one thing, no changes, just a continuous sameness, well, then it becomes boring and hopeless, but change comes to challenge us, to make life interesting and filled with purpose. Living this life is a journey that can be full of adventure and intrigue to keep us interested and interesting, to keep us alert, responsive and growing. We are not usually comfortable with change, with challenge, with discomfort, with hard discipline, but once we accept the necessary changes and we put our ego aside or take control of our ego, we realize that change will take us to a higher place, it will position us to win and to grow, so we accept the change because we know that it will take us to a better place where newness and wisdom coupled with understanding will give us an existence of mental and spiritual freedom. It opens our eyes in incredible ways, and then we grow. It brings us to a higher place of growth, a place of joy, a place of greater understanding of things in life. Be ready for change in your life. Nothing stays the same; we must strive to grow. We will change for the worse, or we will grow great, awesome, better, amazing. As we live, change is inevitable. We have to choose how we will grow. Break bad habits, change some rules, change old norms, think of doing something different and better. Allow good changes in you life.

Wisdom and Understanding
January 2

Hear my cry, O God; attend unto my prayer. From the end of the earth
will I cry unto thee, when my heart is overwhelmed;
lead me to the rock that is higher than I.
—Psalms 61:12 KJV

Today I will call on my Father all day: at work, at play, in the train, in the bus, at home, at the gym, wherever I go. Today I will allow myself to be constantly conscientious of God and His love and sacrifice for me. When I feel overwhelmed, I will whisper His name, Jesus, for strength and peace. This New Year, I will remember Jesus more often.

We present ourselves as strong, smart, handsome, pretty, pleasant to the people we encounter in public places, but inside our minds, hearts, bodies, we know the truth that we are sad, broken, insecure. We have secrets. We think we are ugly. We feel inadequate. We think others are perfect and we are so imperfect. We want to hide in a box or a closet, and yet little do we know the other person feels the same way. When you are feeling down and weary, sad and lonely, then try to quiet your mind. Meditate and breath in deeply and breath out. Take a moment to remember the truth of who you are. You are a magnificent spirit and soul, with a magnificently made body and an awesome mind. Your insecurities are just a tiny part of you. Your insecurities are just a minute part of you. You are breathing through a transformable spiritual being that can cause change at any time. Good change, change your mind and change your life. Give tomorrow a chance to come and shine a new light on your concerns. Say a prayer to the great Spirit, even if you don't believe in Him. If it's your last resort of hope, then just do it. Don't give up on the one and only amazing creation that you are. There is not another one in all the universe. Live to see your great potential. Wake up with great expectations and walk right into it. God is real, He made you, and He is just waiting for you to accept who you are so He can help you fulfill your amazing destiny. Come on, walk into your greatness already. Start living life today.

HUMILITY

Many people, throughout most of their lives, do not exhibit HUMILITY. To not be so caught up with yourself and to be more concerned about others does not come easy for many. But that is one of the main requirements for us humans, as spiritual beings, to do: to consider others more often; to check and see if your fellow man/woman is okay; to make sure your circle, the people in your proximity, are fine; and then to consider the well-being of those not so near. Ponder on this. For this exact reason, I believe many people do not like to connect with their spiritual self, their spiritual side. It will require of you to be more selfless, to reach out to others whether you like them or not, whether you know them or not. To see someone looking sad on the street and to say to that stranger, "Excuse me, but are you okay?" then you are obligated to extend yourself and share a cheerful word with them or smile with them or take them to get some food if they are in need of that, so now you have come out of your selfish self into your selfless self, and you have encouraged your fellowman, such a high calling, such a hard thing to do, such a sacrifice, and yet after you have feared and dared to do it, oh, what a feeling. But mostly we would not take that chance of just loving a stranger, and when we cannot do that, we can't even show that love and encouragement to our own family. We can definitely do that and more for our children, but in that I say, there is no sacrifice, no extra honor in that.

That comes automatically with being a parent. Make an effort to treat others with love and tenderness, with understanding and patience. Therein lies the sacrifice, the growth, the blessing.

Wisdom and Understanding
January 3

Having escaped the corruption that is in the world through lust.
And besides this, giving all diligence, add to your faith virtue;
and to virtue knowledge; and to knowledge temperance; and to
temperance patience; and to patience godliness; and to godliness
brotherly kindness; and to brotherly kindness charity.
—1 Peter 1, p/o 4-7 BRG

In the year 2009, the United States of America saw an African descent; American born man start his year as the president of the nation. Many people believed this would not happen in this country that have for so long ill-treated its citizens of melanin-filled skin. Despite the horrible history, despite the lies of character, the lies of ability or capability of a people, this man still became president, and he earned it. He presented himself to the people as able and worthy of the appointment. When a people, a tribe, a group treat another badly, it's never because the other is indeed lesser or worse or beneath or not as good. It's always because of the oppressor's ego, selfishness, ugly behavior, cowardice, the need for self-aggrandizing, bullying, narcissism, power over others, unwarranted need for control, greed, and complete absence of the true Spirit of God in them. Whether it be a minute or four hundred years of oppression, a lie will never remain forever, the truth will eventually show up and disgrace the lie. Time will expose every deception.

All people are created equal. We have to relearn and train ourselves to love our neighbors, to love everybody—everybody, no exception. We have to teach ourselves to see spirit and soul. The outer physical part is a small percentage of who we are.
Our emotions, our feelings, our intangible heart, our love, our hate, our joy, our peace, our sadness, our soul is always crying out for love— love from others. We know God is real, that He is a spirit that can live in us. We also know He wants us to choose good over wrong. We must also realize that evil and the spirit of evil is also real and can live in us. We have to fight the will to do wrong. It's impossible for us to be perfect, so we have to be intentional about trying to be good and do good.

The strong-willed wicked people coerce the weak people to do wrong, knowing that the weak will perpetrate and pass on the evil for them. In the end, when truth and goodness shows up, speaks up, stands up, all the wicked will be exposed and castigated for their wrongdoings. Although their evil rule lasted a very long time, the end is brutal, embarrassing, terminal, and the results, zero—wasted time, emptiness, and disgrace.

Lies that the fathers and mothers told, their children will have to suffer for it because time will expose the truth and the children of those that behaved badly are left to carry the load of shame and ill-gained inheritance, whether it be financial or emotional.
Some will try to prove the lie to be truth, trying to continue the deception, and some will be emotionally embarrassed, self-harming, and pretending to be like the descendants of the oppressed. It's better to be good while struggling than to present yourself perfect with lots of hidden lies and pretenses.

Wisdom and Understanding
January 4

Without counsel purposes are disappointed:
But in the multitude of counselors they are established.
—Proverbs 15:22 KJV

Oh, Lord, guide me to good counselors so that I may make wise decisions with the finances You give me, with the children You gave me, and with everything You have provided me with so that my life would honor You, in Jesus's name, I pray. Amen.

Young people, trust that you don't know nor do you understand this world or the world around you enough to ignore the counsel of your elders. Find someone you can trust and ask them some life questions. Ask them about life and love and envy and money and real estate and about their life story. Ask them now while you are young so that you may learn early and act sooner on things they delayed and missed in their youth. Ask them today so your tomorrow will be brighter and filled with wisdom, understanding, and smart decisions. Ask them questions about the spirit of man, the mind, the body, even the soul. Listen to their opinions and then form yours as you live life, as you read books, as you scan the Internet, as you learn things of life, and as you experience that unique journey that you alone will know as your life.

Your youth is the time to be mostly silent and learn. It's a time when you will start choosing what kind of grown-up you will be. It's a time to study and learn so your decisions will be founded on your understandings as you apply wisdom. Your ego is still at a stage where it can be disciplined and shaped. Your ego is at a state that if you hone your God Spirit now, which lies inside of you, you will be a great grown-up. Balance should be your objective. Ego balanced with the God Spirit in us makes for a great human being. Everything will be better and brighter, clearer and smoother, for you in your journey if only you acknowledge your ego and your God Spirit self.

This is the writer's understanding of things: You must study to find your own understanding and truth of things. You will agree with the writer, or you will find more truth to share with the writer and the world. It says in 2 Timothy 2:15 KJV, "Study to show thyself approved unto God, a workman that needeth not to be ashamed, rightly dividing the word of truth." (The Bible is amazing. Read it.)

Wisdom and Understanding
January 5

Every good gift and every perfect gift is
from above, and cometh down from the
Father of lights, with whom is no
variableness, neither shadow of turning.
—James 1:17 KJV

Today I will consider my shoes, my clothes, my eyes, my tongue, my hair, my brain, and my home. I will consider the air I breathe, the water I drink, my children, my family, and my friends, and I will remember that every good gift is from God. Today I am just thankful.

What is the ego? I believe the ego is that part of us, we, human beings, that God created to balance our God Spirit. Meaning, that as God created us so amazing and perfect in His sight and in His likeness, He realized that we will automatically love our Creator, our parent, our Maker instinctively; so He, in His amazing, loving, and unselfish ways, did not want us to love Him by force, obligated because we came from Him; so He created the "ego," the self, the part of us where His spirit does not live. The ego is not really a bad element, but by itself, it does not have neither common sense nor goodness. So now we have a choice to live through our ego only or couple it with the Spirit of God that lives in all of us also or ignore the Spirit completely and live only through our ego. Living through our ego causes us to live a selfish, mean, nasty, evil, sometimes demonic life. Living through the ego alone allows the evil spirit of Satan to penetrate our lives and control it, all the while we, self, ego, think it's us that is all-powerful, great, amazing, all-knowing, the only great person alive, etc. But living through the Word of God, the Spirit of God, the wisdom and understanding of God, coupled with our self, ego, we grow into more perfect human beings. We live an enlightened life. We see the roses, the flowers, the rain, the sun, the beauty of life in ourselves and in others. We walk in our assigned amazing journey to our God-assigned destiny. Choose to tap into, to connect to your Spirit self, to the Spirit in you. What a wonderful creature you are.

Wisdom and Understanding
January 6

Thou prepares a table before me in the presence of mine enemies:
thou anointest my head with oil; my cup runneth over.
—Psalms 23:5 KJV

I am confident today. I will not be concerned about my job and its security. I will trust in God. Even in the midst of trouble, I have to remember that God is really in control of my life and of the direction my life will take. God will prepare a table for me wherever He wants to. I am His favored child. Amen.

Imagine you yourself in a mental and spiritual state where you know that you are special and precious to your Maker, that He is real and He holds you in His spiritual arms and He rocks you like a baby, kisses you, and tells you He loves you and will always take care of you as long as you abide with Him and in His counsel. What a comfort. What a great sense of security to feel loved and protected and safe. Well, that's our God. He has great promises with expectations in the Bible for us. What a great joy and peace to know we are never alone, the spirit that God is will always be with us. Amen. Choose God. His Spirit will abide with you always.

Wisdom and Understanding
January 7

A soft answer turns away wrath, but a harsh word stirs up anger.
The tongue of the wise uses knowledge rightly, but the mouth
of fools pours forth foolishness.
—Proverbs 15:1-2 NKJV

Lord, help me to know when to talk and when to keep quiet.
Help me to take the high road and speak softly when others yell, help me to think before I speak, help me to listen more than I speak, and help me to use good judgment at all times. Amen.

The ego, that thing in us that was given no rule or power, knowledge or understanding; that thing so tiny and yet when we don't tap into the ocean of our Spirit self, the ego thinks of itself as powerful and all-knowing, so when it's time to do the RIGHT thing or the thing I (ego) want to do, we have to now do what the tiny foolish ego wants. Do the right thing, or do what I want to do. In the moment of decision, for an instant the problem becomes a great dilemma but because we, the individual, live daily through his or her ego the battle is won by the ego and so what I (ego) want to do is what wins. The bigger the reason, the greater the resolve. Not the right thing but what my wrong and strong ego wants to do. We sharpen our lives daily in the ego state when we refuse to tap into our "God Spirit self and sharpen that part of us by applying wisdom, by studying to acquire understanding, so that by the time we are much older, we are stuck in our failures. Sometimes the failure is not financial, it's emotional and mental, but then now we have to live with ourselves and ask the question, where did I go wrong? We can have lots of money but have no joy, no happiness, no peace. People around us don't care for us because our ego has always ruled in our lives, and now it has no genuine goodness to express. A dead spirit and a very live and limited ego. Please choose the God Spirit in you. Choose and hone your spirit. Sharpen your spirit while you are young, and if you are not so young, it is not too late to start. It's just so much harder when you are older, but you can do it. Start that journey to discover your true self, that spirit self you were brought into this world to be and to make the world a better place, because now on this new journey, if you are true to it, it will make you love your Maker, God. It will teach you to love people. It will make you help people. It will make you peaceful and happy and joyous too. Get ready to meet your true self. Encourage a stranger who is your neighbor. Start by reading and studying God's promises to you in the Bible. cms

Wisdom and Understanding
January 8

*In you, O Lord, I put my trust; Let me never be put to shame. Deliver
me in your righteousness, and cause me to escape; Incline your ear to
me, save me. Be my strong refuge, to which I may resort continually;
You have given the commandment to save me. For you are my ROCK,
and my fortress.*
—Psalm 71:1–3 NKJV

When I faint in my spirit, I know renewed strength is on the way
because God is always looking out for me, even when I lose myself in
distress because of this or because of that. What a wonderful God. If I
do a free fall in my spirit, I know He will catch me.

That is grace and mercy, unwarranted
love. Thank you, Jesus! Amen.

See, the thing is, if you make a cake and the whole world say you did
not make that cake, but you know you made that cake, and you made
it from scratch, bought all the ingredients, toiled in the kitchen, and
came up with a wonderfully-tasting cake. You dressed it with amazing
homemade icing, and then you took the time to decorate it, and when
it was finished, you said, "Ahhhh, wow, this is a beautiful cake, and it
tastes so good. I did a good job. I am so proud of my beautiful cake,"
and then you shared it with others, and it was so good and so lovely
that those you shared it with said to you, "You did not make this cake.
It's too marvelous. You did not make this cake."
Now you are so sad and disappointed that they can't believe you made
this amazing and wonderful cake, so now you wait, hoping that one
day they will realize that there is no one else to thank for the cake but
you. And when they come to you and thank you for the cake, you
simply embrace them with love and say, "You are welcome. I have more
cake for you."

Just because one does not believe the truth does not make it a lie.

Because God the Almighty Spirit made us, He knows us, and He exists, no matter what we do or say. Whether we believe it or not, if the flowers and the trees and the ocean and our nose and our lips and our eyes are too wonderfully made for us to believe the Maker made it all, then just know that whenever we decide to tap into our spirit self and connect with the God Spirit, we will know the truth, and we will accept it and live a more purposeful, joyful, and happy life.

Wisdom and Understanding
January 9

*Add to your faith virtue, to virtue knowledge, to knowledge
self-control, to self control perseverance, to perseverance godliness,
to godliness brotherly kindness, and to brotherly kindness LOVE.*
—2 Peter 1:5b–7 NKJV

All He wants us to do is love one another. Sometimes it's just so hard to love some people, and yet if we dare to obey, we will make that extra effort, extend ourselves, and just love. Sometimes it is actually easy to do it, but we make it hard. Today I will love everybody. I don't have to tell them, I just have to allow love to be in my heart. Today I will even love strangers.

In this life, we have to make a conscious effort to force ourselves to be the best possible human we can be. Every minute of the day, every day, we have to consider our actions and make a choice to do the right thing. Anything other than the right thing is the wrong thing. Sometimes that decision is hard, but doing the easy wrong thing will not make it the right thing to do, or I should say doing the easy ego thing will not make it right.

Wisdom and Understanding
January 10

With All Thy Wisdom Get Understanding

I will lift up my eyes to the hills, from whence cometh my help? My help comes from the Lord, who made heaven and earth. He will not allow your foot to be moved; He who keeps you will not slumber. Behold, He who keeps Israel
shall neither slumber nor sleep. The Lord is your keeper; The Lord is your shade at your right hand.
The sun shall not strike you by day, nor the moon by night.
The Lord shall preserve you from all evil;
He shall preserve your soul.
The Lord shall preserve your going out and your coming in from this time forth,
and even forevermore.
—Psalm 121 KJV

What does all this mean? The Lord's got this. He got this. It's not too great, too big, too large, too deep, too difficult. He got this. I know He got this. He can handle this. He is handling this. Thank You, Lord. Amen.

Ungratefulness is a terrible thing. When someone does something unusual and big and amazing for you, and you pretend as though it's nothing, as though you could have done that for yourself, and so you do not show gratefulness, humility, and appreciation toward that person, you don't say an honest thank you and show them that you appreciate the help, it not only disappoints them, but it also makes you a small person, a small spirit, a small creature with no might. Think about it: You were made to be great and awesome, and you make yourself small and show yourself as insignificant. That is no way to reach your assigned destiny and potential. Your life is waiting for you to rise up and be great. Do the right thing. Just do it. Fight your ego. Tap into your God Spirit self. It's really hard to do, but life will be so much better when you do.

Wisdom and Understanding
January 11

Praise the Lord!
Praise God in His sanctuary;
Praise Him in His mighty firmament!
Praise Him for His mighty acts; Praise Him according to His excellent
greatness!
Praise Him with the sound of the trumpet;
Praise Him with the lute and harp!
Praise Him with the timbrel and dance;
Praise Him with stringed instruments and flutes!
Praise Him with loud cymbals; Praise Him with clashing cymbals!
Let everything that has breath praise the Lord.
Praise the Lord!
—Psalm 150 KJV

To praise the Lord in His sanctuary. *Hhhhmmmmm.* So many of us were raised in the church. Sometimes we felt it was too much church. But today so many parents in our neighborhoods don't take their children to church but are complaining that their children don't listen to them, girls having sex and having babies at thirteen and fourteen and younger, boys packing guns and doing drugs, refusing to listen to their parents. Yet when I ask the parents, "Have you been taking them to church? Do you take your family to church?" the response is "no." It's not to say attending church is going to solve everything, but it will help solve some things. It may give the church community a chance to aid the parents. The preached word may change a heart. The activities may keep the children distracted from mischief. Maybe, if we show them the road, when they lose their way, they will know which road to look for to find their way. Just a thought.

Wisdom and Understanding
January 12

He who has knowledge spares his words,
and a man of understanding is of a calm spirit. Even
a fool is counted wise when he holds his peace;
When he shuts his lips, he is considered perceptive.
—Proverbs 17:27–28 NKJV

On January 20, 2009, we will have a new president. Yes, he looks like Africa, and yet he is America. The world is becoming one people, and we are extremely proud of him. Even in the face of adversary and lies and taunting, he kept calm. He kept his cool. What a difficult thing to do, and yet he is the victor. An aggressive reaction to an aggressive action is almost never the best response. Lord, give me patience and wisdom according to my understanding of who You are as I study Your word. Amen!

Shut up. Yes, shut up. Learn to hush. Close your mouth. Hear it and leave it alone. Show yourself smart and intelligent, mysterious and amazing. Learn when to close your lips. Observe, listen, learn, meditate on it, sleep on it, analyze it, and then tomorrow talk about it, if it will help. Otherwise, shut up about it. Find something else to do rather than talk about it. Leave it alone. Open your mouth to teach, to guide, to have good conversation, to laugh, not to hurt and gossip or lie and destroy. Tomorrow you will see yourself empty and silly. Do good today so tomorrow won't have to talk about your wrongdoings.

Wisdom and Understanding
January 13

A person who has friends must themselves
be friendly,
But
there is a friend who sticks closer
than a brother.
—Proverbs 18:24 NKJV

He who has pity on the poor
lends to the Lord, and He will pay back
what he has given.
—Proverbs 19:17 NKJV

The name of the Lord is a strong tower; T
he righteous run to it and are safe.
—Proverbs 18:10 KJV

So many want friends, but they are soooooooo
mean. Sometimes friends are friendlier than family
members. What a friend we have in Jesus!

It behooves us to be kind and giving. There is
an added benefit; God will repay us.

Jesus, Jesus, Jesus.
Jesus, Jesus.
Jesus.

Wisdom and Understanding
January 14

What is FAITH?
Now Faith is the substance of things hoped for,
the evidence of things not seen.
—Hebrews 11:1 KJV

For by fa (IT) h the elders obtained a good testimony.
—Hebrews 11:2 KJV

But without faith it is impossible to please Him,
for he who comes to God must believe that He is, and that He is
a rewarder of those who diligently seek Him.
—Hebrews 11:6 KJV

To acquire faith, one must become a believer. One must accept that Jesus died for their sins and was resurrected by His Father, by our Father God, in order to experience faith. Faith is that invisible thing that once you accept Christ as your Savior, you then pray for God to give you strength to acquire it—faith. Then through faith, you will begin to see many miracles in your life, big ones and small ones, because you now live in the supernatural realm of hoping for things that do not seem possible, seeing things we cannot see, knowing that the universe was made by God, although we did not see it being made. By faith, we choose to do the right thing, not knowing for sure that we will be blessed and rewarded, but through faith, we know that God will bless us. Having faith, we can accomplish so many things more than others can. Living with faith will allow us to leave a better and greater legacy to our family when we are long gone and living in the spirit world when our flesh world have expired.

Wisdom and Understanding
January 15

But know that the Lord has set apart for Himself him who is godly;
the Lord will hear when I call to Him.

Be angry, and do not sin.
Meditate within your heart on your bed, and be still.

Offer the sacrifices of righteousness,
and put your trust in the Lord.
—Psalm 4:3–5 NKJV

Lord, help us to remember that in our anger, we must not cross that line—that sin line, that error line. Lord, help us as Christians to make a difference in our home, in our communities, at our jobs—everywhere we go. Show us how to represent You. In Jesus's name, I pray. Amen.

God has made known some promises, and those promises are in the Bible, If only we would take the time to read them, to study the Bible, to go to a good church and listen to the preached word for guidance and understanding of the Word of God. So we don't know the promises, and so we don't know how to cash in on them. God is faithful if we live in His word. His promises are for us, and they are promises of wealth, health, joy, peace, and happiness. If you don't have the debit card (knowledge of the word, worship, praise, love, etc.), you cannot go to the God Spirit bank account and withdraw anything. Open an account today. Praise God. Amen.

Wisdom and Understanding
January 16

Oh, that people would give thanks to the Lord for His goodness,
and for His wonderful works to the
children of men!
Let them sacrifice the sacrifices of thanksgiving,
and declare His works with rejoicing.
—Psalm 106:21–22 NKJV

Those who go down to the sea in ships,
who do business on great waters,
they see the works of the Lord,
and His wonders in the deep.
—Psalm 106:23–24 NKJV

I really like that scripture. I always pray for clarity
and interpretation of it. *Hhhhmmmmm.*

Lord, give me the fortitude to do whatever maybe difficult, impossible, daring, challenging, almost impossible that would make me trust You more and will grow my faith in You. If you placed it in my heart, I know I can do it, I know it can be done. Show me how to make this business work, this school, this idea, this invention, this great challenge, this graduate school, this new job. Show me how to raise these children right, to do my best. Be with me in these deep waters. I know I am not alone, You are here with me. Amen.

Wisdom and Understanding
January 17

I will lift up my eyes to the hills—
from whence comes my help?
my help comes from the Lord, Who made heaven and earth.
he will not allow your foot to be moved;
He who keeps you will not slumber.
Behold, He who keeps Israel shall neither slumber nor sleep.
The Lord is your keeper;
The Lord is your shade at your right hand.
The sun shall not strike you by day,
nor the moon by night.
The Lord shall preserve you from all evil;
He shall preserve your soul.
The Lord shall preserve your going out and your coming in
from this time forth, and even forevermore.
—Psalm 121 KJV

The psalmist David wrote so many wonderful psalms that sometimes when my heart is weary, I can find almost any Psalm to read, and it brings me peace. Read a Psalm today. Talk about instant gratification, instant results. Thank God for the Bible, the Word of God.

The promises of our Lord God Almighty, who is able to do all things as He wills, are for everyone that lives upright and that makes an effort to do the right things in life. We are not able to be perfect, but we can strive toward perfection in our daily lives.

God appreciates our efforts to treat others well. Don't tell lies on others. Don't steal. Don't envy others or their possessions. Endure your difficult times with hope while working toward your change, your better times. Strive to learn to love who you are while constantly working on bettering who you are by reading, helping others, praying, etc. Wait on the Lord to make things better as you do your part.

Wisdom and Understanding
January 18

If it had not been for the Lord who was on our side,
when men rose up against us, then they would have swallowed us
alive
—Psalm 124:2–3a KJV

Those who trust in the Lord
are like Mount Zion,
which cannot be moved, but abides forever.
—Psalm 125:1 KJV

I was glad when they said to me
let us go into the house of the Lord!
—Psalm 122:1 KJV

Unless your law had been my delight,
I would then have perished in my affliction.
I will never forget your precepts,
for by them you have given me life.
I am yours, save me;
for I have sought your precepts.
—Psalm 119:92–94 NKJV

Such an unsettling time, so much trouble, and yet for those of us that are called by His name, "Christians," we must believe that our Father will bring us through triumphantly. If the trouble is not with me, it is with my brother or my sister. I feel your pain, you feel my pain. I pray for you, you pray for me. I hope I can shine even in hard times, knowing that God will bring me through. Amen.

Wisdom and Understanding
January 19

Let God arise,
let His enemies be scattered;
let those also who hate Him flee before Him.
As smoke is driven away, so drive them away;
as wax melts before the fire
so let the wicked perish at the presence of God
But let the righteous be glad;
Let them rejoice before God;
Yes, let them rejoice exceedingly.
Sing to God, sing praises to His name;
Extol Him who rides on the clouds, by His name Yah, and
rejoice before
HIM
—Psalm 68:1–4 KJV

Lord, I thank You for Your protection daily. I praise Your name because You abide in my home and You go with me everywhere I go. Without Your protection, I am defenseless. Thanks, Father, for Your loving kindness. Amen.

Proverbs 4:7 King James Version (KJV) Wisdom is the principal thing; therefore get wisdom: and with all thy getting get understanding.

Wisdom and Understanding
January 20

*I will extol You, O Lord, for You
have lifted me up, and have not let my foes
rejoice over me.
Oh Lord my God, I cried out to You, and
you healed me.
Oh Lord, you brought my soul up from the grave;
You have kept me alive, that I should not go down to the pit.
Sing praise to the Lord, you saints of His,
and give thanks at the
remembrance of His holy name,
for His anger is but for a moment, His favor is for life;
Weeping may endure for a night,
but joy comes in the morning.
Now in my prosperity I said,
"I shall never be moved."
—Psalm 30:1–6* **AMPC**

So many have lost their jobs, so many expect to lose their job. And with that comes the loss of housing, food, confidence, and sense of hope, ushering in disappointment and depression.

For those of us that still have our jobs, still continue to feel prosperity in the midst of this economic gloom, still feel some sense of security in our jobs, we must remember to make time often to say, "Thank you, Lord." Thank you, Lord. Thank you, Lord. Amen.

VERSES ON NEIGHBOR
The NIV version
January 21

He answered, "'Love the Lord your God with all your heart and with all your soul and with all your soul and with all your mind'; and, 'Love your *neighbor* as yourself.'"
—*Luke 10:27 NIV*

For the entire law is fulfilled in keeping this one command: "Love your *neighbor* as yourself."
—*Galatians 5:14*

But he wanted to justify himself, so he asked Jesus, "And who is my *neighbor?*"
—*Luke 10:29 NIV*

The commandments, "You shall not commit adultery," "You shall not murder," "You shall not steal," "You shall not covet," and whatever other command there may be, are summed up in this one command: "Love your *neighbor* as yourself."
—*Romans 13:9 NIV*

Therefore each of you must put off falsehood and speak truthfully to your *neighbor*, for we are all members of one body.
—*Ephesians 4:25 NIV*

If you really keep the royal law found in Scripture, "Love your *neighbor* as yourself," you are doing right.
—*James 2:8 NIV*

Each of us should please our *neighbor*s for their good, to build them up.
—*Romans 15:2 NIV*

*There is only one Lawgiver and Judge, the one who is able to save and destroy. But you—who are you to judge your **neighbor**?*
—James 4:12 NIV

*Honor your father and mother, and love your **neighbor** as yourself.*
—Matthew 19:19 NIV

*And the second is like it: "Love your **neighbor** as yourself."*
—Matthew 22:39 NIV

*The second is this: "Love your **neighbor** as yourself." There is no commandment greater than these.*
—Mark 12:31 NIV

*To love him with all your heart, with all your understanding and with all your strength, and to love your **neighbor** as yourself is more important than all burnt offerings and sacrifices."*
—Mark 12:33 NIV

*Her **neighbors** and relatives heard that the Lord had shown her great mercy, and they shared her joy.*
—Luke 1:58 NIV

*With their mouths the godless destroy their **neighbors**, but through knowledge the righteous escape.*
—Proverbs 11:9 NIV

*Whoever derides their **neighbor** has no sense, but the one who has understanding holds their tongue.*
—Proverbs 11:12 NIV

*It is a sin to despise one's **neighbor**, but blessed is the one who is kind to the needy.*
—Proverbs 14:21 NIV

*Do not testify against your **neighbor** without cause— would you use your lips to mislead?*
—Proverbs 24:28 NIV

*do not bring hastily to court, for what will you do in the end if your **neighbor** puts you to shame?*
—Proverbs 25:8 NIV

*If you take your **neighbor** to court, do not betray another's confidence,*
—Proverbs 25:9 NIV

*Seldom set foot in your **neighbor's** house— too much of you, and they will hate you.*
—Proverbs 25:17 NIV

*Like a club or a sword or a sharp arrow is one who gives false testimony against a **neighbor**.*
—Proverbs 25:18 NIV

*Like a maniac shooting flaming arrows of death is one who deceives their **neighbor** and says, "I was only joking!"*
—Proverbs 26:18–19 NIV

*Their tongue is a deadly arrow; it speaks deceitfully. With their mouths they all speak cordially to their **neighbors**, but in their hearts they set traps for them.*
—Jeremiah 9:8 NIV

Wisdom and Understanding
January 22

Give ear to my words, O Lord,
consider my meditation.
Give heed to the voice of my cry,
My King and my God,
for to you I will pray.
My voice You shall hear in the morning, O Lord;
In the morning I will direct it to You, and I will look up.
—Psalm 5:1–3 NKJV

It's good to wake up with a song of praise in my heart. It seems to help my day to start off peacefully, mellow, and with pleasant thoughts. I will sing songs of praise in my heart today. I will think of those songs we sing on Sunday at church and allow them to resonate in my being on Monday, Tuesday, Wednesday, Thursday, Friday, and Saturday too.

Life can be so busy with work and then lots of after-work activities like the gym, going out after work to eat at a restaurant or watching television, a movie, sports, news, so much distraction from having a quiet time, silence, meditation, noticing the flowers, the grass, the butterflies, listening to the birds or just closing your eyes for a moment, noticing the palm trees and their leaves, the mango tree, noticing those beautiful trees with lots of green leaves and lots of purple, red or yellow flowers, sometimes they are orange or blue. Life can be so wonderful, beautiful and amazing if we take the time to enjoy what we are looking at, we should take time to honor nature and what it might be saying to us. Slow down. See, don't just look. Notice the beauty around you to allow your spirit to show you the beauty in this journey called life, your life. Make the best of this one journey you are experiencing, this one journey called your life, my life.

Wisdom and Understanding
January 23

He who walk with integrity walks securely,
but he who perverts his ways, will become known.
—Proverbs 10:9 NKJV

The labor of the righteous leads to life,
the wages of the wicked to sin.
—Proverbs 10:16 NKJV

He who keeps instruction is in the way of life,
but he who refuses correction goes astray.
—Proverbs 10:17 NKJV

Just Some Snippets from Proverbs
Things That Make You Go *Hhhhmmmmm*

When you choose integrity by which to build your character (attributes of integrity includes honesty, strong moral principles, good character, applying ethics, morals, righteousness, morality, decency, virtue, fairness, scrupulousness, sincerity, truthfulness, trustworthiness, etc.), you are choosing a path to build a character that is whole and undivided, good and worthy of honor. This journey will take you on a difficult road. You will find yourself often without a friend to turn to, a friend that understands you. You are likely, though, to find that one or sometimes two friends that will recognize what you are doing; a friend that wants to be around you and grow with you; a friend that sees a great, morally amazing, and unique person in your being, in your person. We are creatures that are forever evolving. We are constantly growing. We will grow bad, or we will grow good. Whatever you decide, that's how you will grow. Even when it seems we are not growing, we are growing from one second to the next into our aging. It's sad to look back and see that we grew ourselves to nothing good. We did not work to earn a better tomorrow (which we are living today). We did not help others other than our own children, our immediate love interest. We did not financially support any institution that supports those in need.

We did nothing but eat and do those things that come with eating. We did not help the world in any way to be a better world. We did nothing for no one else but ourselves.

It never seems like we did enough, though, when we look back and we realize that we did a whole lot for a whole lot of people in our circle, it was a lot from the little we had. We gave at the church. We gave to the school. We gave to a friend in need. We gave to a stranger in need. We checked on another person to make sure they were well, they had enough to eat; to see if they needed someone to talk to, to see if they were feeling down today and needed encouragement. We helped where and when we could. We listened when it was necessary to help heal a broken spirit that needed to share, to cry, to vent. I was present in my journey as I encountered others on their journey, and I lived up to one of Jesus's commandments every time I was able to, and that is to, the second of the law commandments, which is like the first, "love your neighbor as yourself." Yes, we must make an effort to look after others. We must make an effort until it becomes a natural habit. We are to help the world to be a better place every day.

Wisdom and Understanding
January 24

*Receive one who is weak in the faith, but not
to disputes over doubtful things.
For one believes he may eat all things, but he
who is weak eats only vegetables.
Let not him who eats despise him who does not eat,
and let not him who does not eat judge
him who eats; for God has received him.
—Romans 14:1–3 NKJV*

It is amazing how everything we need is in the Word of God, in the Bible. Read and knowhow He wants us to live. More and more, I am learning to accept my fellow man. He is not perfect, but neither am I. I can be great or humble. With prayer and supplication, I learn how to apply myself. It starts with me. Amen. (It's always a prayer away.)

For Mama and Daddy. That's what we called our mother and father. As I get older, I realize more and more that no one have the perfect ingredients as to how a child should be raised, so I appreciate my mother and father more and more. My goodness, they were so flawed. How dare they bring children to this world and they be so flawed. But that's it, that's who have children, the flawed, the not so perfect, the human, and that's all of us. So now I am learning to extract their good intentions in raising me. It was thirteen of us they had. Each one with such a very different personality from the other. Each one have a very different outcome from the upbringing under the same parents. I know now that it's partly because in their humanity, as they evolved and grew, they saw things differently, and they did things differently, and so they affected us differently, and we received it differently. Coupled with that is the unique personality by which each of us were born with. And so we each take all that plus what we learn and our experiences at school and work, and while socializing in the world, we shape our character and build a new person on this earth. I am so glad that my parents felt they should give me teachings of good principles, good manners, good behavior, good morals that would build in me good character. I had to figure it out myself later on, but they thought they would plant in me certain seeds that would bring me to be a good person with a good mind, soul, spirit, even a good and healthy body. I am so glad they chose to teach me the Word of God as a root to guide me in this life's journey, then when I was about nineteen years old and embarking on a road on my own with no parental guidance, I chose the road they brought me up on. I considered other roads, but I liked the road they guided me to, and I accepted it as an adult. It has since been very much worth it, worth the sadness, the loneliness, the joy, the laughter, the lessons, everything. It has been a good choice. What journey are you guiding your children on, your acquaintances, your friends, your circle? What's your conversations like? Are they growing words or just negative, sad, and discouraging words? Consider sharing uplifting words and conversations. Yes, we must talk of the wrongs and the evil around us, but we should also remember to talk about hope, grace, mercy, goodness, prosperity, laughter, joy, and good things and times.

Wisdom and Understanding
January 25

*For the earth which drinks in the rain that
often comes upon it, and bears herbs
useful for those by whom it is cultivated, receives
blessing from God;
BUT
if it bears thorns and briers, it is
rejected and near to being cursed, whose end is to be burned.
But, beloved we are confident of better things concerning you, yes,
things that accompany salvation, though we speak in this manner.
For God is not unjust to forget your work and labor
of love which you have shown toward His name,
in that you have ministered to the saints, and do
minister.
—Hebrews 6:7–10 NKJV*

(Beloved, always remember to read another version
of the scripture if the NKJV is not clear to you.)

It is important to aid others, to share, to give, to pray for others, to reach out to others in whatever way we can and all in the name of God. He remembers and will reward us. He promised.

Wisdom and Understanding
January 26

Beloved,
what manner of love the Father has bestowed on us, that
we should be called children of God!
Therefore the world does not know us,
because it did not know Him.
Beloved,
now we are children of God; and it has not yet been
revealed what we shall be,
but we know that when He is revealed, we
shall be like Him, for we shall see Him as He is.
—1 John 3:1–2 KJV

Potential is never dead while there is life. I have not yet done all the great things I have been sent to do in this life. God is preparing me on my journey to my destiny, to do the amazing works He has for me and all for His honor and His glory that I might bless others and so myself be blessed. I can't wait to see the great things God is going to do through me. Thank you, Lord, You know what's best for me. Help me to do my part and to be open to Your commands. God only asks us to do good things. Amen!

Imagine living close to a fountain, a pool of water that is so crystal clear, sparkling brightly by the rays of the sun. It is said that the rain makes it more potent and the moon's reflection is seen in it every time the moon is full, and it is also said that great inspiration is given to whomever meditates by it, and it is also rumored to be a healing body of water. Now imagine you live a five-minute walk away from this fountain of water, your life is uninspired, you are ailing with all kinds of illnesses, you are bored with life, and you feel you have no hope, but you never even considered walking over to that pool and just going into it just to see if anything new, any good change would come to your life, even as a last resort to try something different, something new. Take a chance for a better existence. Try Jesus. Just do it!

Wisdom and Understanding
January 27

Kind of long today, but . . .
(these are things that really make you go hhhhmmmmm)
The Word of God

For we all stumble in many things,
if anyone does not stumble in word, he is a perfect man,
able also to bridle the whole body.
Indeed, we put bits in horses' mouths that they may obey us,
as we turn their whole body.

Look also at ships: although they are so large
and are driven by fierce winds,
they are turned by a very small rudder
wherever the pilot desires.

Even so the tongue is a little member
and boasts great things.
See how great a forest a little fire kindles!

And the tongue is a fire, a world of iniquity.
The tongue is so set
among our members
that it defiles the whole body,
and sets on fire
the course of nature;
and it is set on fire by hell.
For every kind of beast and bird, of reptile
and creature of the sea, is tamed and has been tamed by mankind.
BUT
no man can tame the tongue. It is an unruly evil,
full of deadly poison. With it we bless our
God and Father, and with it we curse
men, who have been made in the similitude of God.
Out of the same mouth proceed blessing and cursing.

My brethren,
these things ought not to be so.
—James 3:2–10 KJV

Lord, help me to think before I talk. Help me to consider before I join certain conversations. Lord, help me to mind the affairs that will help me to prosper spiritually and financially. Father, thank You for my tongue. Help me to always bless others and not to ruin them with my tongue. Show me how to guide it in Your name and for Your name's sake. Amen.

Wisdom and Understanding
January 28

Oh Lord, You have searched me and known me.
You know my sitting down and my rising up;
You understand my thought afar off.
You comprehend my path and my lying down,
and are acquainted with all my ways.
—Psalm 139:1–3 NKJV

I am so glad that He knows me completely. God understands what I am going through, and I will trust Him to see me through. Today I am thankful that God knows all about my needs, and as I worship and praise Him, He will bring me out of this situation. Thank you, Father, in Jesus's name. My needs are not always financial. Sometimes my need is lack of spirit. Sometimes I am down and depressed, and I need help to lift me up. In Jesus's name. Amen.

So many Christians, people that say they believe in Christ Jesus and His teachings, say they are Christians as they seek to impress the person they speak to, as they seek to impress people yet nothing in their lives shows that behavior. Because of their extreme love of self (their ego), they cannot let go of their own wants and choose Christ's needs for them. They live by flesh and by their physical eyes. They forget that God is a spirit and He gave us His spirit by which to live through. He also gave us flesh, a body that our flesh eyes may see, but our spirit is greater than our body. They forget daily that God knows their heart and their mind. He knows how we are building our soul, good or bad. He judges us by our mind, spirit, soul, and heart, that which cannot be seen by man. Let's choose good over evil. It might be difficult, hard, uncomfortable in the beginning, when you start to change for good, but it becomes easier and sweeter, and you have to start to make that change. Good will always prevail over evil, in your lifetime or the next lifetime after you. Choose life. It lives on after your flesh is past.

Wisdom and Understanding
January 29

*Behold, how good and how pleasant it is
for brethren to dwell together in unity!
It is like the precious oil upon the head,
running down on the beard,
The beard of Aaron,
Running down on the edge of his garments.
It is like the dew of Hermon,
Descending upon the mountains of
Zion;
For there the Lord commanded the blessing—
Life forevermore.
—Psalm 133 KJV*

All that to say, it is so good to be in unity, in harmony, in fellowship, in oneness, one with another, all of us. Let us be of one accord. Amen.

I remember our family worship time. My father and mother would bring us together after dinner, and we would sing a few hymns, read and elaborate on scriptures from the Bible, pray and close. It was my parents' way of bringing the family together in one accord. With so much distraction today, like the Internet, our smart phones, and televisions, it seems that every one in the family is doing their own thing, and so we don't have time to interact and to talk about our day at work, at school, the troubles we experienced, our concerns. We don't have time to seek advice regarding any concerns we may have encountered throughout the day, leaving one another to possibly bad decisions, non-actions for things we should address and fix; leaving one another feeling alone, lonely in the middle of a group setting, home with family, at school with peers, at work with coworkers, at church in a large congregation, etc. How should we change that and make time at the dinner table to sit down and eat together and talk and share and pray and laugh and look one another in the face and see one another again, anew every day, and therefore to make a difference, a better outcome in our lives? Let's just start. Let's just do it. Just begin to do it now, today.

Wisdom and Understanding
January 30

We then who are strong ought to bear with the scruples of the weak,
and not to please ourselves.
Let each of us please his neighbor for his good,
leading to edification.
For even Christ did not please Himself; but as it is written,
"The reproaches
of those who reproached You fell on Me."
For whatever things were written before were written for our
learning, that we through the patience and comfort of the Scriptures
might have hope.

Now may the God of patience and comfort
grant you to be like-minded toward one another,
according to Christ Jesus,
that you may with one mind and one mouth
glorify the God and Father of our Lord Jesus Christ.
Therefore receive one another, just as
Christ also received us, to the glory of God.
—Romans 15:1–7 NKJV

The Word of God

There will always be people stronger than you and people weaker than you. We are instructed and advised to defend, help, and teach the weak. As we walk this journey of life, indeed, giving is sweeter than receiving. Take a chance and help someone else, a stranger, a neighbor. You will be surprised with the feeling you get when you give without expecting in return. The only way this is not true for you is if you raised yourself to be selfish, stingy, and greedy. Outside of that, if you desire to do good, you will enjoy giving to others of your time, talent, and money. The Bible, in Luke 6:37b, says, "Give, and it will begiven to you. A good measure, pressed down, shaken together and running over, will be poured into your lap, For with the measure you use, it will be measured to you.

Wisdom and Understanding
January 31

Those who trust in the Lord are like Mount Zion,
Which cannot be moved, but abides forever.
As the mountains surround Jerusalem,
So the Lord surrounds His people
from this time forth and forever.

For the scepter of wickedness shall not rest
on the land allotted to the righteous,
lest the righteous reach out their hands to iniquity.
Do good, O Lord, to those who are good,
and to those who are upright in
their hearts.

As for such as turn aside to their crooked ways,
The Lord shall lead them away
with the workers of iniquity.

Peace be upon Israel!
—Psalm 125 KJV

King David's pleas to God, even so many eras ago, still apply to our needs today. Just a Psalm to carry you throughout this day. Amen.

Wisdom and Understanding
February 1

Brethren, if a man, is overtaken in any trespass,
you who are spiritual restore such a one in
a spirit of gentleness,
considering yourself lest you also be tempted.
Bear one another's burdens, and so fulfill the
law of Christ.
For if anyone thinks himself to be something, when he is nothing,
he deceives himself.
But let each one examine his own
work, and then he will have rejoicing in himself alone,
and not in another.
For each one shall bear his own load.
Let him who is taught the word
share in all good things with him who teaches.
Do not be deceived,
God is not mocked;
for whatever a man/woman sows,
that he will also reap
—Galatians 6:1-7 KJV

It's not always easy to remember that we too fall short of greatness sometimes when someone else does us wrong.

Father, show me how to be patient with my brothers and sisters in Christ, even with those that are nonbelievers. Help me to be forgiving. Help me to be the bigger person when uncomfortable times with others occur. Help us to apply love and understanding, in Jesus's name. Amen.

Wisdom and Understanding
February 2

Your word is a lamp to my feet and
a light to my path.
I have sworn and confirmed that I will keep
Your righteous judgments.
I am afflicted very much;
Revive me, O Lord,
according to your word.
Accept, I pray, the freewill
offerings of my mouth,
O Lord,
and teach me Your judgments.
My life is continually in my hand,
Yet I do not forget Your law.
The wicked have laid a snare for me,
Yet I have not strayed from Your precepts.
Your testimonies I have taken as
a heritage forever,
For they are the rejoicing of my heart.
I have inclined my heat to perform Your statutes
forever, to the very end
—Psalm 119:105–112 NKJV

Father, please accept my prayers, whether they be in formal words, or in yearnings, or in crying, or in meditation, or in serving, or in my calling Your name, or in thought, or in wonderment, or in supplication, or in adoration, or in thanksgiving. I cry out to you, O Lord. I know no other sure help. Amen.

Wisdom and Understanding
February 3

This is how the story goes . . .

*A certain man had a fig tree planted in
his vineyard, "look, for three years I have come seeking fruit
on this fig three and find none.
Cut it down; why does it use
up the ground?"
But he answered and said to him,
"Sir, let it alone this year also, until I dig around it and
fertilize it.
"And if it bears fruit, well. But if not,
after that you can cut it down.
Jesus spoke this parable
—Luke 13:6–9 NKJV*

The owner wanted to cut it down, but the caretaker asked to give it another chance. That's how our "caretaker" works with us. He always wants to give us another chance. Give someone a second chance today: maybe a child, encourage him or her; maybe a parent, forgive them, thank them; maybe a brother, a sister, be patient; maybe a leader, a teacher, a boss, give them time; maybe a spouse, just a little bit more understanding. Or am I doing enough for others? Do I deserve a second chance? Lord, give me an assignment that I may serve You more, that I maybe more useful on earth for Your purpose and Your kingdom. I want to produce good fruit. Amen.

Wisdom and Understanding
February 4

A Parable of Jesus

"Listen! Behold, a sower went out to sow.
"And it happened, as he sowed, that some seed fell
by the wayside; and the birds of the air came
and devoured it.
"Some fell on stony ground, where it did not have much earth;
and immediately it sprang up because it had no depth of earth.
"But when the sun was up it was scorched, and because
it had no root it withered away.
"And some seed fell among thorns; and the thorns
grew up and choked it,
and it yielded no crop.
"But other seed fell on good ground and yielded a crop that
sprang up, increased and produced: Some thirty fold,
some sixty, and some a hundred."
. . . And He said to them,
"He who has ears to hear, let him hear!"
—Mark 4:3–9 NKJV

Hhhhmmmmm. What type of soil was I? What type of soil am I now? What type of soil will I be? Father, please make me the best soil I can be so that You might be seen in me thirty-fold and sixty and a hundred. Let Your light shine through me. Amen.

Wisdom and Understanding
February 5

The preparations of the heart belong to man,
But the answer of the tongue
is from the LORD.
—Proverbs 16:1 KJV

As Christians, we should let God's word have the last say.

All the ways of a man are pure in his own eyes,
But the LORD weighs the spirits.
—Proverbs 16:2 KJV

As Christians, we should let God's word have the last say.

Commit your works to the LORD,
and your thoughts will be establish.
—Proverbs 16:3 KJV

This is how we make it happen.

When a person's ways
please the LORD,
He makes even his enemies to be
at peace with him.
—Proverbs 16:7 KJV

This is how we make it happen.

A person's heart plans his way,
But the LORD determines his steps.
—Proverbs 16:9 CSB

As Christians, we should let God's word have the last say. This is how we make it happen.

Wisdom and Understanding
February 6

Though I speak with the tongues of men and
of angels, but have not LOVE,
I have become sounding brass or a clanging cymbal.
And though I have the gift of prophecy, and
understand all mysteries and all
knowledge, and though I have
all faith, so that I could remove
mountains, but have not
LOVE,
I am nothing.
And though I bestow all my goods
to feed the poor, and though
I
give my body to be burned,
but have not
LOVE,
it profits me nothing.
LOVE
suffers long and is kind;
LOVE
does not envy;
LOVE
does not parade itself, is not puffed up;
does not behave rudely, does not seek its own,
is not provoked, thinks no evil;
does not rejoice in iniquity,
but rejoices in the truth;
bears all things, believes all things,
hopes all things, endures all things.
LOVE never fails.
—1 Corinthians 13:1–8a ESV

Lord, teach me how to *love* with the love of God. Help me to return to *love* whenever I stray from it; when angered, when provoked, when lied to, when cheated on, when misunderstood, when depressed, when lost, when I do wrong, or even when I think wrong things. Thank You for Your sovereign *love*. In Jesus's name, I pray. Amen.

Wisdom and Understanding
February 7

To everything there is a season,
A time for every purpose under heaven:
A time to be born, and a time to die;
A time to plant, And a time to pluck what is planted;
A time to kill, And a time to heal;
A time to break down, and a time to build up;
A time to weep, and a time to laugh;
A time to mourn, and a time to dance
A time to cast away stones, and a time to gather stones;
A time to embrace,
and a time to refrain from embracing;
A time to gain, and a time to lose;
a time to keep, and a time to throw away;
a time to tear, and a time to sew;

A time to keep silence,
and a time to speak;
a time to love, and a time to hate;
a time of war
and a time of peace.
—Ecclesiastes 3:1–8 NKJV

Lord, help me to discern what time it is, what to do, and when to do it. In Jesus's name, I pray. *Amen.*

Wisdom and Understanding
February 8

Walk prudently when you go to the house of God;
and draw near to hear rather than to give the
sacrifice of fools,
for they do not know that they do evil.
Do not be rash with your mouth,
and let not your heart utter
anything hastily before God.
For God is in heaven, and you on earth;
Therefore let your words be few.
For a dream comes through much activity,
and a fool's voice is known by his many words.
When you make a vow to God, do not
delay to pay it;
For He has no pleasure in fools.
Pay what you have vowed—
Better not to vow than to vow and not pay.
—Ecclesiastes 5:1–5 NKJV

The Bible, the Word of God, it has all the instructions for our daily living here on earth. It's an amazing book. Read the rest of the chapter. Read the Bible.

Listen and hear. Take heed, pay attention. Notice the details. Enter the room and notice the small things others miss. See the expression on each face, read the body language. Hear what is not being said, see what you cannot see with your physical eyes. Smell what others cannot smell, pay keen attention. Don't follow the crowd blindly, find out why you should or should not follow the crowd. Be alert. Know how to follow when necessary, but do not be a follower. Be a leader, a wise and knowledgeable leader. First of all, be a leader to yourself. Follow good leaders.

Wisdom and Understanding
February 9

We have heard with our ears, O God,
Our fathers have told us the deeds You did in their days,
in days of old:
You drove out the nations with your hand,
But them, you planted;
You afflicted the peoples, and cast them out.
For they did not gain possession of the land
by their own sword, nor did their own arms save them;
But it was Your right hand, Your arm, and the light of Your
countenance,
Because You favored them.

You are my King, O God;
Command victories for Jacob.
Through You we will push down our enemies;
Through Your name we will
trample those who rise up
against us.
For I will not trust in my bow,
Nor shall my sword save me.
But You have saved us from our enemies, and have put to
shame those who hated us.

In God we boast all day long,
and praise Your name forever.
—Psalm 44:1–8 NKJV

A Psalm for today, to remind us how David prayed and trusted in God—he trusted God in a bold way. I trust You, Lord. I know You will rescue me. I know You will protect me. I know You will guide me. I know You will bless me indeed. Thank you! Amen.

Wisdom and Understanding
February 10

*For God did not appoint us to wrath,
but to obtain salvation through our Lord Jesus Christ,
who died for us, that whether we wake or sleep, we should
live together with Him.
Therefore comfort each other and edify
one another, just as you also are doing.
And we urge you, brethren, to
recognize those who labor among you, and
are over you in the Lord and admonish you,
and to esteem them very highly in love
for their work's sake. Be at peace among yourselves.
Now we exhort you, brethren, warn
those who are unruly, comfort the
fainthearted, uphold the weak, be patient with all.
See that no one renders evil for evil to anyone,
but always pursue what is good both
for yourselves and for all.
Rejoice always,
pray without ceasing,
in everything give thanks; for this is
the will of God in Christ Jesus for you.
Do not quench the Spirit.
Do not despise prophecies
Test all things; hold fast what is good
Abstain from every form of evil.
—1 Thessalonians 5:9–22 NKJV*

Bless this day in my life, O Lord! Amen.

Wisdom and Understanding
February 11

But as for you, speak the things which are proper
for sound doctrine: That the older men
be sober, reverent, temperate, sound in faith,
in love, in patience;
the older women likewise, that they be
reverent in behavior, not slanderers,
not given to much wine, teachers of good things-
that they admonish the young women to love
their husbands, to love their children,
to be discreet, chaste, homemakers,
good, obedient to their own husbands, that the Word
of God may not be blasphemed.
Likewise, exhort the young men to be sober-minded,
in all tings showing yourself to be a pattern of good works;
in doctrine showing integrity, reverence incorruptibility,
sound speech that cannot be condemned,
that one who is an opponent may be ashamed, having
nothing evil to say of you.
—Titus 2:1–8 NKJV

The Word of God—sometimes it's hard to live by the letter of the word, but thank God for instructions that I may know what to strive for. Father God, give me the strength to grow in Your word and to help and encourage others so that the world may be a better place. In Jesus's name. Amen!

Wisdom and Understanding
February 12

REJOICE in the Lord, O you righteous!
For praise from the upright is beautiful.
Praise the LORD with the harp;
make melody to Him with an instrument of ten strings.
Sing to Him a new song;
Play skillfully with a shout of joy.
For the word of the Lord is right, and all His work is done in truth.
he loves righteousness and justice;
The earth is full of the goodness of the Lord.
By the word of the Lord the heavens were made,
and all the host of them by the
breath of His mouth,
He gathers the waters of the sea
together as a heap;
He lays up the deep in storehouses.
Let all the earth fear the Lord;
Let all the inhabitants of the world
stand in awe of Him.
For He spoke, and it was done;
He commanded, and it stood fast.
The Lord brings the counsel of the nations to nothing;
He makes the plans of the peoples of no effect.
The counsel of the Lord stands forever,
The plans of His heart to all generations.
—Psalm 33:1–11 NKJV

What does my song of praise sound like? Let me think about it for a minute. How can I praise my Lord today? Let me remember the great things He has done for me. Let me remember the beautiful things He has created: the sun, the moon, the morning, the night. What else? Everything else! Thank you, Lord, for indeed You are awesome.

Wisdom and Understanding
February 13

He who dwells in the secret place of the Most High
shall abide under the shadow of the Almighty.
I will say of the Lord, He is my refuge and my fortress;
My God, in Him I will trust.
Surely He shall deliver you from the snare of the Fowler
and from the perilous pestilence.
He shall cover you with His feathers,
and under His wings you shall take refuge;
His truth shall be your shield and buckler.
You shall not be afraid of the terror by night,
nor of the arrow that flies by day,
nor of the pestilence that walks in darkness,
nor of the destruction that lays waste at noonday.
A thousand may fall at your side and
ten thousand at your right hand;
But it shall not come near you.
—Psalm 91:1–7 NKJV

Read the rest of this Psalm. It's rich.

Exalt the Lord our God,
and worship at His holy hill;
For the Lord our God is holy.
—Psalm 99:9 NKJV

My valentine no. 1: Jesus Christ. And look
out for valentine no. 2 tomorrow!

Wisdom and Understanding
February 14

Let him kiss me with the kisses of his mouth—
for your love is better than wine.
Because of the fragrance of your good ointments,
Your name is ointment poured forth;
Therefore the virgins love you.
Draw me away!
—Song of Solomon 1:2–4 NKJV

Behold, you are handsome, my beloved!
Yes, pleasant!
Also our bed is green.
—Song of Solomon 1:16 NKJV

He: Like an apple tree among the trees
of the woods, so is my beloved among the daughters.
She: Like an apple tree among the trees of the woods,
So is my beloved among the sons.
I sat down in his shade with great delight,
and his fruit was sweet to my taste.
He brought me to the banqueting house,
and his banner over me was love.
Sustain me with cakes of raisins,
refresh me with apples,
for I am lovesick.
His left hand is under my head,
and his right hand embraces me.
—Song of Solomon 2:3–6 NKJV

Make haste, my beloved,
and be like a gazelle
or a young stag
On the mountains of spices.
—Song of Solomon 8:14 NKJV

The Word of God, all found in the book of God–the Bible. Check it out! It reads seductive. It's still the Bible. Yeah, for all the valentines, happy valentine's to her and to him. All things done in order and as we understand the word.

Father God, thank You for all the great emotions You have made us with. Thank You for love and husbands and wives, lovers and friends and children, and peace and joy. Thank You for eros love = being in love. Thank You for philia love = brotherly love. Thank You for agape love = Godly love, Your love towards us. Amen!

Wisdom and Understanding
February 15

Wine is a mocker,
strong drink is a brawler,
and whoever is led astray by it is not wise.
—Proverbs 20:1 NKJV

It is honorable for a man to stop striving,
since any fool can start a quarrel.

The lazy man will not plow because of winter;
he will beg during harvest and have nothing.

Counsel in the heart of man is like deep water,
But a man of understanding will draw it out.
—Proverbs 20:3–5 NKJV

Everything that is right should be done in moderation so not to ruin a good thing. It's one of the hardest things to do, but imagine not arguing back, and the arguer walks away with no battle. Hhhhmmmmm. Something to make you go . . .What? Lord, teach me to be like You. Guide me every day, and please bless all my actions. Amen.

Any mind-altering substance, legal or not, when over used over time is a foolish choice. How about moderation? How about picking and choosing what will be your choice of a relaxing substance? How about something that will not ruin your life? Maybe nothing at all if you cannot handle it or if your family have a history of abuse and you have addictive genes. Be the peacemaker, it's not so easy to be the one that keeps the people in the room undivided. It's so very easy to start a fight, but to keep the peace, it takes a real awesome human being.

Wisdom and Understanding
February 16

Blessed is he who considers the poor;
The Lord will deliver him in time of trouble.
The Lord will preserve him and keep him alive,
And he Will be blessed on the earth;
You will not deliver him to the will of his enemies.
The Lord will strengthen him on
his bed of illness;
you Will sustain him on his sickbed.
—Psalm 41:1–3 NKJV

These days, more than ever, there is someone in our proximity whom we need to ask, "Do you have enough to eat? Do you have enough for the children? Can I give you these clothes that I love but cannot fit anymore? Take this coat, I think it's your size." Father, help us to notice others' needs and reach out and help them. Amen.

Do not live a selfish life so that when you are old, you will not have regrets you cannot change. Help someone along the way, not just your immediate family, but neighbors, friends, and strangers too. You don't have to have a whole lot of time, things, or money to help. Just help someone that does not have as much as you.

Wisdom and Understanding
February 17

Unless the Lord builds the house,
they labor in vain who build it;
unless the Lord guards the city,
The watchman stays awake in vain.
It is vain for you to rise up early,
to sit up late,
To eat the bread of sorrows;
for so He gives His beloved sleep.
Behold, children are a heritage from the Lord,
the fruit of the womb is a reward.
Like arrows in the hand of a warrior,
so are the children of one's youth.
Happy is the man who has his quiver full of them;
They shall not be ashamed,
but shall speak with their enemies
in the gate.
—Psalm 127 NKJV

We might as well include God in everything we do, even those things we are not sure if we should do, so that He may guide us. Hhhhmmmmm. He knows anyway, so we might as well confess.

My parents know of the quiver full. They had thirteen children. So love and guide your children well that later they may look out for you and protect you too. Lord, thank You for the brilliant idea of bringing us in the world as children so we may grow in greatness. Amen.

Wisdom and Understanding
February 18

I have done justice and righteousness;
do not leave me to my oppressors.
Be surety for Your servant for good;
Do not let the proud oppress me.
My eyes fail from seeking your salvation
and your righteous word.
Deal with your servant according to your mercy,
and teach me your statutes.
I am Your servant; give me understanding,
that I may know Your testimonies.
It is time for You to act, O Lord,
for they have regarded Your law as void.
Therefore I love your commandments
more than gold, yes, than fine gold!
Therefore all Your precepts concerning all things
I consider to be right;
I hate every false way.
—Psalm 119:121–128 NKJV

Maybe this prayer of David's so many eras ago applies to somebody today. God still hears and cares. Thank You for prayer, Lord, we can come to You with all our troubles, and we know You hear us, and You will address our troubles in your perfect time. Amen.

Wisdom and Understanding
February 19

A Prayer of Moses, the Man of God

Lord, You have been our dwelling place in all
generations.
Before the mountains were brought forth,
or ever you had formed the earth and the world,
even from everlasting to everlasting, You are God.
You turn man to destruction
and say, "Return, O children of men."
For a thousand years in Your sight are like yesterday when it is past,
and like a watch in the night.
You carry them away like a flood;
they are like a sleep. In the morning
they are like grass which grows up:
In the morning it flourishes and grows up;
In the evening it is cut down and withers.
—Psalm 90:1–6 NKJV

He who dwells in the secret place
of the Most High
shall abide under the shadow of the almighty.
—Psalm 91:1 NKJV

God has not changed. He was there for our parents, our grandparents, and our ancestors. He is still here for us. Thank God for grace and mercy, even when we don't deserve it. Amen.

Wisdom and Understanding
February 20

Bits and Bites for Thought

Do not rebuke an older man, but exhort him as a father,
younger men as brothers,
Older women as mothers,
younger women as sisters, with all purity.
—1 Timothy 5:1–2 NKJV

All scripture is given by inspiration
of God, and is profitable for doctrine,
for reproof, for correction, for instruction in righteousness,
That the man of God may be complete, thoroughly
equipped for every good work.
—2 Timothy 3:16–17 NKJV

I have fought the good fight, I have
finished the race,
I have kept the faith.
—2 Timothy 4:7 NKJV

The Lord Jesus Christ be with your spirit.
Grace be with you.
Amen.
—2 Timothy 4:22 NKJV

Wisdom and Understanding
February 21

*You therefore, my son, be strong in the grace that is
in Christ Jesus.
And the things that you have heard from
me among many witnesses, commit
these to faithful men who will be
able to teach others also.
You therefore must endure hardship as a good
soldier of Jesus Christ.
No one engaged in warfare
entangles himself with the affairs of this life,
that he may please him who enlisted him as a soldier.
And also if anyone competes in athletics,
he is not crowned unless he
competes according to the rules.
The hard working farmer must be first to partake of the crops.
Consider what I say, and may the
Lord give you understanding in all things.
—2 Timothy 2:1–7 NKJV*

The Word of God is so efficient, it actually blows my mind sometimes. Even today, it serves a great purpose. Even if someone is not a believer, it will do them so much good to read the word. Imagine how much more for us believers. Lord, I cannot thank You enough for Your wonderful word. Thank You. Amen.

*Remember that Jesus Christ, of the seed of David,
was raised from the dead according to my gospel,
for which I suffer trouble as an evil-doer, even to the point
of chains; but the word of God is not chained.
Therefore I endure all things for the sake of the elect,
that they also may obtain the salvation
which is in Christ Jesus with eternal glory.*

This is a faithful saying:
For if we died with Him,
we shall also live with Him. If we endure,
we shall also reign with Him.
If we deny Him,
He also will deny us.
If we are faithless,
He remains faithful;
He cannot deny Himself.
—2 Timothy 2:8–13 NKJV

To God be the glory, forever and ever. Amen!

Wisdom and Understanding
February 22

Oh, how I love all you've revealed,
I reverently ponder it all the day long.
Your commands give me an edge on my enemies
They never become obsolete. I've even become smarter
than my teacher
Since I've pondered and absorbed your counsel. I've become
wiser than the
Wise old sages simply by doing what you tell me. I watch my step,
Avoiding the ditches and ruts of evil so I can spend all
my time keeping your Word.
I never make detours from the route you laid out, you
gave me such good
Directions. Your words are so choice, so tasty; I prefer
them to the best
Home cooking. With your instruction, I understand life; that's why I
Hate false propaganda.
I stood up for justice and the right; don't leave me to the mercy
Of my oppressors. Take the side of your servant, good God;
don't let the godless
Take advantage of me. I can't keep my eyes open any longer, waiting
For You to keep your promises to set everything right. Let Your love
Dictate how You deal with me; teach me from Your
textbook on life. I'm Your
Servant-help me understand what that means, the inner
meaning of Your
Instructions. It's time to act, GOD; they've made a
shambles of Your revelations!
Yea-Saying God, I love what you command; I love it more
than gold and gemstones;
Yea-Saying God, I honor everything you tell me, I despise
every deceitful detour.
—Psalms 119:121–128 MSG

Amazing and mighty Creator of all things, You who are merciful and kind, enough to share free will with us mortals. Thank You for Your word that is a guide and a mystery at the same time, a guide that holds all the instructions for righteous and joyful living and a mystery that we have to study, meditate on, and pray for inspiration to get what the book is teaching. Open our desire to read the book so we may love You more and one another also. In Jesus's name. Amen.

Wisdom and Understanding
February 23

(These are words Paul spoke.)

There is a message in this scripture. Read slowly
and know the instruction, the Word of God!

Remind them of these things,
charging them before the Lord not to strive
about words to no profit, to the ruin of the hearers.
Be diligent to present yourself approved to
God,
a worker who does not need to be ashamed, rightly
dividing the word of truth. But shun
profane and idle babblings, for they will increase to more
ungodliness. And their message will spread like cancer.
Hymenaeus and Philetus are of this sort.
Who have strayed concerning the truth,
saying that the resurrection is already past; and
they overthrow the faith of some.
Nevertheless the solid foundation of God
stands, having this seal: "The Lord
knows those who are His," and, "Let everyone
who names the name of Christ depart from
iniquity." But in a great house there
are not only vessels of gold and silver, but
also of wood and clay, some for honor
and some for dishonor.
Therefore if anyone cleanses himself from the latter,
he will be a vessel for honor, sanctified
and useful for the Master, prepared for
every good work.
—2 Timothy 2:14–21 NKJV

Wisdom and Understanding
February 24

I Will lift up my eyes to the hills,
from whence comes my help?
My help comes from the Lord,
Who made heaven and earth.
He will not allow your foot to be moved;
He who keeps you will not slumber.
Behold, He who keeps Israel
Shall neither slumber nor sleep.
The Lord is your keeper;
The Lord is your shade at your right hand.
The sun shall not strike you by day,
nor the moon by night.
The Lord shall preserve you from all evil;
He shall preserve your soul.
The Lord shall preserve your
going out and your coming in
from this time forth,
and even forevermore.
—Psalm 121 NKJV

This is the Psalm that I think of when I cannot solve my own troubles. I surrender to You, Lord. You see all, know all, understand all, and can fix it all. I will trust You, and I will rest in You. To God be the glory. Amen.

Wisdom and Understanding
February 25

There are diversities of gifts, but the same Spirit.
There are differences of ministries,
but the same Lord.
And there are diversities of activities,
but it is the same God who works all in all.
But the manifestation of the Spirit
is given to each one for the profit of all:
For to one is given the word of wisdom through the Spirit,
to another the word of knowledge through the same Spirit,
To another the working of miracles,
to another prophecy,
to another discerning of spirits,
to another the interpretation of tongues.
But one and the same Spirit works
all these things,
distributing to each one individually as He wills.
—1 Corinthians 12:3–11 NKJV

Even in the realm of the Spirit, in the world of the Spirit, that larger part of us, that 90 percent part of us, God gives gifts. Lord, show me how to search Your Spirit so that I may master and use the gifts You have given my spirit that not only my physical actions may be seen but that my spirit may be of Your Spirit that others may be encouraged through me. In Jesus's name. Amen!

Wisdom and Understanding
February 26

Oh give thanks to the Lord, for He is good!
For His mercy endures forever.
Let the redeemed of the Lord say so,
Whom He has redeemed from
the hand of the enemy,
and gathered out of the lands,
from the east and from the west,
from the north and from the south.
They wandered in the wilderness
in a desolate way;
They found no city to dwell in. Hungry and thirsty,
their soul fainted in them.
Then they cried out to the Lord in their trouble,
and He delivered them out of their distress,
and He led them forth by the right way,
that they might go to a city for a dwelling place.
Oh, that men would give thanks to the Lord
for His goodness,
and for His wonderful works to the
children of men!
For he satisfies the longing soul,
and fill the hungry soul with goodness.
—Psalm 107:1–9 NKJV

So what am I crying out to the Lord about today? I am glad You hear my cry, Lord. You are the only one I can really hide and trust in. Blessed be Your name forever. Amen.

Wisdom and Understanding
February 27

The Lord by wisdom founded the earth;
by understanding He established the heavens;
By His knowledge the depths were broken up,
and clouds drop down the dew.
My son (daughter) let them not depart
from your eyes—keep sound wisdom and discretion;
So they will be life to your soul
and grace to your neck.
then you Will walk safely in your way,
and your foot will not stumble.
When you lie down, you will not be afraid;
Yes, you will lie down and your sleep will be sweet.
Do not be afraid of sudden terror,
nor of trouble from the wicked when it comes;
For the Lord will be your confidence, and
will keep your foot from being caught.
—Proverbs 3:19–26 NKJV

How lovely is Your tabernacle, O Lord of hosts!
My soul longs, yes, even faints for the
courts of the Lord; My heart and
my flesh cry out for the living God.
—Psalm 84:1–2 NKJV

Amen!

Wisdom and Understanding
February 28

Do not withhold good from those to whom it is due,
When it is in the power of your hand to do so.
Do not say to your neighbor,
"Go, and come back, and tomorrow I will give it,"
when you have it with you.
Do not devise evil against your neighbor,
For he/she dwells by you for safety's sake.
Do not strive with a man/woman without cause,
if he has done you no harm.
Do not envy the oppressor,
and choose none of his ways;
For the perverse person is an
abomination to the Lord,
But His secret counsel is with the upright.
The curse of the Lord is on the
House of the wicked,
But He blesses the home of the just.
Surely He scorns the scornful,
but give grace to the humble.
The wise shall inherit glory,
But shame shall be the legacy of fools.
—Proverbs 3:27–35 NKJV

Righteous are You, O Lord, and upright are Your judgments.
Your testimonies, which You have commanded,
are righteous and very faithful.
—Psalm 119:137–138 NKJV

Flee also youthful lusts; but pursue
Righteousness, faith, love, peace with those
Who call on the Lord out of a pure heart?
But avoid foolish and ignorant disputes,

Knowing that they generate strife.
And a servant of the Lord must not

Quarrel but be gentle to all, able to teach, patient,
In humility correcting those who are in
Opposition, if God perhaps will grant them repentance,
So that they may know the truth, and
That they may come to their senses and escape
The snare of the devil, having been taken captive
By him to do his will.
—2 Timothy 2:22–26 NKJV

Wisdom and Understanding
February 29

Wisdom calls aloud outside;
She raises her voice in the open squares.
She cried out in the chief concourses,
At the openings of the gates in the city
She speaks her words:
"How long, you simple ones, will you love simplicity?"
For scorners delight in their scorning,
And fools hate knowledge.
Turn at my rebuke;
Surely I will pour out my spirit on you;
I will make my words known to you.
Because I have called and you refused,
I have stretched out my hand and no one regarded,
Because you disdained all my counsel,
And would have non of my rebuke,
I also will laugh at your calamity;
I will mock when you terror comes,
When your terror comes like a storm,
And your destruction comes like a whirlwind,
When distress and anguish come upon you.
—Proverbs 1:20–26

Wisdom and Understanding
March 1

*Blessed are the poor in spirit; for theirs is the kingdom
of heaven.
Blessed are they that mourn; for they shall be comforted.
Blessed are the meek; for they shall inherit the earth.
Blessed are they which do hunger and thirst after righteousness;
for they shall be filled.
Blessed are the merciful;
for they shall obtain mercy.
Blessed are the peacemakers; for they
shall be called the children of God.
Blessed are they which are persecuted for
righteousness' sake; for theirs is the kingdom of heaven.
Blessed are ye, when men
shall revile you, and persecute you,
and shall say all manner of evil
against you falsely, for my sake.
Rejoice, and be exceeding glad; for
great is your reward in heaven; for so
persecuted they the Prophets which
were before you.
—Matthew 5:3–12 NKJV*

*Jesus spoke those words.
Hear a just cause, O Lord,
attend to my cry;
Give ear to my prayer which is not
from deceitful lips.
Let my vindication come from your presence;
Let Your eyes look on the things that
are upright.
—Psalm 17:1–2 NKJV*

Amen!

Wisdom and Understanding
March 2

*You are the salt of the earth but if
the salt loses its flavor, how shall it be
seasoned? It is then good for nothing
but to be thrown out and trampled underfoot by men.
You are the light of the world. A city that is set on a hill
cannot be hidden, nor do they light a lamp and put
it under a basket, but on a lamp stand, and
it gives light to all who are in the house.
Let your light so shine before men,
that they may see your good works
and glorify your Father in heaven.
—Mathew 5:13–16 NKJV*

Know that you make a difference wherever you are. Your presence matters. What you say and what you do, even what you don't do or say, makes a difference. Eyes are on you, waiting to see what you think and how you will handle the situation. Somebody is affected by you, by your words and your behavior. Think before you act. Think before you talk. Consider what you are going to say, your tone, your voice, and what you mean to express. Make a good difference, not a negative and mean expression. The salt seasons the food in such a way that it becomes tasty and delicious. Even if you cannot use salt in your food anymore, this metaphor is deep. Use it in your life to bring goodness to your circle, the circle of people that surround you. Love will always be sweeter than bitterness.

Wisdom and Understanding
March 3

If it had not been the Lord who
was on our side,
Let Israel now say,
If it had not been the Lord who was on our side,
when men rose up against us,
then they would have swallowed us alive.
When their wrath was kindled against us;
Then the waters would have overwhelmed us,
The stream would have gone over our soul;
Then the swollen waters
would have gone over our soul.
Blessed be the Lord.
Who has not given us as prey to their teeth.
Our soul has escaped as a bird
from the snare of the fowlers;
The snare is broken, and we have escaped.
Our help is in the name of the Lord,
Who made heaven and earth.
—Psalm 124 KJV

Lord, we thank You for bringing us to a place where our fathers desired to have come. Help us to be thankful daily, to remember how it was and how it is much better now, although there is still yet a lot more that should be better. You, O Lord, defend the least of us. In Jesus's name. Amen.

Rejoice in the Lord, O you righteous!
For praise from the upright is beautiful.
Praise the Lord with the harp;
make melody to Him with an instrument of ten strings.
Sing to Him a new song
Play skillfully with a shout of joy.
For the Word of the Lord is right,
and all His work is done in truth.
—Psalm 33:1–4 NKJV

Those of us who are believers in a higher power, in the one and only God, in knowing that we ourselves are too limited, we don't know everything, and we need guidance every day of our lives; those of us who call on the great Spirit to show us the road to our right journey here on earth; those of us who don't live only through our ego, we know where to go when we need help in desperate moments. Where do those who don't believe or think they don't believe, those who are not sure, those who live only through their ego, go? Who do they go to for reassurance, for hope, and for peace of mind and spirit? Find yourself. Find your spirit. Make contact. It's waiting to unite with you and be one, to be whole and more perfect.

Wisdom and Understanding
March 4

*Speak these things, exhort, and rebuke with all
authority. Let no one despise you.
Remind them to be subject to rulers and
authorities, to obey, to be ready for every good work,
to speak evil of no one, to be peaceable, gentle,
showing all humility to all men.
For we ourselves were also once foolish,
disobedient, deceived, serving various lusts and pleasures
living in malice and envy, hateful and
hating one another.
But when the kindness and the love of God
our Savior toward man appeared,
not by works of righteousness which we
have done, but according to His mercy
He saved us through the washing of
regeneration and renewing of the
Holy Spirit,
whom He poured out on us abundantly through
Jesus Christ our Savior,
That having been justified by His grace we should
become heirs according to the hope of eternal life.*
—Titus 2:15, 3:1–7 NKJV

*Righteous are You, O Lord,
and upright are Your judgments,
Your testimonies, which You have commanded,
are righteous and very faithful.*
—Psalm 119:137–138 NKJV

Amen!

Wisdom and Understanding
March 5

Things That Make You Go *Hhhhmmmmm*

Do not malign a servant to his master,
lest he curse you, and you be found guilty.
—Proverbs 30:10 NKJV

There is a generation that curses its father,
and does not bless its mother.
There is a generation that is pure
in its own eyes,
yet is not washed from its filthiness.
There is a generation whose teeth are
like swords, and whose fangs are like knives,
to devour the poor from off the earth,
and the needy from among men.
—Proverbs 30:11–14 NKJV

The leech has two daughters—
Give and Give!
—Proverbs 30:15a NKJV

(Today the word "servant" can be translated as "worker" or "employee" and the word "master" as "boss" or "leader.")

Oh, sing to the Lord a new song!
Sing to the Lord, all the earth.
Sing to the Lord, bless His name;
proclaim the good news of His salvation
from day to day.
Declare His glory among the nations,
His wonders among all peoples.
—Psalm 96:1–3 NKJV

Wisdom and Understanding
March 6

Things That Make You Go *Hhhhmmmmm*

There are three things that are never satisfied,
Four never say "Enough!"; The grave, the barren womb,
the earth that is not satisfied with water
and the fire never says, "enough!"
—Proverbs 30:16 NKJV

There are three things which are too wonderful
for me, yes, four which I do not understand;
The way of an eagle in the air, the way
of a serpent on a rock, the way of a ship in the
midst of the sea, and the way of a man with a virgin.
—Proverbs 30:18–19 NKJV

For three things the earth is perturbed,
yes, for four it cannot bear up;
for a servant when he reigns, a fool when he is
filled with food, a hateful woman when she is married,
and a maidservant who
succeeds her mistress.
—Proverbs 30:21–23 NKJV

There are four things which are little on the earth,
but they are exceedingly wise;
The ants are a people not strong, Yet
they prepare their food in the summer;
The rock badgers are a feeble folk, Yet they
make their homes in the crags; the locusts have
no king, yet they all advance in ranks;
The spider skillfully grasps with its hands,
and it is in kings' palaces.
There are three things which are
majestic in pace, yes, four which are stately in walk;

a lion, which is mighty among beasts
and does not turn away from any;
a greyhound, a male goat also,
a king whose troops are with him.
—Proverbs 30:24–31 NKJV

O Lord, our Lord,
how excellent is Your name in all the earth,
who have set Your glory above the heavens!
—Psalm 8:1 NKJV

Wisdom and Understanding
March 7

The Lord is my shepherd;
I shall not want.
He makes me to lie down in green pastures;
He leads me beside the still waters.
He restores my soul;
He leads me in the paths of righteousness
For His name's sake.
Yea, though I walk through the valley of the
Shadow of death, I will fear no evil;
For you are with me;
Your rod and your staff, they comfort me.
You prepare a table before me in the
Presence of my enemies;
You anoint my head with oil;
My cup runs over.
Surely goodness and mercy shall follow me
All the days of my life;
And I will dwell in the house of the Lord
Forever.
—Psalms 23 NKJV

The Lord is my shepherd, I shall not want. Yeah, we are like sheep to our Maker. He knows us and will take care of us. Our destiny is already decided upon, we simply have to walk into it. Live good, do the right thing as much as possible, help others, praise God, work hard, and trust that your journey will be better than if you did wrong, steal, lie, give false witness against your neighbor, cheat, behave like a con artist, living a life plotting your next trick, trick and trap against another human being, seeking to ruin and destroy, behaving just like the evil one that was cast out of heaven to hell and now hates God's best love, us humans. Don't treat your neighbors with disdain as though you are different from the rest of the world. Stop it and behave with love. Surely goodness and mercy shall follow me all the days of my life; and I will dwell in the house of the Lord forever. Amen.

Wisdom and Understanding
March 8

The Lord is my light and my salvation;
Whom shall I fear?
The Lord is the strength of my life;
Of whom shall I be afraid?
When the wicked came against me to eat
Up my flesh, my enemies and foes,
They stumbled and fell.
Though an army may encamp against me,
My heart shall not fear;
Though war may rise against me,
In this I will be confident.
One thing I have desired of the Lord,
That will I seek:
That I may dwell in the house of the Lord
All the days of my life,
To behold the beauty of the Lord,
And to inquire in His temple.
For in the time of trouble He shall
Hide me in His pavilion;
In the secret place of His tabernacle
He shall hide me;
He shall set me high upon a rock.
And now my head shall be lifted up above
My enemies all around me;
Therefore I will offer sacrifices of joy in His tabernacle;
I will sing, yes, I will sing praises to the Lord.
—Psalms 27:1–6 NKJV

Wisdom and Understanding
March 9

Praise the Lord!
Oh, give thanks to the Lord, for He is good!
For His mercy endures forever.
Who can utter the mighty acts of the Lord?
Who can declare all His praise?
Blessed are those who keep justice,
and he who does righteousness at all times!
Remember me, O Lord, with the
favor You have toward Your people.
Oh, visit me with Your salvation,
that I may see the benefit of Your
chose ones, that I may rejoice in
the gladness of Your nation, that I
may glory with Your inheritance.
—Psalm 106:1–5 NKJV

Father God, I thank you for Your daily protection toward me. I thank You for Your word and Your shield over me. Blessed be the name of the Lord forever, world without end! Amen.

Remember to be grateful and thankful. Have a presence of someone that knows they are blessed and special. Each person is an awesome creation, a human art, a living one-and-only art piece, no copy nowhere on earth. Even if you have a look alike, that's just external. No other person have ever or will ever have the same mind, soul, spirit, character, and personality as you. You alone can shape, change, and grow your person, so do a good job. Be the best you possible. It takes hard work daily, but it's worth it. You will be happier, and your joy will be inside out, not just expressed outside. Your joy will be genuine, and it will spread and make others happy too.

Wisdom and Understanding
March 10

A soft answer turns away wrath,
But a harsh word stirs up anger.

The tongue of the wise uses knowledge rightly,
but the mouth of fools pours forth foolishness.

The eyes of the Lord are in every place,
keeping watch of the evil and the good.

A wholesome tongue is a tree of life,
but perverseness in it breaks the spirit.

A fool despises his father's instruction,
but he who receives correction is prudent.

In the house of the righteous there is much treasure,
but in the revenue of the wicked is trouble.
—Proverbs 15:1–6 NKJV

Oh, sing to the Lord a new song!
For He has done marvelous things;
His right hand and His holy arm
have gained Him the victory.
The Lord has made known His salvation;
His righteousness,
He has revealed
in the sight of the nations.
—Psalms 98:1–2 NKJV

Amen!

Wisdom and Understanding
March 11

Top 10 Heart-Healthy Foods

Fish; salmon, tuna, sardines, etc.
Beans— black, white, red, kidney, etc.
Oats—a great source of soluble fiber,
Milk and yogurt are high in calcium which are good for bones
and heart,
Berries, blackberries, blueberries, strawberries,
lingonberries, raspberries, etc.
Walnuts and other nuts—high in omega-3
but high in calories so just a few.
Flaxseeds—high in omega-3 and soluble fiber
Brussels sprouts and other green vegetables, high in soluble
fiber, research your foods and know their nutritional
value for your body and your children's bodies.
Olive oil (my favorite)—good oil. Lord help us
to eat healthy foods, natural foods so our bodies
and our minds would be healthy also.
Body, mind, soul and spirit, they are all connected, we must
purpose to keep all parts of our being healthy and happy.

And their father Israel said unto them, If it must be so now,
do this; take of the best fruits in the land in your vessels,
and carry down the man a present, a little balm, and a little honey,
*spices, and myrrh, **nuts**, and almonds:*
—Genesis 43:11 NKJV

And sow the fields, and plant vineyards,
*which may yield **fruits** of increase.*
—Psalm 107:37 KJV

Lord, help me to eat better foods for my health. I know I should not eat so much fried foods, although they are tasty. Help me to learn how to choose more healthy foods. Help me to discipline my mind and my spirit. With Your help, I know I can do what is good for me. In Jesus's name, I pray. Amen!

Wisdom and Understanding
March 12

Kind of long today, a hard word from Paul to us.

For you, brethren, have been called to liberty;
only do not use liberty as an opportunity for the flesh,
but through love serve one another.
For all the law is fulfilled in one word, even in this: "You shall
love your neighbor as yourself."
But if you bite and devour one another,
beware lest you be consumed by one another!
I say then: Walk in the Spirit, and you shall not
fulfill the lust o the flesh. For the flesh lusts against
the Spirit and the Spirit against the flesh; and
these are contrary to one another so
that you do not do the things that you wish.
But if you are led by the Spirit, you
are not under the law.
Now the works of the flesh are evident, which are:
adultery, fornication, uncleanness, lewdness,
idolatry, sorcery, hatred, contentions,
jealousies, outbursts of wrath,
selfish ambitions, dissensions, heresies,
envy, murders, drunkenness, revelries *and the like;*
of which I tell you beforehand, just as I also told you in
time past, that those who practice such things
will not inherit the kingdom of God.
But the fruit of the Spirit is love, joy, peace,
long suffering, kindness, goodness, Faithfulness,
gentleness, self-control, *against such there is no law.*
—*Galatians 5:1–23 NKJV*

(Please check the dictionary for words that are
not clear or different in another version.)

The thing about this word is, why is it that we concentrate on the words like "adultery" and "fornication" since they seem easiest to accuse others of, but we don't concentrate and or take seriously those words that I have emphasized? We don't take time to ask God to remove envy, jealousy, outbursts of wrath, selfish ambitions, etc., out of our behavior. Father God, it's not easy for me, but with Your help, I can be a better Christian. Amen.

I cannot emphasize enough—it is our obligation, our charge, to love our neighbor and find time to care for one another.

Wisdom and Understanding
March 13

(A prayer)

Vindicate me, O God,
and plead my cause against an ungodly nation;
Oh, deliver me from the deceitful
and unjust man!/woman!
For You are the God of my strength:
Why do You cast me off?
Why do I go mourning because of the
oppression of the enemy?
Oh, send out Your light and Your truth!
Let them lead me; Let them bring me to Your holy hill
and to Your tabernacle.
Then I will go to the altar of God,
to God my exceeding joy;
And on the harp I will praise you,
O God, my God.
Why are you cast down, O my soul?
And why are you disquieted within me?
Hope in God:
For I shall yet praise Him,
The help of my countenance and
my
God.
—Psalm 43 NKJV

Get wisdom, and with all your getting, get understanding. I really like this saying, it makes a lot of sense to me. Sometimes we think we are so wise, and yet the Bible says wisdom must be coupled with understanding. Understanding is acquired. You have to do the work to get understanding. You have to do the research, investigate, ask questions, etc. You have to care, you have to want. You have to give it time, be patient, wait for clarity, see the facts or see what the spirit says and then apply wisdom. Now you have the complete recipe. Make a beautiful cake of life. Enjoy.

Wisdom and Understanding
March 14

God be merciful to us and bless us,
and cause His face to shine upon us,
that Your way may be known on earth,
Your salvation among all nations.
Let the people praise You O God;
Let all the peoples praise You.
Oh, let the nations be glad and sing for joy!
For You shall judge the people righteously,
and govern the nations on earth,
Let the peoples praise You, O God;
let all the peoples praise You.
Then the earth shall yield her increase;
God, our own God, shall bless us.
God shall bless us,
and all the ends of the earth shall fear Him.
—Psalm 67 NKJV

Wisdom and Understanding
March 15

The lips of the wise disperse knowledge,
but the heart of the fool does not do so.
The sacrifice of the wicked is an abomination to the Lord,
but the prayer of the upright is His delight.
The way of the wicked is an abomination to the Lord,
But He loves him who follows righteousness.
Harsh discipline is for him who
forsakes the way,
and he who hates correction will die.
Hell and destruction are before the Lord;
So how much more the hearts of the
sons of men.
A scoffer does not love one who corrects him,
Nor will he go to the wise.
A merry heart makes a cheerful countenance,
but by sorrow of the heart the spirit is broken.
—Proverbs 15:7–13 NKJV

I waited patiently for the Lord;
and He inclined to me,
and heard my cry.
He also brought me up out of a horrible pit,
out of the miry clay,
and set my feet upon a rock,
and established my steps.
He has put a new song in my mouth—
praise to our God;
many will see it and fear,
and will trust in the Lord.
—Psalm 40:1–3 NKJV

Wisdom and Understanding
March 16

And when he had apprehended him, he put
him in prison, and delivered him to four quaternions
of soldiers to keep him; intending after
Easter
to bring him forth to the people.
—Acts 12:4 KJV

(This is the only time Easter is mentioned in the Bible.)

*Howbeit this kind goeth not out but by **prayer and fasting**.*
—Mathew 17:21 KJV

And I will give you pastors according to mine heart, which
*shall **feed you** with knowledge and understanding.*
—Jeremiah 3:15 KJV

And he gave some, apostles; and some, prophets; and some,
*evangelists; and some, **pastors** and teachers;*
—Ephesians 4:11 KJV

Unto you I lift up my eyes,
O You who dwell in the heavens.
Behold, as the eyes of servants
look to the hand of their masters,
as the eyes of the maid to the hand of her mistress,
So our eyes look to the Lord our God,
until He has mercy on us.
—Psalm 123:1–2 NKJV

Wisdom and Understanding
March 17

I will bless the LORD at all times:
his praise shall continually be in my mouth.
My soul shall make her boast in the LORD:
the humble shall hear thereof, and be glad.
O magnify the LORD with me,
and let us exalt his name together.
I sought the LORD, and he heard me,
and delivered me from all my fears.
They looked unto him, and were lightened:
and their faces were not ashamed.
This poor man/woman cried, and the LORD heard him,
and saved him out of all his troubles.
The angel of the LORD encampeth round about them that fear him,
and delivereth them.
O taste and see that the LORD is good:
blessed is the man that trusteth in him.
O fear the LORD, ye his saints:
for there is no want to them that fear him.
The young lions do lack, and suffer hunger:
but they that seek the LORD shall not want any good thing.
—Psalm 34:1–10 KJV

Father, we thank You for Your love and kindness toward us, Your grace and Your mercy every day. We thank You for our jobs in such a time as we are in. We thank You for our joy and for accepting our worship and praise even in such a difficult economy. Thank You for You, our defender and our presenter. You make us look good, in Jesus's name. Amen!

Wisdom and Understanding
March 18

Do not fret because of evildoers,
nor be envious of the workers of iniquity.
For they shall soon be cut down like the grass,
and wither as the green herb.
Trust in the Lord, and do good;
dwell in the land, and feed on His faithfulness.
Delight yourself also in the Lord,
and He shall give you the desires of your heart.
Commit your way to the Lord,
trust also in Him,
and He shall bring it to pass.
He shall bring forth your righteousness
as the light, and your justice as the noonday.
Rest in the Lord, and wait
patiently for Him; do not fret
because of him who prospers in his way,
because of the man who brings
wicked schemes to pass.
Cease from anger, and forsake wrath;
do not fret—it only causes harm.
For evildoers shall be cut off;
but those who wait on the Lord,
they shall inherit the earth.
For yet a little while and the wicked shall be no more;
indeed, you will look carefully for
his place, but it shall be no more.
—Psalm 37:1–10 NKJV

Father God, sometimes it seems that after one storm passes, just after a short while of clear skies, here comes another storm. Help me to trust in You, Lord, and to know that my storms will make me stronger and better and that You will bring me through again and again and again and I will be better and better and better and stronger and stronger, and I can serve You better and help others better because You brought me through. In Jesus's name. Amen!

Wisdom and Understanding
March 19

(This is a word for some rich folks today.)

Come now, you rich, weep and howl
for your miseries that are coming upon you!
Your riches are corrupted, and your
garments are moth-eaten.
Your gold and silver are corroded,
and their corrosion will be a witness against you
and will eat your flesh like fire. You have
heaped up treasure in the last days.
Indeed the wages of the laborers who
mowed your fields, which you kept back
by fraud, cry out; and the cries of
the reapers have reached the ears of
the Lord of Sabaoth.
You have lived on the earth in pleasure and luxury;
you have fattened your hearts as in a day of slaughter.
You have condemned, you have
murdered the just; he does not resist you.

(Then a word for the rest of us.)

Therefore be patient, brethren until
the coming of the Lord. See how the farmer
waits for the precious fruit of the earth,
waiting patiently for it until it
receives the early and latter rain.
You also be patient. Establish your hearts,
for the coming of the Lord is at hand.
Do not grumble against one another, brethren,
lest you be condemned. Behold, the
judge is standing at the door!
My brethren, take the prophets,

who spoke in the name of the Lord, as an
example of suffering and patience.

Indeed we count them blessed who endure.
You have heard of the perseverance of Job
and seen the end intended by the Lord—that the Lord
is very compassionate and merciful.
But above all, my brethren, do not
swear, either by heaven or by earth or with
any other oath. But let your "Yes" be "Yes,"
and your "No," No,"
lest you fall into judgment.
—James 5:1–12 NKJV

Praise the name of the Lord forever! Amen.

Wisdom and Understanding
March 20

And so I insist—and God backs me up on this—that
there be no going along with the crowd, the empty-headed,
mindless crowd. They've refused
for so long to deal with God that they've lost touch
not only with God but with reality itself.
They can't think straight anymore.
Feeling no pain, they let themselves go
in sexual obsession, addicted to
every sort of perversion. But that's no life
for you. You learned Christ! My
assumption is that you have
paid careful attention to Him, been well
instructed in the truth precisely as we
have it in Jesus. Since, then, we do not have
the excuse of ignorance, everything—and
I do mean everything—connected with that old way of life has to go.
It's rotten through and through. Get rid of it!
And then take on an entirely new way of life—a God—fashioned
life, a life renewed from the inside and
working itself into your conduct as God accurately
reproduces his character in you.
What this adds up to, then, is this: No more LIES,
no more PRETENSE. Tell your neighbor
the TRUTH. In Christ's body
we're all connected to each other, after all.
When you lie to others, you end up
lying to yourself.
—Ephesians 4:17–25 MSG

Father God, please help us to start over, to try anew, to be truthful, to be honest, to be sincere, without games and tricks and without false promises though large or small. Help us to dare, to trust You, so we don't feel we have to lie to one another just to look good for the moment, yet knowing we will not or cannot do what we have promised. All of us, leaders and followers, Father, we need Your power so we can rest in You and not in ourselves. In Jesus's name, we pray. Amen.

Wisdom and Understanding
March 21

The Lord reigns, He is clothed with
majesty; The Lord is clothed,
He has girded Himself with strength.
Surely the world is established, so
that it cannot be moved.
your throne is established from of old;
You are from everlasting.
The floods have lifted up, O Lord,
The floods have lifted up their voice;
The floods lift up their waves.
The Lord on high is mightier
Than the noise of many waters,
than the mighty waves of the sea.
Your testimonies are very sure;
Holiness adorns Your house,
O Lord, forever.
—Psalm 93 NKJV

I am so glad that I am a friend of God!

Those of us that are admitted believers in God the Father, Jesus the Son, and the Holy Spirit who intercedes for us, let us be reminded to make time to worship, praise, and thank God for all His benefits toward us, for His grace and mercy daily given to us, all unmerited but gracefully given, things like eyes to see, nose, hands, ears, lips, tongue, flowers, trees. Mix them all up, consider all the things we don't often think about that are practically automatically given to us as we are born, things that if we lose them, we then realize how valuable they are. Let's not only remember to go to God in prayer and adoration when we need things, when we have troubles, or when the storms in life come. Let's also worship and thank Him on purpose, when nothing extraordinary is happening. Let's bring worshipping to our consciousness more so that it will be part of our existence to praise God and just think about Him when we wake up in the mornings or when we see children going to school or playing or when we are at work, just any time and all the time. Let's remember our Maker always. Let's live a life of gratefulness, a life of thanksgiving. Let's send a sweet fragrance to God's nostrils from the way we live our lives for Him, put a big smile on the heavens by the way we live our lives! Amen.

Wisdom and Understanding
March 22

How long, O Lord? Will You forget me forever?
How long will You hide Your face from me?
How long shall I take counsel in my soul,
having sorrow in my heart daily?
How long will my enemy be exalted over me?
Consider and hear me, O Lord my God:
enlighten my eyes,
lest I sleep the sleep of death;
Lest my enemy say, "I have prevailed
against him"; Lest those who trouble
me rejoice when I am moved.
But I have trusted in Your mercy;
My heart shall rejoice in Your salvation.
I will sing to the Lord,
because He has dealt
bountifully with me.
—Psalm 13 NKJV
Amen!

Wisdom and Understanding
March 23

She opens her mouth with wisdom,
and on her tongue is the law of kindness.
She watches over the ways of her household,
and does not eat the bread of idleness.
Her children rise up and call
her blessed;
her husband also, and he praises her:
"Many daughters have done well, but
you excel them all."
Charm is deceitful and beauty is passing,
but a woman who fears the Lord,
she shall be praised.
Give her of the fruit of her hands,
and let her own works praise her
in the gates.
—Proverbs 31:26–31 NKJV

During March, "Women's Month," a word to the women, how about showing love to a sister before we judge a sister? She looks so pretty on the outside, but she is crying on the inside. Just because all you see is the fancy clothes, the pretty face, the gorgeous, smooth, jet-black, tan, peach, honey, light, light skin, natural 'fro, weave, curly hair, wig, long, short, sexy styles doesn't mean that the sister, the next woman, is not going through hard times too, whether it be financial, spiritual, physical, or psychological. "Love a sister before you judge a sister." Who knows the great things that can happen when girl talk becomes God talk? We have a nation to build, not to tear down. In Jesus's name. Amen.

Wisdom and Understanding
March 24

Grace to you and peace from God
our Father and the Lord Jesus Christ.
Blessed be the God and Father of
our Lord Jesus Christ, the Father of mercies
and God of all comfort,
who comforts us in all our tribulation, that
we may be able to comfort those
who are in any trouble, with the comfort with
which we ourselves are comforted by God.
For as the sufferings of Christ abound in us,
so our consolation also abounds through Christ.
—2 Corinthians 1:2–5 NKJV

Our Father, who art in heaven, please protect us here on earth. Keep us in Your will and focused on You, no matter what trials and tribulations we face. Help us to concentrate on You. Help us to be strong for the weak. Shower us with Your grace and mercy. We need you, Lord. In Jesus's name, we pray. *Amen!*

Wisdom and Understanding
March 25

Praise the Lord!
Praise the Lord from the heavens;
Praise Him in the heights!
Praise Him, all His angels;
Praise Him, all His hosts!
Praise Him, sun and moon;
Praise Him, all you stars of light!
Praise Him, you heavens of heavens,
and you waters above the heavens!
Let them praise the name of the Lord,
for He commanded and they were created,
He also established them forever and ever;
He made a decree which shall not
pass away.
—Psalm 148:1–6 NKJV

Father and God, we thank You and praise You for You are our consciousness. Your teachings make us know Your will. Guide us daily as we grow in Your word. You are an awesome God. Praise Your name forever. Amen!

Wisdom and Understanding
March 26

*I charge you therefore before God
and the Lord Jesus Christ, who will
judge the living and the dead at His
appearing and His kingdom:
Preach the word! Be ready in season
and out of season. Convince, rebuke, exhort,
with all long suffering and teaching.
For the time will come when they
will not endure sound doctrine, but
according to their own desires,
because they have itching ears,
they will heap up for themselves teachers;
and they will turn their ears away from the truth,
and be turned aside to fables.
But you be watchful in all things,
endure afflictions, do the work of an
evangelist, fulfill your ministry.
—2 Timothy 4:1–5 NKJV*

Father God, I want to behave as a Christian should every day of the week, at work, at home, walking down the street, at the party, in a meeting, everywhere, and all the time. It's not easy to do when I am angry or when things don't seem to be going in my favor, but with Your Spirit abiding in me, I will make an effort, a conscious effort, to be more like You always, even when dealing with vulnerable children, or strangers, or those who don't really like me. Show me how, Lord, in Jesus's name. Amen.

Wisdom and Understanding
March 27

(Sorry, kinda long today. Check out how God spoke to the
descendants of Jacob, and He is speaking to us today. I figured
I would print it from the clearest version I know of.)

"I am GOD—
yes, I AM.
I haven't changed. And because I haven't changed,
you, the descendants of Jacob, haven't
been destroyed. You have a long history
of ignoring my commands. You haven't done a thing
I've told you. Return to me so I can
return to you," says God-of-the-Angel-Armies
(hyphened as per the version).
"You ask, 'But how do we return?'
"Begin by being honest. Do honest people rob God?
But you rob me day after day.
"You ask, 'How have we robbed you?'
"THE TITHE AND THE OFFERING—
that's how! And now you are under a curse—
the whole lot of you—because you're robbing me.
Bring your full tithe to the Temple
treasury so there will be ample provisions in my
Temple. Test me in this and see if I
don't open up heaven itself to you and pour out
blessings beyond your wildest dreams.
For my part, I will defend you against marauders,
protect your wheat fields and vegetable gardens
against plunderers. "The Message of God-of-the-Angel-Armies.
—Malachi 3:6–12 MSG

This came clear to me when I realized that God was challenging me. I
love a good challenge, and when it's from God, please, it's on. He has
been so true to His word that if I were to share the amazing miracles He
has done in my life, some would think this is not a daily word anymore

but a "show-off" word. For about ten years now, God has boldly made me look good when I was supposed to be sinking in a mess. I say all this to dare you to take Him on. Pay your tithes and offerings. God is God Almighty. He wants to bless you even more than He already has. *Just do it.* Amen!

Wisdom and Understanding
March 28

Therefore, laying aside all malice,
all deceit, hypocrisy, envy, and all evil
speaking, as newborn babies, desire the
pure milk of the word, that you may
grow thereby, if indeed you have tasted
that the Lord is gracious. Coming to Him
as to a living stone, rejected indeed by men,
but chosen by God and precious, you also,
as living stones, are being built
up a spiritual house, a holy
priesthood, to offer up spiritual sacrifices
acceptable to God through
Jesus Christ.
—1 Peter 2:1–5 NKJV

Sometimes I forget who I am. I forget that my whole purpose of existence is that I am special to God and that He is always preparing me, building me into a "spiritual house." Sometimes, when others reject me, I forget who I am: after a bad interview, or when I flunked that test, or when I did not get that position, or when they did not choose me, or when I lost that game or, when I feel down, sad, or lonely, or when my child did not do so well, or . . . or . . . or . . . I forget that I am still very special to You, God. Father, help me to remember that I am Yours and You are in me. Let me rejoice always because You live in me. Amen!

Wisdom and Understanding
March 29

Remember the word to Your servant,
upon which You have caused me to hope.
This is my comfort in my affliction,
for your word has given me life.
The proud have me in great derision,
yet I do not turn aside from Your law.
I remember Your judgments of old, O Lord,
and have comforted myself.
Indignation has taken hold of me
because of the wicked, who forsake
Your law. Your statutes have been my
songs in the house of my pilgrimage.
I remember Your name in the night, O Lord
and I keep Your law.
This has become mine,
because I kept Your precepts.
—Psalm 119:49–56 NKJV

At my bedtime, my sleeping time, I lay there, I let go a great sigh. Before I fall asleep, I consider You, O Lord, how You have kept me throughout the day. Then I ask You to protect me and my friends, my neighbors, my family, and all those who love You as we sleep, even those who don't know You yet. Then I have to smile and consider how great and awesome You are, my Lord, my Savior, and my protector. Amen!

Wisdom and Understanding
March 30

*Your hands have made me and
fashioned me; Give me understanding,
that I may learn Your commandments.
Those who fear You will be glad when
they see me, because I have hoped
in Your word.
I know, O Lord, that Your
judgments are right, and that in
faithfulness You have afflicted me.
Let, I pray, Your merciful kindness
be for my comfort,
according to Your word to Your servant.
Let Your tender mercies come to me,
that I may live; for Your law is my delight.
—Psalm 119:73–77 NKJV*

Father, I pray that You bring me out of all my troubles because I am Your servant and I need You always. I know You allow my afflictions that I may become stronger and better, and as preparation for something better, give me strength to carry on and to persevere. In Jesus's name. Amen!

Wisdom and Understanding
March 31

Oh, give thanks to the Lord, for He is good!
For His mercy endures forever.
Let Israel now say,
"His mercy endures forever."
Let the house of Aaron now say,
His mercy endures forever.
Let those who fear the Lord now say,
His mercy endures forever.
I called on the Lord in distress;
The Lord answered me and set me
in a broad place.
The Lord is on my side;
I will not fear.
What can man do to me?
The Lord is for me among those who help me;
Therefore I shall see my desire on those
who hate me. It is better to
trust in the Lord than to put
confidence in princes.
—Psalm 118:1–9 NKJV

Although I cannot see the light at the end of the tunnel as yet, I will be still and trust You, Lord. Thank You for Your word. Amen.

Wisdom and Understanding
April 1

The king's heart is in the hand of the Lord,
like the rivers of water;
He turns it wherever He wishes.
Every way of a man is right in his
own eyes,
but the Lord weighs the hearts.
To do righteousness and justice
is more acceptable to the Lord
than sacrifice.
—Proverbs 21:1–3 NKJV

We could say the "president's" heart is in the hand of the Lord. Let's continue to pray for our president, our government, our state, city, and our neighborhood. With God's help, we can bring positive change.

Wisdom and Understanding
April 2

Things That Make You Go *Hhhhmmmmm*

A person who bears false witness
against his neighbor is like a club,
a sword, and a sharp arrow.
Confidence in an unfaithful man/woman
in time of trouble is like a bad tooth
and a foot out of joint.
—Proverbs 25:18–19 NKJV

If your enemy is hungry, give him
bread to eat; and if he/she is thirsty,
give him/her water to drink;
for so you will heap coals of fire
on his/her head, and the Lord will reward you.
—Proverbs 25:21–22 NKJV

Father God, we ask for wisdom and understanding each day so that we may walk in truth and honesty. Help us to lessen our ego and put You first that we may do our very best while on earth. Your will be done. Amen.

Wisdom and Understanding
April 3

Things That Make You *Hhhhmmmmm*

The rich and the poor have this in common,
The Lord is the maker of them all.
A prudent man/woman foresees evil and
hides himself, but the simple pass
on and are punished.
—Proverbs 22:23 NKJV
Train up a child in the way he/she should go,
and when he is old he will not
depart from it.
The rich rules over the poor,
and the borrower is servant to the lender.
He who sows iniquity will reap sorrow,
and the rod of his anger will fail.
He who has a generous eye will be
blessed, for he gives of his bread to the poor.
Cast out the scoffer, and contention
will leave;
Yes, strife and reproach will cease.
—Proverbs 22:6–10 NKJV

I will lift up my eyes to the hills—
from whence comes my help?
My help comes from the Lord,
Who made heaven and earth.
He will not allow your foot to be moved:
He who keeps you will not slumber.
—Psalm 121:1–3 NKJV

Hallelujah!

Wisdom and Understanding
April 4

Therefore do not be unwise,
but understand what the will of the Lord is.
And do not be drunk with wine,
in which is dissipation; but be
filled with the Spirit,
speaking to one another in psalms
and hymns and spiritual songs,
singing and making melody in your heart
to the Lord,
giving thanks always for all things
to God the Father in the name of
our Lord Jesus Christ,
submitting to one another in the fear of
God.
—Ephesians 5:17–21 NKJV

Everything should be done in moderation,; Lord, give us more grace and mercy, joy and laughter. Put a song in our hearts always. Help us to maintain a thankful and grateful spirit even in the midst of problems. Show us how to be patient with one another even when we disagree and to lovingly express our disagreement. Thank You for Your word. In Jesus's name, we pray. Amen!

Wisdom and Understanding
April 5

Wisdom and Knowledge and Understanding

On that night God appeared to Solomon,
and said to him, "Ask! What shall I give you?"
—2 Chronicles 1:7 NKJV

"Now, give me wisdom and knowledge,
that I may go out and come in before this people;
for who can judge this great people of Yours?
Then God said to Solomon: "Because this
was in your heart, and you have not asked
riches or wealth or honor or the life
of your enemies, nor have you asked
long life—but have asked
wisdom and knowledge for yourself,
that you may judge My people
over whom I have made you king—
"wisdom and knowledge
are granted to you; and I will give
you riches and wealth and honor,
such as none of the kings have had
who were before you, nor shall any
after you have the like."
—2 Chronicles 1:10–12 NKJV

"But seek first the kingdom of God and His
righteousness and all these things
shall be added to you.
—Matthew 6:33 NKJV

When I go to the altar, I humble myself before His presence. I hope I ask for the right things, the things that will grow me spiritually, because I know that He will add all those other things that I want. I hope I ask for the things I really need. Accept my meditation, O Lord, my God. Amen.

Wisdom and Understanding
April 6

That I may know HIM and the
Power of
HIS RESURRECTION,
and the fellowship of HIS
sufferings, being conformed to
HIS death.
If, by any means, I may attain to the
RESURRECTION
from the dead.
Not that I have already attained,
or am already perfected; but I press on
that I may lay hold of that for which
Christ Jesus has also laid hold of me.
—Philippians 3:10–12 NKJV

I gave up all that inferior stuff so I could know
Christ
personally, experience His RESURRECTION power,
be a partner in his suffering, and go all the way
with Him to death itself. If there was any
way to get in on the RESURRECTION
from the dead, I wanted to do it.
I'm not saying that I have this all together, that
I have it made. But I am well on my way,
reaching out for Christ, who has so
wondrously reached out for me.
—Philippians 3:10–12 MSG

Father and God, we thank You for Your Son, Jesus the Christ. We are so glad You sent Him to redeem us, and today we serve a risen Savior. He rose from the dead, and now with all power in His hands, He blesses us all the time. In Jesus's name. Amen.

Wisdom and Understanding
April 7

As the deer pants for the water brooks,
so pants my soul for You, O God.
My soul thirsts for God, for the
living God.
When shall I come and appear
before God?
My tears have been my food day and night,
while they continually say to me,
"Where is your God?"
When I remember these things,
I pour out my soul within me.
For I used to go with the multitude;
I went with them to the house of God,
with the voice of joy and praise,
with a multitude that kept a pilgrim feast.
Why are you cast down, O my soul?
And why are you disquieted
within me?
HOPE IN GOD, for I shall yet praise Him
for the help of his countenance.
—Psalm 42:1–5 NKJV

Sometimes I feel like King David. I step back, look at my circumstance, feel sad, pitiful, lost, alone, and then in the third person, I speak to my soul and ask her, "Why are you cast down, oh my soul?" Then I have to remind her (him for the he's), "Hope in God, for I shall yet praise Him."

But those who wait on the Lord
shall renew their strength;
they shall mount up with wings
like eagles,
they shall run and not be weary,
they shall walk and not faint.
—Isaiah 40:31

Help, Lord, help. Amen.

Wisdom and Understanding
April 8

When wisdom enters your heart,
and knowledge is pleasant to your soul,
discretion will preserve you;
understanding will keep you,
to deliver you from the way of evil,
from the man/woman who speaks perverse things,
from those who leave the paths of
uprightness to walk in the ways of
darkness;
—Proverbs 2:10–13 NKJV

So you may walk in the way of
goodness, and keep to the paths of
righteousness.
—Proverbs 2:20 NKJV

Praise the Lord, all you gentiles!
Laud Him, all you peoples!
For His merciful kindness is great
toward us, and the truth of the
Lord endures forever.
—Psalm 117 NKJV

Amen.
("Amen" means "It is so" or "Let it be so.")

Wisdom and Understanding
April 9

Therefore, as the elect of God, holy
and beloved, put on tender mercies,
kindness, humility, meekness, longsuffering;
bearing with one another,
and forgiving one another, if anyone has
a complaint against another; even
as Christ forgave you, so you
also must do.
But above all these things put on
love, which is the bond of perfection. And let the peace of God rule in
your
hearts, to which also you were called in one body;
and be
THANKFUL
—Colossians 3:12–15 NKJV

Father, we thank You for Your word, Your teachings, Your guidance. We know You are calling us to be wiser, to be better in a bad situation, to be the one to pursue peace, to be the one to teach by example, and to be the one to represent You. Remind us how to do so each time we face a challenge. Show us how to be angry but not to sin in that anger, send us Your Holy Spirit to intercede for us in every situation and let us remember to be thankful. In Jesus's name, we pray. Amen.

Wisdom and Understanding
April 10

*Therefore we were buried with Him
through baptism into death,
that just as Christ was raised from the dead
by the glory of the Father,
even so we also should walk in
newness of life.
For if we have been united together
in the likeness of His death, certainly
we also shall be in the likeness of
His Resurrection,
Knowing this, that our old man was
crucified with
Him,
that the body of sin might be done
away with, that we should no longer be slaves of sin.
—Romans 6:4–6 NKJV*

*I have been crucified with Christ:
it is no longer I who live,
but Christ lives in me; and the life
which I now live in the flesh I live
by faith in the Son of God,
who loved me and gave Himself for me.
—Galatians 2:20 NKJV*

Father God, I thank You for sending Your Son to die on the cross in my place. Jesus, we thank You for accepting that horrible death in our place. I can brag that my old person died with You on that cross, and yet I did not suffer that death on a cross with nails piercing my feet and hands and a cruel crown of thorns and anguish, and how great Thou art! How great You are. My redemption came just with my confession and my acceptance of Your only begotten Son. What a merciful God You are! I pray for my entire community and family that they will all hunger for You and accept You. Thank You, God. In the name of Jesus. Amen!

Wisdom and Understanding
April 11

Wisdom and Understanding, Easter Season

*But Christ came as High Priest of the
good things to come, with the greater and more
perfect tabernacle not made with hands,
that is, not of this creation.
Not with the blood of goats and calves,
but with HIS OWN BLOOD HE entered the Most
Holy Place once for all, having obtained
eternal redemption.
For if the blood of bulls and goats and
the ashes of a heifer, sprinkling the unclean,
sanctifies for the purifying of the flesh,
how much more shall the BLOOD OF CHRIST,
who through the eternal Spirit
offered Himself without spot to GOD,
cleanse your conscience from dead works
to serve the living God?
And for this reason He is the mediator of the
new covenant, by means of death,
for the redemption of the transgressions
under the first covenant, that those who
are called may receive the promise of the
eternal inheritance.
For where there is a testament there must also
of necessity be the death of the testator.
For a testament is in force after men are dead,
since it has no power at all
while the testator lives.
—Hebrews 9:11–17 NKJV*

The English dictionary describing the word testament: (law) a solemn, authentic instrument in writing by which a person declares his or her will as to disposal of his or her estate and effects after his or her death. Note: This is otherwise called a will and sometimes a last will and testament. A testament, to be valid, must be made by a person of sound mind, and it must be executed and published in due form of law. A man or woman, in certain cases, may make a valid will by word of mouth only. See nuncupative will under nuncupative. One of the two distinct revelations of God's purposes toward man; a covenant; also, one of the two general divisions of the canonical books of

the sacred scriptures in which the covenants are respectively revealed; as the Old Testament; the New Testament; often limited, in colloquial language, to the latter. He is the mediator of the New Testament for the redemption of the transgressions that were under the Old Testament. Only a God that loves me, loves you, loves us individually and specially would leave such a testament for us. Thank God for the blood of Jesus.

Wisdom and Understanding
April 12

For it is better, if it is the will of God,
to suffer for doing good than for doing evil.
For Christ also suffered once for sins,
the just for the unjust, that He
might bring us to God, being put
to death in the flesh but made alive by the Spirit,
by whom also He went and preached to the
Spirits in prison, who formerly were
disobedient, when once the Divine
longsuffering waited in the days
of Noah, while the ark was being prepared,
in which a few, that is eight souls, were
saved through water.
There is also an antitype which now saves us
—baptism (not the removal of
the filth of the flesh, but the answer of a
good conscience toward God), through the
Resurrection of Jesus Christ,
who has gone into heaven and is
at the right hand of God, angels and
authorities and powers having been made
subject to Him.
—1 Peter 3:17–21 NKJV

He arose, He arose, Hallelujah. Christ arose. He has the victory.
We have the victory because of Him. Thank You, Jesus!

Wisdom and Understanding
April 13

Whoever believes that Jesus is the
Christ is born of God, and
everyone who loves Him who begot
also loves him who is begotten of Him.
By this we know that we love the children
of God, when we love God and
Keep His commandments.
For this is the love of God, that we
keep His commandments. And His
commandments are not burdensome.
For whatever is born of
God
overcomes the world. And this is the
Victory
that has overcome the world—our faith.
—1 John 5:1–4 NKJV

Our Father in Heaven, we thank You again for the victory that You have honored Your Son Jesus with, the victory of overcoming death. So as we are victorious because of Him, teach us to love one another because we are all Your children. Thank You for Easter, for the ultimate resurrection, Jesus's resurrection, and for our daily resurrection from the difficulties of life until You resurrect us from death with a new body. In Christ Jesus. Amen.

Wisdom and Understanding
April 14

Snippets of Wisdom and Understanding

Ears that hear and eyes that see—
we get our basic equipment from God!
Don't be too fond of sleep; you'll end
up in the poorhouse. Wake up and
get up; then there'll be food on the table.
The shopper says, "That's junk—I'll take it off
your hands," then goes off boasting of the bargain.
Drinking from the beautiful chalice of
knowledge is better than adorning
oneself with gold and rare gems.
hold tight to collateral on any loan to a stranger;
beware of accepting what a transient has pawned.
Stolen bread tastes sweet,
but soon your mouth is full of gravel.
Form your purpose by asking for counsel,
then carry it out using all the help you can get.
Gossips can't keep secrets,
so never confide in blabbermouths.
Anyone who curses father and mother
extinguishes light and exists benighted.
—Proverbs 20:12–20 The Message/Remix Version

Wisdom and Understanding
April 15

Snippets of Wisdom and Understanding

*Better to live alone in a tumbledown shack
than share a mansion with a nagging spouse.*

*Wicked souls love to make trouble;
they feel nothing for friends and neighbors.*

*Simpletons only learn the hard way,
but the wise learn by listening.*

*A God-loyal person will see right through
the wicked and undo the evil they've planned.*

*If you stop your ears to the cries of the poor,
your cries will go unheard, unanswered.*

*A quietly given gift soothes an irritable person,
a heartfelt present cools a hot temper.
—Proverbs 21:9–14 MSG*

*Wise men and women are always learning,
always listening for fresh insights.*

*A gift gets attention;
it buys the attention of eminent people.*

*The first speech in a court case is always
convincing—until the cross-examination starts!*

*You may have to draw straws
when faced with a tough decision.*

Do a favor and win a friend forever,
nothing can untie that bond.

Words satisfy the mind as much as fruit
does the stomach;
good talk is as gratifying as a good harvest.
—Proverbs 18:15–20 MSG

Wisdom and Understanding
April 16

No one has seen God at any time. If we
love one another, God abides in us,
and His love has been perfected in us.
By this we know that we abide in Him,
and He in us, because He has given
us of His Spirit. And we have seen and
testify that the Father has sent the Son
as Savior of the world.
Whoever confesses that Jesus is the
Son of God, God abides in him,
and he in God.
And we have known and believed
the love that God has for us. God is love,
and he who abides in love abides in God,
and God in him.
Love has been perfected among us
in this; that we may have boldness in the
day of judgment; because as He is, so
are we in this world.
There is no fear in love; but perfect
love casts out fear, because fear
involves torment. But he who fears has
not been made perfect in love.
We love Him because He first loved us.
—1 John 4:12–19 NIV

Father God, we need more of Your Spirit. No, we have Your Spirit. We just need to own it and acknowledge it. We need to understand that we must be bold in Your name. Give us the audacity to speak up for You, to chastise one another in love for You, to encourage each one in love for You, to make this world a better place even if just in our circles of interacting with others. Help us to represent You in deed and in truth. In Jesus's name. Amen!

Wisdom and Understanding
April 17

*Grace to you and peace from God our
Father and the Lord Jesus Christ.
Blessed be the God and Father of our
Lord Jesus Christ, who has blessed us
with every spiritual blessing in the
heavenly places in Christ, just as He chose us
in Him before the foundation of the world,
that we should be holy and without blame
before Him in love,
having predestined us to adoption as sons
by Jesus Christ to Himself, according
to the good pleasure of His will,
to the praise of the glory of His
grace, by which He made us accepted
in the Beloved.
In Him we have redemption through His
blood, the forgiveness of sins, according
to the riches of His grace which
He made to abound toward us in
all wisdom and prudence, having made
known to us the mystery of His will, according
to His good pleasure which He purposed in
Himself, that in the dispensation of the fullness of
the times He might gather together in one all things
in Christ, both which are on earth-in Him.
—Ephesians 1:2–10 NASB*

When I think of my Savior and His love for me, how my redemption was obtained through His sacrifice, how He cancelled all my debt of iniquity, how He forgives me daily and loves me again and again, how I am invited to the table to enjoy His grace and mercy, I feel special. I know I am special. Lord, help me to stay in the path of righteousness for Your name's sake. Amen.

Wisdom and Understanding
April 18

I will love You, O Lord, my strength.
The Lord is my rock and my fortress
and my deliverer;
My God, my strength, in whom I will
trust; My shield and the horn of my
salvation, my stronghold.
I will call upon the Lord, who is
worthy to be praised; So shall
I be saved from my enemies.
The pangs of death surrounded me,
and the floods of ungodliness
made me afraid.
The sorrows of Sheol surrounded me;
in my distress I called upon the
Lord,
and cried out to my
God;
He heard my voice from His temple,
and my cry came before Him,
even to His ears.
—Psalm 18:1–6 NKJV

Behold, bless the Lord, all you servants of the Lord,
who by night stand in the house of the Lord!
Lift up your hands in the sanctuary,
and bless the Lord.
The Lord who made heaven and earth
bless you from Zion!
—Psalm 134 NKJV

Wisdom and Understanding
April 19

(Sorry it's so long today.) Hear the Word of God

The Ark
And the Lord spoke to Moses, saying;
—Exodus 25:1

"And they shall make an ark of acacia wood;
two and a half cubits shall be its length,
a cubit and a half its width, and a cubit and a
half its height. And you shall overlay it with
pure gold, inside and out you shall overlay it,
and shall make on it a molding of gold all around.
you shall cast four rings of gold for it, and
put them in its four corners; two rings shall be on
one side, and two rings on the other side.
And you shall make poles of acacia wood, and overlay
them with gold. You shall put the poles into the
rings on the sides of the ark, that the ark may be
carried by them. The piles shall be in the
rings of the ark; they shall not be taken from it.
And you shall put into the ark the Testimony which
I will give you. You shall make a MERCY SEAT of
pure gold; two and a half cubits shall be its
length and a cubit and a half its width.
And you shall make two cherubim of gold; of
hammered work you shall make them at the two
ends of the mercy seat. Make one cherub at one end,
and the other cherub at the other end; you shall make
the cherubim at the two ends of it of
one piece with the mercy seat. You shall put the mercy seat
on top of the ark, and in the ark you
shall put the Testimony that I will give you.
And there I will meet with you, and I will
speak with you from above the mercy seat,

from between the two cherubim which are
on the ark of the Testimony, about everything
which I will give you in commandment to the
children of Israel."
—Exodus 25:10–22 NIV

Then God went on to elaborate in incredible detail how Moses and the people should make the table, the lampstand, the tabernacle, the altar, the courtyard, the vestments, the ephod, the breastpiece, the robe, the turban, tunic, and underwear. God was so specific and detailed. It seems to me as though He was "micromanaging." He wanted these things done just right, so He told Moses how to get it right in detail. Read it and see how God teaches. Father, teach us as leaders, as parents, and as guardians to be specific, detailed, and clear as we lead Your people, Your/our children, and our subordinates. If we don't talk clearly about sex, about crime, about life, about good and bad, and about how we want things done in Your name, then how can we expect things to be done correctly? Lord, teach us to "micromanage" if we have to until it is understood how things should be done. Help us to dare to walk the road less traveled to lay it all on the line for You because You will pave the way for us. In Jesus's name, we pray. Amen!

Wisdom and Understanding
April 20

My son/daughter, do not forget my law,
but let your heart keep my commands;
For length of days and long life and peace
they will add to you. Let not mercy and truth
forsake you; bind them around your neck,
write them on the tablet of your heart,
and so find favor and high esteem in the sight
of God and man. Trust in the Lord
with all your heart, and lean not on your
own understanding; In all your
ways acknowledge Him, and He shall direct your
paths. Do not be wise in your own eyes;
fear the Lord and depart from evil.
It will be health to your flesh, and
strength to your bones.
—Proverbs 3:1–8 NKJV

Praise the Lord!
I will praise the Lord with my whole heart,
In the assembly of the upright and
in the congregation. The works of the Lord
are great, studied by all who have pleasure in them.
His work is honorable and glorious,
and His righteousness endures forever.
—Psalm 111:1–3 KJV

Wisdom and Understanding
April 21

Prayer and Supplication

*"The Spirit of the Lord God is upon Me, because the
Lord has anointed Me to preach good tidings to the poor;
He has sent Me to heal the brokenhearted, to proclaim liberty
to the captives, and the opening of the prison to those who
are bound; to proclaim the acceptable year of the Lord, and
the day of vengeance of our God; to comfort all who mourn, to console
those who mourn in Zion, to give them beauty for ashes,
the oil of joy for mourning, the garment of praise for the spirit of
heaviness; that they may be called trees of righteousness.
The planting of the Lord, that He may be glorified." And they shall
rebuild the old ruins, they shall raise up the former desolation,
and they shall repair the ruined cities, the desolation of many
generations. Strangers shall stand and feed your flocks, and the sons
of the foreigner shall be your plowmen and your vine dressers. But
you shall be named the priests of the Lord, they shall call you the
servants of our God. You shall eat the riches
of the Gentiles, and in their
glory you shall boast. Instead of your shame you shall have double
honor, and instead of confusion they shall rejoice in their portion.
Therefore in their land they shall possess double;
Everlasting joy shall be theirs.
—Isaiah 61:1–7 NKJV*

*Save me, O God!
For the waters have come up to my neck.
I sink in deep mire, where there is no standing;
I have come into deep waters, where the floods
overflow me. I am weary with my crying; my throat is dry;
my eyes fail while I wait for my God. Those who hate me
without a cause are more than the hairs of my head;
they are mighty who would destroy me, being my enemies
wrongfully; though I have stolen nothing, I still must restore it.*

O God, You know my foolishness; and my sins are not hidden from
You. Let not those who wait for You, O Lord God of hosts,
be ashamed because of me; let not those who seek you be
confounded because of me, O God of Israel.
—Psalm 69:1–6 NKJV

It's good to cry out to the Lord. Who else will have pity on me? It is good to go to God in prayer and tell Him all our concerns and our needs. God hears, and He cares, and in due time, He will send help to those who trust Him and wait on Him. Thank You, Father, for You take good care of us, your children. Amen.

Wisdom and Understanding
April 22

Honor the Lord with your possessions,
and with the firstfruits of all your increase;
So your barns will be filled with plenty,
and your vats will overflow with new wine.
My son, do not despise the chastening of the Lord,
nor detest His correction;
for whom the Lord loves He corrects,
just as a father the son in whom he
delights. Happy is the man/woman who
finds wisdom, and the woman/man who gains
understanding; for her proceeds are
better than the profits of silver,
she is more precious than rubies,
and all the things you may desire
cannot compare with her.
Length of days is in her right hand,
in her left hand riches and honor. Her
ways are ways of pleasantness,
and all her paths are peace.
She is a tree of life to those who
take hold of her, and happy are all
who retain her.
The Lord by wisdom founded the earth;
by understanding He established the heavens;
by His knowledge the depths were broken up,
and clouds drop down the dew.
—Proverbs 3:9–20 NKJV
Praise, O servants of the Lord,
praise the name of the Lord!
Blessed be the name of the Lord
from this time forth and forevermore!
From the rising of the sun to
its going down
The Lord's name is to be praised.
—Psalm 113:1–3 NKJV

Wisdom and Understanding
April 23

Things That Make You Go *Hhhhmmmmm*

*Dishonest scales are an abomination to
the Lord, but a just weight is His delight.*

When pride comes, then comes shame: but with the humble is wisdom.

*The integrity of the upright will guide them,
but the perversity of the unfaithful
will destroy them.*

*Riches do not profit in the day of wrath,
but righteousness delivers from death.*

*The righteousness of the blameless
will direct his way aright,
but the wicked will fall by his own
wickedness.*

*The righteousness of the upright will
deliver them, but the unfaithful
will be caught by their lust.*
—Proverbs 11:1–6 KJV

*Let God arise, let His enemies be scattered;
let those also who hate Him flee before Him.
As smoke is driven away, so drive them away;
as wax melts before the fire,
so let the wicked perish at the presence of God.*

*But let the righteous be glad; let them rejoice
before God; Yes, let them rejoice
exceedingly. Sing to God, sing praises to His
name; extol Him who rides on the clouds,
by His name YAH, and rejoice before Him.*
—Psalm 68:1–4 NKJV

Wisdom and Understanding
April 24

To everything there is a season,
a time for every purpose under heaven:
A time to be born, and a time to die;
a time to plant, and a time to pluck what is planted;
a time to kill, and a time to heal;
a time to break down, and a time to build up
a time to weep and a time to laugh,
a time to mourn, and a time to dance;
a time to cast away stones,
and a time to gather stones;
a time to embrace, and a time to refrain
from embracing; a time to gain, and a time to lose;
a time to keep and a time to throw away;
a time to tear, and a time to sew;
a time to keep silence, and a time to speak;
a time to love, and a time to hate;
a time of war, and a time of peace.
What profit has the worker from that in which
he labors? I have seen the God-given task with which the
sons of men are to be occupied. He has made everything
beautiful in its time. Also He has put eternity in their hearts, except
that no one can find out the work that God does
from beginning to end.
I know that nothing is better for them
than to rejoice, and to do good in their lives,
and also that every man should eat and
drink and enjoy the good of all his labor-it
is the gift of God.
—Ecclesiastes 3:1–13 KJV

Amen!

Wisdom and Understanding
April 25

Things That Make You Go *Hhhhmmmmm*

Vanity of vanities, says the preacher; vanity
of vanities, all is vanity.
What profit has a man/woman from all his/her labor
in which he/she toils under the sun?
One generation passes away, and another
generation comes; but the earth abides
forever. The sun also rises,
and the sun goes down, and hastens to the
place where it arose. The wind goes toward
the south, and turns around to the north;
the wind whirls about continually,
and comes again on its circuit.
All the rivers run into the sea,
yet the sea is not full; to the place from
which the rivers come, there they return again.
All things are full of labor;
man cannot express it.
The eye is not satisfied with seeing,
nor the ear filled with hearing.
That which has been is what will be,
that which is done is what will be done,
and there is nothing new under the sun.
—Ecclesiastes 1:2–9

Praise the Lord!
praise the Lord from the heavens;
praise Him in the heights!
Praise Him, all His angels;
Praise Him, all His hosts!
Praise Him, sun and moon;
Praise Him, all you stars of light!
Praise Him, you heavens of heavens,

and you waters above the heavens!
Let them praise the name of the Lord,
for he commanded and they were created.
—Psalm 148:1–5 NKJV

Amen!

Wisdom and Understanding
April 26

In you, O Lord, I put my trust;
let me never be put to shame. Deliver me
in Your righteousness, and cause me
to escape; incline Your ear to me, and save me.
Be my strong refuge, to which I may
resort continually; You have given the
commandment to save me, for You are my
rock and my fortress. Deliver me,
O my God, out of the hand of the wicked,
out of the hand of the unrighteous and
cruel man/woman. For you are
my hope, O Lord God; You are my trust
from my youth. By You I have been upheld
from birth; You are He who took me
out of my mother's womb.
My praise shall be continually of You.
I have become as a wonder to many,
but You are my strong refuge. Let my
mouth be filled with Your praise and with
Your glory all the day.
Do not cast me off in the time of old age;
Do not forsake me when my strength fails.
—Psalm 71:1–9 NKJV

Make a joyful shout to God, all
the earth!
Sing out the honor of His name;
make His praise glorious. Say to God,
"How awesome are Your works!"
Through the greatness of Your power
Your enemies shall submit themselves to You.
—Psalm 66:1–3 NKJV

Wisdom and Understanding
April 27

*Therefore if there is any consolation
in Christ, if any comfort of love, if any
fellowship of the Spirit, if any affection and mercy,
fulfill my joy by being like-minded,
having the same love, being of one accord,
of one mind. Let nothing be done through selfish
ambition or conceit, but in lowliness of
mind let each esteem others better than himself.
Let each of you look out not only for his own interests,
but also for the interest of others. Let
this mind be in you which was also
in Christ Jesus, who, being in the form of God,
did not consider it robbery to be equal with God,
but made Himself of no reputation, taking
the form of a bondservant, and coming in the
likeness of men. And being found in
appearance as a man, He humbled Himself
and became obedient to the point of death,
even the death of the cross.
Therefore God also has highly exalted Him
and given Him the name which is
above every name, that at the name of Jesus
every knee should bow, of those in heaven, and of
those on earth, and of those under the earth,
and that every tongue should confess that
Jesus Christ is Lord, to the
glory of God the Father.
—Philippians 2:1–11 KJV*

Oh! That we should be more like Jesus. Father, we praise You and thank You for Your favor toward us, Your loving kindness, grace, and mercy. We want to hear Your word and adhere to it. I pray we love one another more and more as You love us with such a great sacrifice. Jesus Christ, thank You, we say thank You. In Jesus's name. Amen.

Wisdom and Understanding
April 28

(Have you ever heard this said?)
Children, obey your parents in the Lord,
for this is right. "Honor your father and mother,"
which is the first commandment with promise:
"that it may be well with you and you may
live long on the earth."
—Ephesians 6:1–3 NKJV

(But did you know it also says)
And you, fathers (and mothers) do not
provoke your children to wrath, but
bring them up in the training and
admonition of the Lord.
—Ephesians 6:4 NKJV

Peace to the brethren, and love with faith,
from God the Father and the Lord
Jesus Christ.
—Ephesians 6:23 NKJV

God be merciful to us and bless us,
and cause His face to shine upon us,
That Your way may be known on earth,
Your salvation among all nations.
Let the peoples praise You, O God;
let all the peoples praise You.
—Psalm 67:1–3 NKJV

Amen.

Wisdom and Understanding
April 29

Things That Make You Go *Hhhhmmmmm*

*It is honorable for a man/woman to
stop striving, since any fool
can start a quarrel.*

*The lazy woman/man will not plow because of winter;
He/she will beg during harvest and have nothing.*

*Counsel in the heart of woman/man is like deep water, but a woman/
man of understanding will draw it out.*

*Most women/men will proclaim each his
own goodness, but who
can find a faithful woman/man?*

*The righteous woman/man walks in his integrity;
His/her children are blessed after him/her.*

*A king who sits on the throne of judgment
scatters all evil with his eyes.*

*Who can say, "I have made my
heart clean, I am pure from my sin"?
—Proverbs 20:3–9 NKJV*

*Come and see the works of God;
He is awesome in His doing toward the
sons of men. He turned the sea into dry land;
they went through the river on foot.
There we will rejoice in Him.
—Psalm 66:5–6 NKJV*

Wisdom and Understanding
April 30

Things That Make You Go *Hhhhmmmmm*

God delights in concealing things;
scientists delight in discovering things.

Like the horizons for breadth and the ocean for depth,
the understanding of a good leader is broad and deep.

Remove impurities from the silver
and the silversmith can craft a fine chalice;
remove the wicked from leadership
and authority will be credible and God-honoring.

Don't work yourself into the spotlight;
don't push your way into the place of prominence.
It's better to be promoted to a place of honor
than face humiliation by being demoted.

Don't jump to conclusions—there may be
a perfectly good explanation for what you just saw.

In the heat of an argument,
don't betray confidences;
word is sure to get around, and
no one will trust you.

The right word at the right time
is like a custom-made piece of jewelry,
and a wise friend's timely reprimand
is like a gold ring slipped on your finger.
Reliable friends who do what they say
are like cool drinks in sweltering heat-refreshing!

Like billowing clouds that bring no rain
is the person who talks big but never produces.

Patient persistence pierces through indifference;
gentle speech breaks down rigid defenses.
—*Proverbs 25 2-15 The Message/Remix Version*

Silence is praise to you,
Zion-dwelling God,
and also obedience.
You hear the prayer in it all.
—*Psalm 65:1-2 The Message/Remix Version*

As you are growing up from a child into adolescence and into adulthood, many times in this progression, you will come to a point where you have to take stock on your life and choose what kind of person you want to grow into. Oftentimes you will face choices, the right but hard choices, the right but difficult roads, versus the wrong, exciting-for-now, easy road. What you need to know is that difficult and unpleasant times are going to come, no matter what road you choose, so it is better to choose the right, unpleasant, but correct road now so that tomorrow you will benefit from the discipline you practiced today. You see, doing things the right way, making the right choice, is not always easy. It takes discipline, wisdom, understanding. It takes a heart that wants to do good and the sense to make yourself stick to what's right, no matter what others do or say or how you look by doing the right thing. The benefits will come tomorrow after you honed yourself, after sharpened your control over self, after you studied, after you endured the time it takes for you to grow strong and wise, after you suffered loneliness for doing the right thing, after you allowed life to teach you great lessons that will guide you to make better choices so you can have better and happier outcomes. Make the right choice. Only you can make that decision that's needed to shape your life into a person of great character, honor, discipline, and into a winner—a winner in everything you do, a positive and well-rounded human being. Praise God!

Wisdom and Understanding
May 1

And be renewed in the spirit of your mind,
and that you put on the new man
which was created according to God,
in true righteousness and holiness.
Therefore, putting away lying, "let each one of you
speak truth with his neighbor," for we are members of
one another. "Be angry, and do not sin."
Do not let the sun go down on your wrath,
nor give place to the devil.
Let him who stole steal no longer, but
rather let him labor, working with his hands
what is good, that he may have something
to give him who has need.
Let no corrupt word proceed out of your
mouth, but what is good for necessary edification,
that it may impart grace to the hearers.
And do not grieve the Holy Spirit of God,
by whom you were sealed for the day of redemption.
Let all bitterness, wrath, anger, clamor, and evil
speaking be put away from you, with all malice.
And be kind to one another, tender-hearted,
forgiving one another, even as God in Christ forgave you.
—Ephesians 4:23–32 NKJV

Father God, I thank You for my brothers and my sisters, I mean, even those from another mother and father, since we are all brothers and sisters in Christ Jesus. Teach me how to see with Your eyes and act with Your spirit, and when my brother offends me or my sister disrespects me, help me to remember Your statutes and bring me back to the place where I can forgive, even as I hide behind the cross. Help me to emerge strong and loving still, and maybe those who offend me may learn and do better by seeing my strength in You. In Jesus's name, I pray. Amen.

Wisdom and Understanding
May 2

*And we urge you, brethren, to recognize
those who labor among you, and are over you
in the Lord and admonish you, and to esteem them
very highly in love for their work's sake.
Be at peace among yourselves.
Now we exhort you, brethren, warn those
who are unruly, comfort the fainthearted, uphold
the weak, be patient with all. See that no one
renders evil for evil to anyone, but always
pursue what is good both for yourselves and for all.
Rejoice always,
pray without ceasing,
in everything give thanks; for this is
the will of God in Christ Jesus for you.
Do not quench the Spirit.
Do not despise prophecies.
Test all things; hold fast what is good.
abstain from every form of evil.
Now may the God of peace Himself sanctify you completely,
and may your whole spirit, soul, and body be preserved
blameless at the coming of our
Lord Jesus Christ.
He who calls you is faithful, who also will do it.*
—1 Thessalonians 5:12–24 NKJV

*Oh, sing to the Lord a new song!
For He has done marvelous things;
His right hand and His holy arm have
gained Him the victory. The Lord has
made known His salvation; His righteousness He
has revealed in the sight of the nations.*
—Psalm 98:1–2 NKJV

Wisdom and Understanding
May 3

*In the beginning God created the
heavens and the earth.
The earth was without form, and
void; and darkness was on the face of the deep.
And the Spirit of God was hovering over the
face of the waters.
Then God said,
"Let there be light"; and there was light.
And God saw the light, that it was good;
and God divided the light from the darkness.
God called the light Day, and the darkness
He called Night. So the evening and
the morning were the first day.
—Genesis 1:1–5 NKJV*

*Then the word of the Lord came to me, saying;
"Before I formed you in the womb I knew you;
Before you were born I sanctified you;
I ordained you a prophet to the nations.
Then said I: "Ah, Lord God!
Behold, I cannot speak, for I am a youth."
But the Lord said to me: "Do not say,
'I am a youth,' For you shall go to all to whom I
send you, and whatever I command you, you
shall speak.
Do not be afraid of their faces.
For I am with you to deliver you," says the Lord.
—Jeremiah 1:4–8 NKJV*

Father, we thank You because You know the secrets of our hearts. You
made us, You love us, and You know us. Teach us how to love You back.
In Jesus's name, we pray. Amen.

Wisdom and Understanding
May 4

*Now faith is the substance of things
hoped for, the evidence of things not seen.
For by it the elders obtained a good testimony.
By faith we understand that the worlds were
framed by the word of God, so that the things which
are seen were not made of things which are visible.
—Hebrews 11:1–3 NKJV*

*By faith Noah, being divinely warned
of things not yet seen, moved with godly fear,
prepared an ark for the saving of his
household, by which he condemned the world and
became heir of the righteousness which is
according to faith.
—Hebrews 11:7 NKJV*

*By faith Sarah herself also received strength to conceive seed,
and she bore a child when she was past the age,
because she judged Him faithful who had promised.
—Hebrews 11:11 NKJV*

*Therefore we also, since we are surrounded
by so great a cloud of witnesses, let us lay aside
every weight, and the sin which so easily ensnares us,
and let us run with endurance the race
that is set before us, looking unto Jesus, the
author and finisher of our faith, who for the joy that was
set before Him endured the cross, despising the shame,
and has sat down at the right hand of the throne of
God.
—Hebrews 12:1–2 NKJV*

Father God, we ask You to breathe Your Spirit in us so that our faith
may be great, so that we may apply faith when we cannot see yet the

things that we hope for; faith when we feel weak, faith when our hearts are breaking, faith that I will find a job, a career; faith that my children will do the right thing after having been taught the right thing; faith that I will be able to pay my bills even as I pay my tithes; faith in You, Lord God, that You will fix it all as I do my best to do the right thing. In Jesus's name, I pray. Amen.

Wisdom and Understanding
May 5

*Let brotherly love continue
Do not forget to entertain strangers, for
by so doing some have unwittingly
entertained angels.*

*Remember the prisoners as if
chained with them—those who are
mistreated—since you yourselves are in the body also.*

*Marriage is honorable among all,
and the bed undefiled; but fornicators
and adulterers God will judge.*

*Let your conduct be without covetousness;
be content with such things as you have.
For He Himself has said, "I will never
leave you nor forsake you."
So we may boldly say;
"The Lord is my helper;
I will not fear.
What can man do to me?"*

*Remember those who rule over you,
who have spoken the word of God to you,
whose faith follow, considering the
outcome of their conduct.*

*Jesus Christ is the same yesterday,
today,
and forever.
—Hebrews 13:1–8 NKJV*

Praise the Lord, O my soul!
While I live I will praise the Lord;
I will sing praises to my God while I have my being.
—Psalm 146:1–2 NKJV

Wisdom and Understanding
May 6

Deal bountifully with Your servant,
that I may live and keep Your word.
Open my eyes, that I may see wondrous
things from Your law.
I am a stranger in the earth; do not hide
Your commandments from me, my soul
breaks with longing for Your
judgments at all times.
You rebuke the proud—the cursed,
who stray from Your commandments.
Remove from me reproach and
contempt, for I have kept Your
testimonies.
Princes also sit and speak against me,
but your servant meditates on Your statutes.
Your testimonies also are my delight
and my counselors.
My soul clings to the dust;
Revive me according to Your word.
I have declared my ways, and You answered me;
Teach me Your statutes.
Make me understand the way of
your precepts; so shall I meditate
on Your wonderful works.
My soul melts from heaviness; Strengthen me
according to Your word.
Remove from me the way of lying,
and grant me Your law graciously.
—Psalm 119:17-29

Lord, I just want to be "in" with You. I just want to walk the right way with You. I just want do the right thing by You because if I please You, Lord, I know I will be right by my fellow man. Thank You for all Your blessings. I humble myself, and I say thank you. In Jesus's name. Amen.

This is a prayer asking God to bless me with plenty, make me comfortable and happy with the things I need and with some of the things I want, so that I may be able to keep His word. Let me see Your miracles and great things from You, O Lord, my God. I need your guidance and your teachings so I can be the best me possible. Let me understand your ways and your laws so I can grow and be useful on this earth. Teach me what you want from me, how you want me to live. Pray to God. Whatever is on your mind, you can tell Him, ask him. If it's good and honorable, you will see it come about at the right and ripe time. It may not happen until you are really ready. God knows when. All that matters is that it's honest and prayed for in earnest.

Wisdom and Understanding
May 7

Give ear to my words, O Lord,
consider my meditation.
Give heed to the voice of my cry,
My King and my God, for to You I will pray.
My voice You shall hear in the morning,
O Lord;
In the morning I will direct it to You,
and I will look up.
For You are not a God who takes
pleasure in wickedness,
Nor shall evil dwell with You.
—Psalm 5:1-4

But You, O Lord, are a shield for me,
my glory and the One who lifts up my head.
I cried to the Lord with my voice,
and He heard me from His holy hill.
I lay down and slept; I awoke, for the Lord
sustained me.
—Psalm 3:3-5

Hear me when I call, O God of my righteousness!
You have relieved me in my distress;
Have mercy on me, and hear my prayer.
—Psalm 4:1

Amen!

Wisdom and Understanding
May 8

Don't envy bad people;
don't even want to be around them.
All they think about is causing a disturbance;
all they talk about is making trouble.

It takes wisdom to build a house,
and understanding to set it on a firm foundation;
It takes knowledge to furnish its rooms
with fine furniture and beautiful draperies.

It's better to be wise than Strong;
intelligence outranks muscle any day.

Strategic planning is the key to warfare;
to win, you need a lot of good counsel.

Wise conversation is way over the head of fools;
in a serious discussion they haven't a clue.

The person who's always cooking up some evil
soon gets a reputation as prince of rogues.
Fools incubate sin;
cynics desecrate beauty.

If you fall to pieces in a crisis,
there wasn't much to you in the first place.

Rescue the perishing;
don't hesitate to step in and help.
If you say, "Hey, that's none of my business,"
will that get you off the hook?
Someone is watching you closely, you know—
Someone not impressed with weak excuses.
—Proverbs 24:1–12 The Message/Remix Version

I will bless the Lord at all times;
His praise shall continually be in my mouth.
My soul shall make its boasts in the Lord;
The humble shall hear of it and be glad
O magnify the Lord with me,
and let us exalt His name together.
—Psalm 34:1–3

Wisdom and Understanding
May 9

A man/woman who wanders from the way
of understanding
will rest in the assembly of the dead.

He who loves pleasure will be a poor woman/man;
He who loves wine and oil will not be rich.
The wicked shall be a ransom for
the righteous, and the unfaithful for the upright.

Better to dwell in the wilderness,
than with a contentious and angry woman/man.

There is desirable treasure,
and oil in the dwelling of the wise,
but a foolish man/woman squanders it.

He/she who follows righteousness and mercy
finds life, righteousness, and honor.

A wise man/woman scales the city of the might,
and brings down the trusted stronghold.

Whoever guards his/her mouth and tongue
keeps his soul from troubles.

A proud and haughty woman/man—"Scoffer" is his/her name;
He acts with arrogant pride.

The desire of the lazy man kills him,
for his hands refuse to labor.
He covets greedily all day long,
but the righteous gives and does not spare.
—Proverbs 21:16–26

Father God, please give us clear understanding of Your word. Guide us as we study and discover the deep mysteries, rich with wisdom and understanding in Your word. We want to live a righteous life, so teach us to seek out Your direction and Your guidance. In Jesus's name, we pray. Amen.

Wisdom and Understanding
May 10

Dare any of you, having a matter
against another, go to law before the
unrighteous, and not before the saints?
Do you not know that the saints will
judge the world? And if the world will
be judged by you, are you unworthy to judge
the smallest matters?
Do you not know that we shall judge
angels? How much more, things that
pertain to this life?
If then you have judgments concerning things
pertaining to this life, do you appoint those who
are least esteemed by the church to judge?
I say this to your shame. Is it so, that there is
not a wise man/woman among you, not
even one, who will be able to judge between his
brethren? But brother goes to law against brother,
and that before unbelievers!
—1 Corinthians 6:1–6

It's amazing how this old book, this ancient book, this wisdom book written so, so long ago still has the rules and regulations for living a right life with God and with one another today. It is up to us to adhere to the Word of God. Whether we are Christians or not, we have no excuse for not knowing right from wrong, even in intense situations. The answers are in the word/the book, the Bible. Thank You, Lord, for not leaving us without a daily guide. In Jesus's name. Amen.

Wisdom and Understanding
May 11

*What shall we say then? Shall we
continue in sin that grace may abound?
Certainly not! How shall we who died to sin
live any longer in it? Or do you not
know that as many of us as were baptized into
Christ Jesus were baptized into His death?
Therefore we were buried with Him
through baptism into death, that just as
Christ was raised from the dead by the glory of
the Father, even so we also should
walk in newness of life.
For if we have been united together in the
likeness of His death, certainly we also shall
be in the likeness of His resurrection.
—Romans 6:1–5*

*It is good to give thanks to the Lord,
and to sing praises to Your name,
O Most High;
To declare Your loving-kindness in the morning,
and Your faithfulness every night, on an
instrument of ten strings, on the lute, and on the
harp, with harmonious sound.
—Psalm 92:13*

Father, we thank You for renewing our hope each day. We praise You for Your Son, who was sacrificed so that we did not have to suffer forever. You are an awesome God. There is none like You, none who loved so amazingly. Thank you, Lord. In the name of Jesus, Your Son. Amen.

Wisdom and Understanding
May 12

Strength and honor are her clothing;
she shall rejoice in time to come.
She opens her mouth with wisdom,
and on her tongue is the law of kindness.
She watches over the ways of her household,
and does not eat the bread of idleness.
Her children rise up and call her blessed;
her husband also, and he praises her:
"Many daughters have done well,
but you excel them all."
Charm is deceitful and beauty is passing,
but a woman who fears the Lord,
she shall be praised.
Give her of the fruit of her hands,
and let her own works praise her in the gates.
—Proverbs 31:25–31

Every day is mother's day. I thank God for my mother, my great defender. I thank God for my grandmother. She treated me as though I was so special. I thank God for mothers all over the world who know they are babysitters for God, for God's babies, and so they are charged to do a good job with the children. How do you remember your mother today? Lord, we thank You for all the mothers in our lives. In Jesus's name. Amen.

Wisdom and Understanding
May 13

Things That Make You Go *Hhhhmmmmm*

Better is a dry morsel with quietness,
than a house full of feasting with strife.

A wise servant will rule over a son
who cause shame, and will share an inheritance
among the brothers.

The refining pot is for silver and the furnace
for gold, but the Lord tests the hearts.

An evildoer gives heed to false lips;
a liar listens eagerly to a spiteful tongue.

He who mocks the poor reproaches
his Maker; he who is glad at calamity
will not go unpunished.

Children's children are the crown of old men,
and the glory of children is their father.

Excellent speech is not becoming to a fool,
much less lying lips to a prince.
—Proverbs 17:1–7

Do not fret because of evildoers,
nor be envious of the workers of iniquity.
For they shall soon be cut down like the grass,
and wither as the green herb.
Trust in the Lord, and do good;
dwell in the land, and feed on His faithfulness.
Delight yourself also in the Lord,
and He shall give you the desires of your heart.
—Psalm 37:1–4

Why wisdom and understanding, you ask? How then would we know how He wants us to live? Lord God, we even thank You for the word, the teachings that make us think and wonder and ponder until You send Your Spirit, Your Holy Spirit, to translate for us. Thank You for the mystery of Your word until we are ready to receive it. In Jesus's name, we pray. Amen.

Wisdom and Understanding
May 14

Brethren, if a man/woman is overtaken in
any trespass, you who are spiritual
restore such a one in a spirit of gentleness,
considering yourself lest you also be tempted.
Bear one another's burdens, and so
fulfill the law of Christ.
For if anyone thinks himself to be
something, when he is nothing, he
deceives him/herself.
But let each one examine his/her own work,
and then he/she will have rejoicing in
himself alone, and not in another.
For each one shall bear his own load.
Let him/her who is taught the word
share in all good things with him/her who teaches.
Do not be deceived, God is not mocked;
for whatever a man/woman sows,
that he will also reap.
—Galatians 6:1–7

I am starting with me. I too have fallen short of the glory of God. Father God, help me to consider my brother or my sister when they do not seem righteous in my eyes. Show me how to be merciful, forgiving, and helpful, even as you are toward me. In Jesus's name. Amen.

Wisdom and Understanding
May 15

Jesus Spoke These Words

I am the true vine, and My Father
is the vinedresser.
"Every branch in Me that does not
bear fruit He takes away; and every branch
that bears fruit He prunes, that it may bear more fruit.
You are already clean because of the word which
I have spoken to you.
Abide in Me, and I in you. As the branch cannot bear fruit
of itself, unless it abides in the vine, neither can you,
unless you abide in me.
"I am the vine, you are the branches. He who
abides in Me, and I in him, bears much fruit; for
without Me you can do nothing.
If anyone does not abide in Me, he is
cast out as a branch and is withered; and
they gather them and throw them into the fire, and
they are burned. If you abide in Me, and My words
abide in you, you will ask what you desire,
and it shall be done for you.
By this My Father is glorified, that you bear much
fruit; so you will be My disciples.
As the Father loved Me, I also have
loved you; abide in My love.
—John 15:1-9

Father God, we thank You for including us at every step of the way. I want to be a branch in Your vine. I am a branch in Your vine. What a privilege it is to be invited to be a branch in Your vine. I want to bear fruit for You. I know I am a VIP with You, Lord. Thank You, thank You. I pray that many more will accept this invitation. In Jesus's name. Amen!

Wisdom and Understanding
May 16

*Therefore, leaving the discussion of
the elementary principles of Christ,
let us go on to perfection, not laying again
the foundation of repentance from dead works
and of faith toward God, of the doctrine of baptisms,
of laying on of hands, of resurrection of the
dead, and of eternal judgment. And this we will do if
God permits. For it is impossible for those
who were once enlightened, and have tasted
the heavenly gift, and have become partakers of the
Holy Spirit,
and have tasted the good word of God and the
powers of the age to come, if they fall
away, to renew them again to repentance, since they
crucify again for themselves the Son of God,
and put Him to an open shame.
—Hebrews 6:1–6 NKJV*

*God is our refuge and strength,
a very present help in trouble. Therefore
we will not fear, even though the earth be
removed, and though the mountains be carried into the
midst of the sea; though it's waters roar and be
troubled, though the mountains shake with its swelling.
There is a river whose streams shall make
glad the city of God, the holy place of the tabernacle of
the Most High.
—Psalm 46:1–4 NKJV*

Blessed be the name of the Lord Jesus Christ forever and ever! Amen.

Wisdom and Understanding
May 17

Oh come, let us sing to the Lord!
Let us shout joyfully to the Rock of our salvation.
Let us come before His presence
with thanksgiving;
Let us shout joyfully to Him with psalms.
For the Lord is the great God,
and the great King above all gods.
in His hand are the deep places of the earth;
The heights of the hills are His also.
The sea is His, for He made it;
and his hands formed the dry land.
Oh come, let us worship and bow down;
Let us kneel before the Lord our Maker.
For He is our God,
and we are the people of His pasture,
and the sheep of His hand.
Today, if you will hear His voice;
Do not harden your hearts, as in
the rebellion, as in the day of trial in the
wilderness, when your fathers tested Me;
They tried Me, though they saw My work.
—Psalm 95:1–9 NKJV

My soul belongs to my Maker, my heart belongs to my Maker, my hopes are according to my Maker, my joy is because of my Maker, and my future is in the hands of my Maker. Do you know your Maker? Blessed is the Lord God Almighty. Hallelujah!

Wisdom and Understanding
May 18

There is a river whose streams
shall make glad the city of God,
the holy place of the tabernacle of
the Most High.
God is in the midst of her, she shall
not be moved;
God shall help her, just at the break of dawn.
The nations raged, the kingdoms were moved;
He uttered His voice, the earth melted.
The Lord of hosts is with us;
The God of Jacob is our refuge.
Come, behold the works of the Lord,
who has made desolations in the earth.
He makes wars cease to the end of
the earth; He breaks the bow and cuts the
spear in two; He burns the chariot in the fire.
Be still, and know that I am God;
I will be exalted among the nations,
I will be exalted in the earth!
The Lord of hosts is with us;
The God of Jacob is our refuge.
—Psalm 46:5–11 NKJV

When the storm is raging and the sunshiny day seems to be a cloudy day, when traveling through the rough part of my journey, I need to remember that God is still God. The calm might change to raging storm, and peace might turn into havoc, but God is still God, and He is still in charge. Give me strength to hold on, to learn the lesson, and bring me to a better day when I will be wiser because of my past tribulations. Thank You, Father, for You are a present help in times of need. Amen!

Wisdom and Understanding
May 19

The Word of God to His People

Now therefore, thus says the Lord of hosts;
"Consider your ways!"
You have sown much, and bring in little;
You eat, but do not have enough;
You drink, but you are not filled
with drink; you clothe yourselves, but no
one is warm; and he who earns wages,
earns wages to put into a bag with holes."
—Haggai 1:5-6 NKJV

I urge you to read the rest of the story, how we get and get and yet we have nothing. Some of us work hard and have nothing to show for it. We should remember to pay our tithes and offerings. We should remember the hungry and the needy. Some of us never consider giving to the house of God, with our presence, our finances, our volunteer help, and yet we never stop to think about how the church helps clothe and feed the poor and hungry. When did I last give to charity or give to the church, feed my mind and spirit with God's word? Do I live selfishly, just for myself? God has a way that even if you make a lot of money, He will make it so that you don't see it. Read the book of Haggai in the Bible. Read the Bible and get wisdom and understanding, and then put it to practice and live a better life, in Jesus's name, God's promise to us.

I was glad when they said unto me,
"let us go into the house of the Lord."
—Psalm 122:1 NKJV

Wisdom and Understanding
May 20

Praise Him, praise Him.

Behold, how good and how pleasant it is
for brethren to dwell together in unity!
It is like the precious oil upon the head,
running down on the beard, the beard
of Aaron, running down
on the edge of his garments. It is like the
dew of Hermon, descending upon
the mountains of Zion;
for there the Lord commanded
the blessing—
Life forevermore.
—Psalm 133 NKJV

When you are sad, call on Jesus. When you are happy, call on Jesus. When you are in trouble, call on Jesus. When you are confused, call on Jesus. When you are lonely, call on Jesus. When you are in need, call on Jesus. When you are not sure, call on Jesus. How do you call on Jesus? Just say Jesus. Say more if you want to, but I dare you to say Jesus. Thank You, Lord, for the healing power in Your name. Amen.

Wisdom and Understanding
May 21

God is our refuge and strength,
a very present help in trouble. Therefore
we will not fear, even though the earth be removed,
and though the mountains be carried into
the midst o the sea; though its waters roar and be
troubled, though the mountains shake with its swelling.
—Psalm 46:1–3 NKJV

Oh, clap your hands, all you peoples!
Shout to God with the voice of triumph!
For the Lord Most High is awesome;
He will subdue the peoples under us,
and the nations under our feet.
—Psalm 47:1–3 NKJV

Great is the Lord, and greatly to be praised
in the city of our God, in His holy mountain.
Beautiful in elevation, the joy of the whole earth,
is Mount Zion on the sides of the north,
the city of the great King.
God is in her palaces;
He is known as her refuge.
—Psalm 48:1–3 NKJV

Hear this, all peoples;
Give ear, all inhabitants of the world,
both low and high, rich and poor together.
My mouth shall speak wisdom,
and the meditation of my heart shall
give understanding.
—Psalm 49:1–3 NKJV

No matter what happens, I will praise the Lord God, my Maker. When I rise, I will purposely think of Him. I will say in my mind, "Thank

You for a new day, Lord. Amen." When at last I lay in bed at the end of the evening, I will say, "Lord, thank You for another day completed and for all the ways you protected me from dangers seen and unseen." Every now and then, throughout the day, I will consider my Maker and the amazing thing that life is, His gift to us. I will also thank Him for eternal life with Him after this life. Jesus bridged the gap for us. Thank you, Lord! Amen.

Wisdom and Understanding
May 22

Things That Make You Go *Hhhhmmmmm*

The wicked flee when no one pursues,
but the righteous are bold as a lion.

Because of the transgression of a land,
many are its princes;
but by a man/woman of understanding and
knowledge right will be prolonged.

A poor man who oppresses the poor
is like a driving rain which leaves no food.

Those who forsake the law praise the wicked,
but such as keep the law contend with them.

Evil men do not understand justice,
but those who seek the Lord understand all.

Better is the poor who walks in his integrity
than one perverse in his ways,
though he be rich.

Whoever keeps the law is a discerning son,
but a companion of gluttons shames his father.

One who increases his possessions by usury
and extortion gathers it for him
who will pity the poor.

one who turns away his ear from hearing
the law, even his prayer is an abomination.
Whoever causes the upright to go astray
in an evil way, he himself will fall into his own pit;

but the blameless will inherit good.
—Proverbs 28:1–10 NKJV

Have mercy upon me, O God,
according to your loving-kindness;
according to the multitude of Your tender mercies,
blot out my transgressions.
wash me thoroughly from my iniquity,
and cleanse me from my sin.
For I acknowledge my transgressions,
and my sin is always before me.
Against You, and You only, have I sinned,
and done this evil in Your sight-
that You may be found just when You speak
and blameless when You judge.
—Psalm 51:1–4

Father God, thank You for Your forgiveness. It is never too late with You. Forgive me of all my wrongdoings today, and help me to do better from now on. In Jesus's name, I ask. Amen.

Just because a person is rich or beautiful to the local standards or charming does not mean that they are fulfilled, they are happy, their lives are complete. A happy spirit is richer than a miserable and mean rich person. Find the joy in your heart even if, at the moment, your finances are not so good. Find peace and contentment while you work on making a change. Yes, it will be better when finances and life and circumstances are all at a good place, but in the meantime, it's up to you to be thankful for everything you have, physical, spiritual, and emotional.

Wisdom and Understanding
May 23

Things That Make You Go *Hhhhmmmmm*

The rich man is wise in his own eyes,
but the poor who has understanding
searches him out.

When the righteous rejoice, there is great glory;
but when the wicked arise, men hide themselves.

He who covers his sins will not prosper,
but whoever confesses and forsakes them will
have mercy.

Happy is the man who is always reverent,
but he who hardens his heart will
fall into calamity.

Like a roaring lion and a charging bear
is a wicked ruler over poor people.

A ruler who lacks understanding is
a great oppressor,
but he who hates covetousness will
prolong his days.

A man burdened with bloodshed
will flee into a pit; let no one help him.
—Proverbs 28:11–17 NKJV

Truly my soul silently waits for
GOD;
From Him comes my salvation.
He only is my rock and my
Salvation;

He is my defense;
I shall not be greatly moved.
—Psalm 62:1–2 NKJV

Lord God, help us to consider these sayings in Your Bible, in Proverbs. They may even cause us to say hhhhmmmmm, that we may apply them to our daily living, and that they may cause us to attain wisdom and understanding so that we may live better lives and enjoy the benefits of a more prosperous life. In Jesus's name. Amen!

Wisdom and Understanding
May 24

Prayer and Supplication

May the Lord answer you in the day of trouble;
May the name of the God of Jacob defend you;
May He send you help from the sanctuary.
and strengthen you out of Zion;
May He remember all your offerings,
and accept your burnt sacrifice.
May He grant you according to your
heart's desire,
and fulfill all your purpose.
We will rejoice in your salvation,
and in the name of our God we will set up our
banners! May the Lord fulfill all your petitions.
Now I know that the Lord saves His anointed;
He will answer him from His holy heaven
with the saving strength of His right hand.
Some trust in chariots, and some in horses;
but we will remember the name of the
Lord our God.
They have bowed down and fallen;
but we have risen and stand upright.
Save, Lord!
May the King answer us when we call.
—Psalm 20 NKJV

Wisdom and Understanding
May 25

But God, who is rich in mercy,
because of His great love with which He
loved us, even when we were dead in
trespasses, made us alive together
with Christ (by grace you have been saved)
and raised us up together, and made
us sit together in the heavenly places in
Christ Jesus,
That in the ages to come He might show
the exceeding riches of His grace in
His kindness toward us in
Christ Jesus.
For by grace you have been saved through faith,
and that not of yourselves; it is the gift of God,
not of works, lest anyone should boast.
For we are His workmanship, created in
Christ Jesus
for good works, which God prepared beforehand
that we should walk in them.
—Ephesians 2:4-9 NKJV

Not unto us, O Lord, not unto us,
but to Your name give glory,
because of Your mercy,
because of Your truth.
Why should the gentiles say,
"So where is their God?"
But our God is in heaven;
He does whatever He pleases.
—Psalm 115:1-3 NKJV

Lord, we thank You for Your Holy Spirit that abides with us always. Help us to acknowledge the presence of the Holy Spirit and ask for Your guidance in everything we do. In Jesus's name. Amen.

Wisdom and Understanding
May 26

*And the Lord God formed man of the dust of
the ground, and breathed
in to his nostrils the breath of life; and
man became a living being.
The Lord God planted a garden
eastward in Eden, and there He put the
man whom He had formed.
And out of the ground the Lord God made
every tree grow that is pleasant to
the sight and good for food. The tree of
life was also in the midst of the garden,
and the tree of the knowledge of good and evil.
—Genesis 2:7–9 NKJV*

Let's read these stories in the Bible again, let's
remember our history, and let's refresh our
knowledge of who we are and of Whom we are.

*Your hands have made me and
fashioned me; give me understanding,
that I may learn Your commandments.
Those who fear You will be glad when
they see me, because I have hoped in Your
word.
I know, O Lord, that Your judgments are right,
and that in faithfulness You have afflicted me.
Let, I pray, Your merciful kindness be
for my comfort, according to Your word to Your servant.
Let Your tender mercies come to me,
that I may live; for your law is my delight.
—Psalm 119:73–77 NKJV*

Wisdom and Understanding
May 27

Get wisdom! Get understanding!
Do not forget, nor turn away from the
words of my mouth.
Do not forsake her, and she will
preserve you; Love her, and she will
keep you. Wisdom is the principal thing;
Therefore get Wisdom.
And in all your getting, get understanding.
Exalt her, and she will promote you;
She will bring you honor, when you
embrace her. She will place on your
head an ornament of grace;
A crown of glory she will deliver to you.
Hear, my son/daughter and receive my sayings,
and the years of your life will be many.
I have thought you in the way of wisdom;
I have led you in right paths.
When you walk, your steps will not
be hindered, and when you run, you
will not stumble.
Take firm hold of instruction, do not let go;
keep her, for she is your life.
—Proverbs 4:5–13 NKJV

I pray for wisdom for the people of the inner city, the people in the projects, the people in the ghettos, the people in the hood, the poor people, the homeless people, the struggling people, the forgotten people, the Christian people, and for all the peoples of the world. I pray we attain wisdom and understanding so that we may unite and help one another more. In Jesus's name. Amen!

Wisdom and Understanding
May 28

The Word of God to His People
(I could not stop, sorry it's so long, it's so rich.)

*"Ho! Everyone who thirsts,
Come to the waters; and you who have no
money, Come, buy and eat.
Yes, come, buy wine and milk without
money and without price. Why do you
spend money for what is not bread, and
your wages for what does not satisfy?
Listen carefully to me, and eat what is
good, and let your SOUL delight itself in
abundance. Incline your ear, and come to Me.
Hear, and your SOUL shall live;
and I will make an everlasting covenant with you—The
sure mercies of David, indeed I have given him
as a witness to the people, a leader and
commander for the people.
Surely you shall call a nation you do not know,
and nations who do not know you shall run to you,
because of the Lord your God, and
the Holy One of Israel;
For He has glorified you."
Seek the Lord while He may be found,
call upon Him while He is near.
Let the wicked forsake his way,
and the unrighteous man his thoughts;
Let him return to the Lord, and He will
have mercy on him; and to our God,
for He will abundantly pardon. "
For My thoughts are not your thoughts,
Nor are your ways My ways," says the Lord.
" for as the heavens are higher than the earth,
so are My ways higher than your ways,*

and My thoughts than your thoughts.
" for as the rain comes down, and
the snow from heaven, and do not return there,
but water the earth, and make it bring forth and bud,
that it may give seed to the sower and bread
to the eater, so shall my word be that goes
forth from My mouth; It shall not return
to Me void. But it shall accomplish what I
please, and it shall prosper in the thing
for which I sent it.
"For you shall go out with joy, and be led out
with peace; the mountains and the hills
shall break forth into singing before you, and
all the trees of the field shall clap their hands.
Instead of the thorn shall come up the
cypress tree, and instead of the brier
shall come up the myrtle tree;
And it shall be to the Lord for a name,
for an everlasting sign that shall not be cut off."
—Isaiah 55 NKJV

Father, we thank you for Your word and Your
promises and Your grace and mercy upon us every
day. In Jesus's name, we pray. Amen!

Wisdom and Understanding
May 29

Who then is Paul, and who is Apollos,
but ministers through whom you believed,
as the Lord gave to each one? I planted,
Apollos watered, but God gave the increase.
So then neither he who plants is anything,
nor he who waters, but God
who gave the increase.
Now he who plants and he who waters are one,
and each one will receive his own reward
according to his own labor.
For we are God's fellow workers;
you are God's field, you are God's
building. According to the grace of
God which was given to me, as a wise
master builder I have laid the foundation,
and another builds on it. But let each one
take heed how he build on it.
For no other foundation can anyone lay
than that which is laid, which is
Jesus Christ.
Now if anyone builds on this foundation
with gold, silver, precious stones,
wood, hay, straw, each ones' work will
become clear; for the day will declare it,
because it will be revealed by fire; and the fire will
test each ones' work, of what sort it is.
If anyone's work which he/she has built
on it endures, he/she will receive a reward.
If anyone's' work is burned, he/she will
suffer loss; but he/she him/herself will
be saved, yet so as through fire.
Do you not know that you are
the temple of God and that the Spirit of God dwells in you?
—1 Corinthians 3:5–16 NKJV

Lord God, give us the mind and determination to do our part, help us to rise up and make an effort, give us the strength and the presence of mind to do our very best at all that we do, that we might do it in Your name, and we know that You will complete the work in us, for we are not able to do it well without You. We praise Your name, and we thank You, for You make us look good for Your purpose on earth and in heaven. In Jesus's name, we pray. Amen!

Wisdom and Understanding
May 30

Praise Him, Praise Him

God be merciful to us and bless us,
and cause His face to shine upon us,
that Your way may be known on earth,
Your salvation among all nations.
Let the peoples praise You, O God;
let all the peoples praise You.
Oh, let the nations be glad and
sing for joy!
For You shall judge the people
righteously,
and govern the nations on earth.
Let the peoples praise You, O God,
let all the peoples praise You.
Then the earth shall yield her increase;
God, our own God, shall bless us,
God shall bless us,
and all the ends of the earth shall fear Him.
—Psalm 67 NKJV

When the praises go up, the blessings come down. May we always praise the Lord in happiness and in sadness, for richer or for poorer, in health and in sickness, and that until death. Amen!

Wisdom and Understanding
May 31

Praise Him, Praise Him.

Let God arise,
let His enemies be scattered;
let those also who hate Him flee
before, Him. As smoke is driven away,
So drive them away;
as wax melts before the fire,
so let the wicked perish at the presence of God.
But let the righteous be glad;
let them rejoice before God;
yes, let them rejoice exceedingly.
Sing to God, sing praises to His name;
Extol Him who rides on the clouds,
by His name YAH, and rejoice before Him.
—Psalm 68:1–4 NKJV

Let the praises go up. Let the blessings come down. Blessed be the name of our Lord Jesus Christ. Amen.

Beware of blockers, distracters, and preventers. Those are people I identify as angry, mean, jealous, negative not only with themselves but also with others. They live their lives plotting and planning how to disrupt, distract, block, and prevent the progress of the happy, hopeful, and capable people around them from ever advancing and shinning.

Your job, if you choose to accept it, is to learn who you are and for what purpose you were sent here on planet earth. Research your ancestors' history, your history. Know who you are and continue to build and fix yourself to create a better you from that history.

Start building in you who you will be in your future. When you work on these things, the blockers, distracters, and preventers will have limited power and eventually no power over you. They will not be able to distract you from your assigned and amazing destiny. Initially, this daily task of working on being the greatest you ever will feel difficult and almost impossible at times, but eventually, it will be a natural and instinctive way of life for you. You will begin to shine and not even know it. Others will remind you that you are shinning and that you are great, awesome, and amazing. Others will let you realize that the good work you did within yourself is paying off. Others will see in you the great work you have done in yourself as they benefit from it, and that's when it really matters. Your neighbors will thank you for seeing them, helping them, encouraging them. Then you will know, "I did my best, and my best was good, very good." You will then thank the great Spirit that abides in you, that's greater than you, and who knows, He will say, "Well done, my servant, well done." Amen!

Wisdom and Understanding
June 1

Praise Him, Praise Him.

I love the Lord, because He has heard
my voice and my supplications.
Because He has inclined His ear to me,
therefore I will call upon Him as long
as I live. The pains of death surrounded me,
and the pangs of Sheol laid hold of me;
I found trouble and sorrow.
Then I called upon the name of the Lord:
"O Lord, I implore You, deliver my soul!"
Gracious is the Lord, and Righteous;
Yes, our God is merciful.
The Lord preserves the simple;
I was brought low, and He save me.
Return to your rest, O my soul,
for the Lord has dealt bountifully with you.
For You have delivered my soul from death,
my eyes from tears, and my feet from falling.
—Psalm 116:1–8 NKJV

Stop everything for a moment and just think of the times when most everything in your life was great, when you had a great job, great friends, and the family was rather okay, and you did not have any major concerns. Then think of all the problems and heartaches and difficult times and joblessness and sickness in the family and all the troubles that existed in your life at one time. Now think of how you overcame them, how the Lord changed your life and made things better again, and how, in due time, they passed away and, in due time, things changed again and got better, the pain was forgotten or subsided, and joy came back in your life. Now consider the troubles that are in your life right now . . . Can God bring you out of them again? Have He not done it before? Did you not learn great and valuable lessons in your sorrows? Have you not become a better person because of your sorrows? God will do it again. He will bring you out like pure gold. Endure the troubled waters, for God will speak soon, and they will be still.

And we know that all things work
together for good to those who love God,
to those who are the called according
to His purpose.
—Romans 8:28 NKJV

Amen!

Wisdom and Understanding
June 2

*As you therefore have received
Christ Jesus the Lord, so walk in Him,
rooted and built up in Him and established
in the faith, as you have been taught
abounding in it with thanksgiving.
Beware lest anyone cheat you through
philosophy and empty deceit, according to the
tradition of men/women, according to the basic
principles of the world, and not according to Christ.
For in Him dwells all the fullness of the
Godhead bodily; and you are complete in Him,
who is the head of all principality and power.
—Colossians 2:6–10 NKJV*

*Hear my cry, O God; attend to my prayer.
From the end of the earth I will cry to You,
when my heart is overwhelmed;
Lead me to the rock that is higher than I.
For You have been a shelter for me,
a strong tower from the enemy.
I will abide in Your tabernacle forever; I will trust
in the shelter of Your wings. For You, O God, have
heard my vows; You have given me the heritage of
those who fear Your name. You will prolong the
king's life, His years as many generations.
He shall abide before God forever. Oh,
prepare mercy and truth, which may preserve him!
So I will sing praise to Your name forever,
that I may daily perform my vows.
—Psalm 61 NKJV*

That is King David speaking. We also can proclaim God's greatness in our lives. Some of us have the legacy of folks that prayed for us, grandparents and parents, aunts and uncles. Some of us may not have had parents who knew how to pray for us, but thank God, it can start with us, with me. Create a great Christian legacy for your children, for your nieces and nephews, and for the generations to come. They will speak of you greatly, and they will be great because of your prayers. In Jesus's name, we pray. Amen!

Wisdom and Understanding
June 3

Therefore, laying aside all malice,
all deceit, hypocrisy, envy, and all evil
speaking, as new born babes, desire the
pure milk of the word, that you may grow
thereby, if indeed you have tasted that the Lord
is gracious. Coming to Him as to a living stone,
rejected indeed by men, but chosen by
God and precious, you also, as living stones,
are being built up a spiritual house, a holy priesthood,
to offer up spiritual sacrifices acceptable
to God through Jesus Christ.
Therefore it is also contained in the Scripture,
"Behold, I lay in Zion
A chief cornerstone, elect, precious,
and he who believes on Him will
by no means be put to shame."
Therefore, to you who believe, He is precious;
but to those who are disobedient,
"The stone which the builders rejected
Has become the chief cornerstone," and
"a stone of stumbling and a rock of offense."
They stumble, being disobedient to the word,
to which they also were appointed.
But you are a chosen generation, a
royal priesthood, a holy nation, His own
special people, that you may proclaim
the praises of Him who called you out of darkness
into His marvelous light;
who once were not a people but are now the
people of God, who had not
obtained mercy but now have obtained mercy.
—*1 Peter 2:1–10 NKJV*

Father God, when I consider that I am a child of the greatest King ever, a child of the Creator of this whole world, and a child beloved to the one and only God Almighty, and that I have accepted His reign over me; when I remember that You are in charge and that my destiny, even tomorrow and the years to come, are all in Your hands, and that You love me, I will not fret, I will not worry. I thank You for Your presence in my life. In Jesus's name. Amen.

Wisdom and Understanding
June 4

Wisdom has built her house,
she has hewn out her seven pillars;
she has slaughtered her meat,
she has mixed her wine,
she has also furnished her table.
She has sent out her maidens,
she cries out from the highest
places of the city,
"Whoever is simple, let him/her turn in here!"
As for him/her who lacks
understanding, she says to him/her,
"Come, eat of my bread
and drink of the wine I have mixed."
—Proverbs 9:1–6

The fear of the Lord is the
beginning of wisdom,
and the knowledge of the Holy
One is understanding.
For by me your days will be
multiplied, and years of life will
be added to you.
—Proverbs 9:10–11 NKJV

O God, teach us how to live by Your word daily. Instill more of that wisdom from the Bible in us and help us to guide our children in Your word that we, as Christians, will represent You better and the world will know that You live in us and they may want to join the body of Christ, in Jesus's name. Amen.

Wisdom and Understanding
June 5

Praise is awaiting You, O God, in
Zion; and to You the vow shall
be performed. O You who hear prayer,
to You all flesh will come.
—Psalm 65:1–2 NKJV

By awesome deeds in righteousness
You will answer us, O God of our salvation,
You who are the confidence of all
the ends of the earth, and of the far-off seas;
who established the mountains by
His strength, being clothed with power;
You who still the noise of the seas,
the noise of the waves, and the tumult
of the peoples.
—Psalm 65:5–7 NKJV

You visit the earth and water it,
You greatly enrich it;
the river of God is full of water;
You provide their grain, for so You
have prepared it. You water its ridges abundantly,
You settle its furrows; You make it soft
with showers, You bless its growth.
You crown the year with Your goodness,
and Your paths drip with abundance.
They drop on the pastures of the wilderness,
and the little hills rejoice on every side.
The pastures are clothed with flocks;
The valleys also are covered with grain;
They shout for joy, they also sing.
—Psalm 65:9–13 NKJV

Today I will say a prayer of thanksgiving to my great Creator. I will simply thank Him for everything that is good and pleasant: water, clothes, bread, my family, roses, rain, my friends, money in my pocket, my socks, a smile . . . and just everything. Today I will say a quick word of thanksgiving to my Lord. Amen.

Wisdom and Understanding
June 6

I have chosen the way of truth;
Your judgments I have laid before me.
I cling to your testimonies;
O Lord, do not put me to shame!
I will run the course of Your commandments,
For You shall enlarge my heart.
Teach me, O Lord, the way of Your statutes,
and I shall keep it to the end.
Give me understanding, and I shall keep your law;
Indeed, I shall observe it with my whole heart.
Make me walk in the path of Your commandments,
for I delight in it.
Incline my heart to Your testimonies,
and not to covetousness.
Turn away my eyes from looking at worthless things,
and revive me in Your way.
Establish Your word to Your servant,
who is devoted to fearing You.
Turn away my reproach which I dread,
for Your judgments are good.
Behold, I long for Your precepts;
Revive me in Your righteousness.
—Psalm 119:30–40 NKJV

Father, Your word is so wonderful, even as my ancestor, Your servant David, worshipped You and praised You. So does my soul yearn for Your glory and Your power in my life. I am so glad I know You. Thank You for Your commandments, Your testimonies, and Your blessings. In Jesus's name. Amen.

Wisdom and Understanding
June 7

Not unto us, O Lord, not unto us,
but to Your name give glory,
because of Your mercy,
because of Your truth.
Why should the Gentiles say, "So where
is their God?" But our God is in heaven;
He does whatever He pleases.
Their idols are silver and gold, the work of men's hands.
they have mouths, but they do not speak;
eyes they have, but they do not see;
they have ears, but they do not hear;
noses they have, but they do not smell;
they have hands, but they do not handle;
feet they have, but they do not walk;
nor do they mutter through their throat.
Those who make them are like them;
so is everyone who trusts in them.
O Israel, trust in the Lord;
He is their help and their shield.
O house of Aaron, trust in the Lord;
He is their help and their shield.
You who fear the Lord, trust in the Lord;
He is their help and their shield.
—Psalm 115:1–11 NKJV

Father, we pray for spiritual mouth, eyes, ears, noses, hands, and feet so that we may indeed take heed of Your word, so that we may be more like our Maker, more like You. Show us how to live more out of our spiritual self and not only out of our carnal self so we may understand more of Your mysteries, and we may live with wisdom and understanding. In Jesus's name, we pray. Amen!

Wisdom and Understanding
June 8

*No temptation has overtaken you
except such as is common to man; but
God is faithful, who will not allow you to be
tempted beyond what you are able, but with the
temptation will also make the way of escape,
that you may be able to bear it.
Therefore, my beloved, flee from idolatry.
I speak as to wise men; judge for
yourselves what I say. The cup of blessing which we bless,
is it not the communion of the blood of
Christ? For we, though many, are one bread and one body;
for we all partake of that one bread.
—1 Corinthians 10:13–17 NKJV*

*You cannot drink the cup of the Lord and
the cup of demons; you cannot partake of the
Lord's table and of the table of demons.
Or do we provoke the Lord to jealousy? Are we
stronger than He?
—1 Corinthians 10:21–22 NKJV*

*The Lord has been mindful of us;
He will bless us;
He will bless the house of Israel;
He will bless the house of Aaron.
He will bless those who fear the Lord,
both small and great.
May the Lord give you increase more and more,
You and your children.
May you be blessed by the Lord, who made heaven and earth.
—Psalm 115:12–15 NKJV*

I, myself, need renewal often. Every now and then, I need renewal of my spirit. I need new hope, new purpose, new energy, and a new vision. I need newness again and again. I know only God can give that newness I need in my spirit, so I seek Him all the day long. Thank You, Father, for Your presence in our lives. In the name of Your Son, Jesus, we pray. Amen!

So often we go through things in life that make us feel very bad. Sometimes we feel disappointed in ourselves in the choices we made or the things we did, and it makes us feel so bad that we think we are the only person in the whole world to make such a bad decision, such a terrible choice that brought about such an awful outcome, but the scripture reminds us in 1 Corinthians 10:13 that no, I am not the only person who made bad decisions, bad choices. It is actually a human flaw, a part of being a normal person on earth, to make mistakes, and then it goes on to remind us that no matter how bad our mistake is, if we call on God, He is aware of it, He is able, and He wants to help us fix the problem and bring us through it. We just have to ask Him for help. Let us remember to be humble in spirit and reach out to the great Spirit for help. Let us remember to say thank you to the great Spirit when we are saved from our troubles. Amen.

Wisdom and Understanding
June 9

*For the word of God is living and
powerful, and sharper than any two-edged
sword, piercing even to the division of soul
and spirit, and of joints and marrow,
and is a discerner of the thoughts and
intents of the heart.
And there is no creature hidden from
His sight, but all things are naked and open
to the eyes of Him to whom we must give account.
Seeing then that we have a great
High Priest who has passed through the
heavens, Jesus the Son of God, let us
hold fast our confession. For we do not
have a High Priest who cannot
sympathize with our weaknesses, but was
in all points tempted as we are, yet
without sin. Let us therefore come boldly
to the throne of grace, that we may obtain
mercy and find grace to help in time of need.
—Hebrews 4:12–16 NKJV*

*Praise the Lord, all you Gentiles!
Laud Him, all you peoples!
For His merciful kindness is great toward us,
and the truth of the Lord endures forever.
Praise the Lord!
—Psalm 117 NKJV*

Father, we thank You because You are great. We thank You for Your mighty power, love, grace, and mercy. We know You know and see everything, and we are grateful that You are able to protect us from harm and trouble. We bless Your name, in Jesus's name. Amen.

Wisdom and Understanding
June 10

*My little children, let us not love in
word or in tongue, but in deed and in truth.
And by this we know that we are of the truth, and
shall assure our hearts before Him.
For if our heart condemns us, God is greater
than our heart, and knows all things.
Beloved, if our heart does not condemn us, we have
confidence toward God. And whatever we ask
we receive from Him, because we keep
His commandments and do those things that are
pleasing in His sight. And this is His
commandment: That we should believe on the
name of His Son Jesus Christ and love one
another, as He gave us commandment.
Now he who keeps His commandments abides
in Him, and He in him. And by this we know
that He abides in us, by the Spirit whom He has given us.
—1 John 3:18–24 NKJV*

*Praise the Lord!
Oh, give thanks to the Lord, for He is good!
For His mercy endures forever.
Who can utter the mighty acts of the Lord?
Who can declare all His praise:
Blessed are those who keep justice, and
he who does righteousness at all times!
Remember me O Lord, with the favor You
have toward Your people. Oh visit me with Your salvation.
—Psalm 106:1–4 NKJV*

Wisdom and Understanding
June 11

Praise Him, Praise Him

Oh, give thanks to the Lord! Call upon
His name; make known His deeds among
the peoples! Sing to Him, sing psalms to Him;
talk of all His wondrous works!
Glory in His holy name; let the hearts of those
rejoice who seek the Lord!
Seek the Lord and His strength;
seek His face evermore!
—1 Chronicles 16:8–11 NKJV

God be merciful to us and bless us,
and cause His face to shine upon us,
that Your way may be known on the earth,
your salvation among all nations.
Let the peoples praise You, O God;
let all the peoples praise You.
—Psalm 67:1–3 NKJV

Make haste O God, to deliver me!
Make haste to help me, O Lord!
Let them be ashamed and confounded
who seek my life;
Let them be turned back and confused who
desire my hurt. Let them be turned
back because of their shame, who say, "Aha, aha!"
Let all those who seek You rejoice
and be glad in You;
and let those who love Your salvation
say continually, "Let God be magnified!"
But I am poor and needy;
Make haste to me, O God!
You are my help and my deliverer;

O Lord, do not delay.
—Psalm 70 NKJV

Father, we praise You, and we worship You. We love You, and we adore You. We know You can help us on our journey to a better self. Help us not to gossip about others. Show us how to encourage one another that if we speak of one another's shortcomings, it's in preparation to pray for each one. Help us not to judge a situation of which we know nothing of, judging our neighbor on gossip. Help us to bless, encourage, and pray for one other. We praise You, and we know You are able to perfect this prayer in our lives. In Jesus's name, we pray. Amen!

Wisdom and Understanding
June 12

*So if you're serious about living this new resurrection
life with Christ, act like it. Pursue the things
over which Christ presides. Don't shuffle along,
eyes to the ground, absorbed with the things
right in front of you. Look up, and be alert to what is
going on around Christ—that's where the action is.
See things from His perspective.
Your old life is dead. Your new life, which is your real life—
even though invisible to spectators—is with
Christ in God. He is your life.
When Christ (your real life, remember) shows up again
on this earth, you'll show up, too—the real you, the
glorious you. Meanwhile, be content with obscurity,
like Christ. And that means killing off everything connected with that
way of death: Sexual promiscuity,
impurity, lust, doing whatever you feel like whenever you
feel like it, and grabbing whatever attracts your fancy.
That's a life shaped by things and feelings instead of by God.
—Colossians 3:1–6 MSG*

*O my soul, bless God.
From head to toe, I'll bless His holy name!
O my soul, bless God,
Don't forget a single blessing!
He forgives your sins—every one.
He heals your diseases—every one.
He redeems you from hell—save your life!
He crowns you with love and mercy—a paradise crown.
He wraps you in goodness—beauty eternal.
He renews your youth—you're always young in his presence.
—Psalm 103:1–5 MSG*

Encourage a new Christian who needs a word and send this along. The
word today is mainly for new Christians, but it certainly applies to us

"old" Christians. It's for those who are rightfully drinking Christian milk, but it applies to those of us who are drinking milk but should be eating Christian meat by now. It certainly applies to those of us who are rightfully eating Christian meat as we continue to nurture our spirits on God's rich word. In Jesus's name, we pray. Amen!

Wisdom and Understanding
June 13

Things that make you go *hhhhmmmmm*

*In all labor there is profit, but idle chatter
leads only to poverty.*

*The crown of the wise is their riches,
but the foolishness of fools is folly.*

*A true witness delivers souls, but a
deceitful witness speaks lies.*

*In the fear of the Lord there is strong confidence,
and His children will have a place of refuge.*

*The fear of the Lord is a fountain of life,
to turn one away from the snares of death.*

*In a multitude of people is a kings honor,
but in the lack of people is the downfall of a prince.*

*He who is slow to wrath has great understanding,
but he who is impulsive exalts folly.*

*A sound heart is life to the body,
but envy is rottenness to the bones.*

*He who oppresses the poor
reproaches his Maker,
but he who honors Him has mercy on the needy.
—Proverbs 14:23–31 NKJV*

To know or not to know, not knowing I should seek to know, knowing I should do better.

Wisdom and Understanding
June 14

Praise Him, Praise Him

I will bless the Lord at all times;
His praise shall continually be in my mouth.
My soul shall make its boast in the Lord;
the humble shall hear of it and be glad.
Oh, magnify the Lord with me,
and let us exalt His name together. I sought the
Lord, and He heard me, and delivered me
from all my fears. They looked to Him and were
radiant, and their faces were not ashamed.
This poor man/woman cried out, and the
Lord heard him/her, and saved him/her out of all
his/her troubles, the angel of the Lord
encamps all around those who fear Him,
and delivers them.
Oh, taste and see that the Lord is good;
Blessed is the man who trusts in Him!
Oh, fear the Lord, you His saints!
There is no want to those who fear Him.
The young lions lack and suffer hunger;
but those who seek the Lord shall not
lack any good thing.
—Psalm 34:1–10 NKJV

When you are sad and weary, when you cannot find a friend, when an answer is not before you, pick up the Bible and read a Psalm and find some peace, even for the moment, so that it may carry you on to the next moment in the meantime until change comes. Blessed be the name of the Lord God Almighty. Amen.

Wisdom and Understanding
June 15

Therefore, having been justified by faith,
we have peace with God through
our Lord Jesus Christ,
through whom also we have access by faith into
this grace in which we stand, and
rejoice in hope of the glory of God.
And not only that, but we also glory in tribulations,
knowing that tribulation produces
perseverance; and perseverance, character;
and character, hope.
Now hope does not disappoint, because
the love of God has been poured out
in our hearts by the Holy Spirit
Who was given to us. For when we were
still without strength, in due time
Christ died for the ungodly.
For scarcely for a righteous man will one die;
yet perhaps for a good man someone
would even dare to die. But
God demonstrates His own love toward us, in that
while we were still sinners
Christ died for us.
—Romans 5:1–8 NKJV

Father, my prayer today is on gratefulness. I am grateful for the way You provide for those who call Your name and even for those who don't know you. The sun shines on the just and the unjust. Your grace and mercy, even in the middle of trouble, is available when we call on you, and then You walk with us in the trouble and bring us out in due time. Help us to remember to say thank You after having dealt with unhappy situations and then seeing a better day. We thank You for Your amazing word that teaches us how to walk and trust and abide in faith. In Jesus's name, we pray. Amen!

Wisdom and Understanding
June 16

Praise Him, Praise Him

Bless the Lord, O my soul!
O Lord my God, You are very great:
You are clothed with honor and majesty,
Who cover Yourself with light as with a garment,
Who stretch out the heavens like a curtain.
He lays the beams of His upper
chambers in the waters, Who makes the clouds
His chariot, Who walks on the wings of the wind,
Who makes His angels spirits,
His ministers a flame of fire.
You who laid the foundations of the earth,
You covered it with the deep as with a garment;
The waters stood above the mountains.
At Your rebuke they fled; at the voice of Your thunder
they hastened away. They went up over the
mountains; they went down into the valleys,
to the place which You founded for them.
You have set a boundary that they may not pass over.
That they may not return to cover the earth.
He sends the springs into the valleys;
they flow among the hills. They give drink to every
beast of the field; The wild donkeys quench
their thirst. By them the birds of the heavens
have their home; They sing among the branches.
He waters the hills from His upper chambers;
The earth is satisfied with the fruit of
Your works.
—Psalm 104:1–13 NKJV

Sometimes I have to put all my troubles aside and just consider those things that sometimes I take for granted, like how majestic His work is on this earth. I Thank God for a wonderful and breathtaking nature all around the world, He made beauty all around us, rivers, butterflies, mountains, valleys, trees, flowers and so much more. What else can you see all around you that is wonderful, awesome, and amazing in nature? Thank You, Lord. Amen.

Wisdom and Understanding
June 17

I, therefore, the prisoner of the Lord,
beseech you to walk worthy of the calling with
which you were called, with all lowliness
and gentleness, with longsuffering, bearing with one
another in love, endeavoring to keep the unity
of the Spirit in the bond of peace.
There is one body and one Spirit, just as you
were called in one hope of your calling;
one Lord, one faith, one baptism;
one God and Father of all, who is
above all, and through all, and in you all.
But to each one of us grace was given
according to the measure of Christ's gift.
Therefore He says;
"when He ascended on high, He led captivity
captive, and gave gifts to men."
—Ephesians 4:1–8 NKJV

(To be continued tomorrow)

In the meantime . . . have you discovered your special gifts? Some can sing, and some can preach, and some can teach, and yet some can encourage and listen. Some can pray for others, some can mentor others, and yet some can just be a good example in their daily walk. What are your gifts, and are you giving of your gifts?

Everybody doesn't have to see or know when you give your gifts, only God in heaven and those you give your gifts to. But God may publicly or privately reward you. Lord, we thank You for making each and every one of us unique and with unique gifts. Amen.

Wisdom and Understanding
June 18

(continuation from yesterday's word)

(Now this, "He ascended" what does it mean but that
He also first descended into the lower parts of the earth?
He who descended is also the One who ascended far above
all the heavens, that He might fill all things.)

And He Himself gave some to be apostles, some prophets,
some evangelists, and some pastors and teachers,
for the equipping of the saints for the work of
ministry, for the edifying of the body of Christ,
till we all come to the unity of the faith and of the knowledge
of the Son of God, to a perfect man, to the measure
of the stature of the fullness of Christ;
that we should no longer be children, tossed to and fro
and carried about with every wind of doctrine,
by the trickery of men, in the cunning craftiness of
deceitful plotting, but, speaking the truth in love, may
grow up in all things into Him who is the head
—CHRIST—
from whom the whole body, joined and knit together
by what every joint supplies, according
to the effective working by which every part does its share,
causes growth of the body for the edifying of itself in
LOVE.
—Ephesians 4:9–16 NKJV

Now we can clearly see that I need you and you need me. There is just no making it on my own. If the hand does its job, the ears do its job, the eyes do its job, and so on, then the whole body will be better because each part does its part. Apparently, that's what God expects of all of us since we are of the same body of Christ. We must pray to know for sure what gifts we have so that we will grow into our gifts. That way, we may do our part to help the body of the church, the body of the household, the body of the workplace, the body of the sports team, the body of the class, the body of the business, etc., to work better or to its best ability. Lord, help me to do my part well to enhance all the bodies I belong to. In Jesus's name, I pray. Amen.

Wisdom and Understanding
June 19

Jesus Spoke These Words

*If you keep My commandments, you will abide in My
love, just as I have kept My Father's commandments
and abide in His love.
These things I have spoken to you, that My
joy may remain in you, and that your joy may be full.
This is My commandment, that you love one
another as I have loved you.
Greater love has no one than this, than to lay
down one's life for his friends.
You are my friends if you do whatever
I command you. No longer do I call you servants,
for a servant does not know what his master
is doing; but I have called you friends, for all things that
I heard from My Father I have made known to you.
You did not choose me, but I chose you and
appointed you that you should go and bear fruit,
and that your fruit should remain,
that whatever you ask the Father in My name
He may give you. These things I command you,
that you love one another.*
—John 15:10–17 NKJV

*It is good to give thanks to the Lord,
and to sing praises to Your name,
O Most High;
To declare Your loving-kindness in
the morning, and Your faithfulness every night.*
—Psalm 92:1–2 NKJV

Wisdom and Understanding
June 20

Owe no one anything except to LOVE
one another, for he/she who LOVES
another has fulfilled the law.
For the commandments, "You shall
not commit adultery," "You shall not murder,"
"You shall not steal," "You shall not
bear false witness," "You shall not covet," and if
there is any other commandment, are all
summed up in this saying, namely, "You
shall LOVE your neighbor as yourself."
LOVE does no harm to a neighbor;
therefore LOVE is the fulfillment of the law.
And do this, knowing the time, that now it is
high time to awake out of sleep; for now our
salvation is nearer than when we first believed.
The night is far spent, the day is at hand.
Therefore let us cast off the works of darkness, and
let us put on the armor of light. Let us walk
properly, as in the day, not in revelry
and drunkenness, not in lewdness and lusts, not in strife and
envy. But put on the Lord Jesus Christ, and
make no provision for the flesh, to fulfill its lusts.
—Romans 13:8–14 NKJV

Is the world going crazy, and has the rules changed? The rules still apply. All the "thou shalt nots" are still the order of the day. Father God, compel us to revisit Your word, the Bible, and reread the rules and reapply them to our daily lives that we may be held accountable for treating one another with love and respect. Even when we don't read the Bible, You have placed it in our spirits to know the difference between right and wrong. Bring our conscience back to us that we may consider deeply and gravely before hurting our fellow human being: all this killing and stealing and envy in our neighborhoods, in our families, in the government, and in the world. Help us to be "God-conscious" again. In Jesus's name, we pray. Amen.

Wisdom and Understanding
June 21ˢᵗ

Praise Him, Praise Him

Oh, give thanks to the Lord, for He is good!
For His mercy endures forever.
Let the redeemed of the Lord say so,
Whom He has redeemed from the hand of the enemy.
And gathered out of the lands,
from the east and from the west, from the north
and from the south. They wandered
in the wilderness in a desolate way;
They found no city to dwell in. Hungry and thirsty,
their soul fainted in them.
Then they cried out to the Lord in their trouble,
and He delivered them out of their distresses.
And He led them forth by the right way,
that they might go to a city for a dwelling place.
Oh, that men/women would give thanks to
the Lord for His goodness,
and for His wonderful works to the
children of men!
For He satisfies the longing soul,
and fills the hungry soul with goodness.
—Psalm 107:1–9 NKJV

Praise Him, Praise Him

Wisdom and Understanding
June 22

How precious is Your loving kindness,
O God!
Therefore the children of men put their trust
under the shadow of Your wings.
They are abundantly satisfied with the
fullness of Your house,
and You give them drink from the river of
Your pleasures. For with You is the fountain
of life; in Your light we see light.
Let not the foot of pride come against me,
and let not the hand of the wicked drive me away.
There the workers of iniquity have fallen;
They have been cast down and are
not able to rise.
—Psalm 36:7–12 NKJV

Do not fret because of evildoers, nor
be envious of the workers of iniquity.
For they shall soon be cut down
like the grass, and wither as the green herb.
Trust in the Lord, and do good;
dwell in the land, and feed on His faithfulness.
Delight yourself also in the Lord,
and He shall give you the desires of
your heart.
—Psalm 37:1–4 NKJV

Sometimes it's hard to understand why mean and ungodly people seem to have all the money and all the comforts of this world. But the sun shines, and the rain falls on the good and the bad. Father, we thank You for all Your blessings. We thank You for giving us material things that give us comfort, but most of all we thank You for Your Son Jesus Christ who died for us that we may also have spiritual richness, spiritual joy, spiritual understanding, and that we may live with You forever after death. In Jesus's name, we pray and give thanks. Amen!

Wisdom and Understanding
June 23

*My son, (my daughter) do not forget my
law, but let your heart keep my commands;
for length of days and long life
and peace they will add to you.
Let not mercy and truth forsake you;
bind them around your neck,
write them on the table of your heart, and so
find favor and high esteem in the sight of
God and man.
Trust in the Lord with all your heart,
and lean not on your own understanding;
In all your ways acknowledge Him,
and He shall direct your paths.
—Proverbs 3:1–6*

*The fool has said in his/her heart,
"there is no God" they are corrupt, and
have done abominable iniquity; there is none
who does good. God looks down from heaven
upon the children of men, to see if there are any
who understand, who seek God.
—Psalm 53:1–2 NKJV*

To live only through our flesh, to eat food and drink wine, to play and dance and talk and behave intelligently, to have great jobs, to have great friends and all those things, and yet to not know Jesus Christ, to not know God, to not connect with our soul and our spirit, what good is all that if your life has no joy and happiness? It is an amazing joy and pleasure when you connect your spirit with God. Lord, I want to know You more. In Jesus's name. Amen.

Wisdom and Understanding
June 24

O Lord, You have searched me and known me.
You know my sitting down and my rising up;
You understand my thought afar off.
You comprehend my path and my lying down,
and are acquainted with all my ways.
But behold, O Lord, You know it altogether.
You have hedged me behind and before,
and laid Your hand upon me.
Such knowledge is too wonderful for me;
it is high, I cannot attain it.
Where can I go from Your Spirit?
Or where can I flee from Your presence?
If I ascend into heaven, You are there;
If I make my bed in hell, behold, You are there.
If I take the wings of the morning,
and dwell in the uttermost parts of the sea,
even there Your hand shall lead me,
and Your right hand shall hold me.
—Psalm 139:1–10 NKJV

Lord, Your word tells me that I am so special to You, that you love me and you carefully formed me and you knew me even before you formed me in my mother's womb. Father, teach me to love myself as You love me, and then for sure, I will know how to love my neighbor. I bless Your name because You are my greatest and best example of how to love. Thank you, Father, in Jesus's name. Amen.

Wisdom and Understanding
June 25

The righteous cry out, and the Lord hears,
and delivers them out of all their troubles.
The Lord is near to those who
have a broken heart,
and saves such as have a contrite spirit.
Many are the afflictions of the righteous,
but the Lord delivers him out of
them all. He guards all his bones;
not one of them is broken.
Evil shall slay the wicked,
and those who hate the righteous
shall be condemned.
The Lord
redeems the soul of His servants,
and none of those who trust in
Him
shall be condemned.
—Psalm 34:17–22 NKJV

There is a word from heaven for me when my heart is sad. Lord, I thank You for hearing my cry, morning, noon, and night. I thank You for letting me see a sunshiny day after a rainy day. I thank You for hope when trouble is raging, and I thank You for saving my soul. In Jesus's name, I thank You, Amen.

Wisdom and Understanding
June 26

Through the Lord's mercies we are
not consumed, because His compassions fail not.
They are new every morning;
Great is Your faithfulness.
"The Lord is my portion," says my soul,
"Therefore I hope in Him!"
The Lord is good to those who wait for Him,
to the soul who seeks Him.
It is good that one should hope and wait quietly
for the salvation of the Lord.
It is good for a man/woman to bear
the yoke in his/her youth.
—Lamentations 3:22–27 NKJV

Oh, that men/women would give thanks to
the Lord for His goodness, and for His wonderful
works to the children of men!
Let them exalt Him also in the assembly of the people,
and praise Him in the company of the elders.
—Psalm 107:31–32 NKJV

Life is indeed short. We just don't know when our Maker will escort us out of this life and into "forever." Let's be our best selves, let's worship and obey our Maker, and then one day it will be our turn as today it has been MJ's passing day. Lord, I want to accomplish my assignment on this earth. I want to leave a good mark. I want to help people. I want to make a difference even as MJ left his legacy in music and great talent. I want to do my part with You as my guide. In Jesus's name. Amen.

Remembering MJ

Wisdom and Understanding
June 27

Jesus Said These Words

*Take heed, and beware of covetousness: For one's
life consists not in the
abundance of the things he possesses.
And He spoke a parable unto them, saying, The ground
of a certain rich man brought forth plentifully: and he
thought within himself, saying, what shall I do, because I have
no room where to bestow my fruits?
And he said, this will I do: I will pull down my barns,
and build greater; and there will I bestow all my
fruits and my goods. And I will say to my
soul, soul, thou hast much goods laid up for many
years; take thine ease, eat drink, and be merry.
But God said unto him, thou fool, this night
thy soul shall be required of thee: Then whose
shall those things be, which thou hast provided?
So is he that layeth up treasure for himself,
and is not rich toward God.
—Luke 12:15–21 NKJV*

Father in heaven, who sees everything on earth, please help me to remember to always help someone who might be in need. Help me to remember that all these material goods are not worth hoarding, that it's better to share it all. Help me to remember not to make money or jewelry or food or earthly pleasures more important than human beings. With Your power, grace, and mercy in my life, I know I will always reach out and help others. Thank You for Your blessings in my life. In Jesus's name, I pray. Amen.

Wisdom and Understanding
June 28

Praise Him, Praise Him

Bless the Lord, oh my soul; and all that is within me, bless
His holy, name! Bless the Lord, o my soul, and forget not all
His benefits: Who forgives all your iniquities, Who heals all your
diseases, who redeems your life from destruction, Who crowns
you with loving kindness and tender mercies, Who satisfies your
mouth with good things, so that your youth is renewed like
the eagle's. The Lord executes righteousness and justice
for all who are oppressed.
—Psalm 103:1–6 NKJV

God always makes a way for His people. He makes sure we have access to everything we need in order to accomplish His mission here on earth. When one door closes, He makes another one available, even if it's a window or a new path or a new idea or a new source. We have but to open our eyes and our minds and see the next opening God provides. Father, we thank You for Your steadfast protection and guidance, in Jesus's name. Amen.

Wisdom and Understanding
June 29

*For we were saved in this hope, but hope that is seen is not hope;
for why does one still hope for what he/she sees?
But if we hope for what we do not see,
we eagerly wait for it with perseverance.
Likewise the Spirit also helps in our weaknesses.
For we do not know what we should pray for as we ought,
but the Spirit Himself makes intersection for us
with groanings which cannot be uttered.
Now He who searches the hearts knows what the mind of the Spirit is,
because He makes intercession for the saints
according to the will of God.
And we know that all things work together
for good to those who love God,
to those who are the called according to His purpose.
—Romans 8:2428 NKJV*

Gracious Father, teach us to exercise patience as You perfect Your will in our lives. Remind us daily that we have but to endure the hard, rough times until You see us through, and You bring us to a better day, a joyful day; when we can look back and say, thank You, Lord for all my rough days because today I am a better person. I have grown spiritually, and I am the better because of my trials. Now life is better, and I can stand tall in Your name. It's in Jesus's name that I thank you. Amen!

Wisdom and Understanding
June 30

*Blessed is the man who endures
temptation; for when he has been
approved, he will receive the crown of life
which the Lord has promised to those who
love Him.
Let no one say when he is tempted,
"I am tempted by God"; for God cannot be tempted by
evil, nor does He Himself tempt anyone.
Then, when desire has conceived, it gives birth to sin;
and sin, when it is full-grown, brings forth death.
Do not be deceived, my beloved brethren.
Every good gift and every perfect gift
is from above, and comes down from the
Father of lights, with whom there is no variation
or shadow of turning.
—James 1:12–17 NKJV*

*The Might One, God the Lord,
has spoken and called the earth from the rising of the sun
to its going down. Out of Zion, the perfection of beauty,
God will shine forth.
—Psalm 50:1–2 NKJV*

Now I know what the older folks mean when they say "the devil is a liar." Four or five years and no problem with the computer, but now that I am dedicated to this "daily word," every minute, there is a problem. So I say, "He/she is a liar." I am back up and running, but I thank God for "BB," that's BlackBerry. Father, we thank You for always making another way, opening another door when one is closed. In Jesus's name. Amen.

Wisdom and Understanding
July 1

The Rules and the Laws

*"At the end of every seven years you shall
grant a release of debts. "And this is the form of the
release: Every creditor who has lent anything to
his/her neighbor shall release it; he shall not require it of his
neighbor or his brother, because it is
called the Lord's release.
"Of a foreigner you may require it;
but you shall give up your claim to what is owed by
your brother, "except when there may
be no poor among you; for the Lord will greatly
bless you in the land which the Lord your God
is giving you to possess as an inheritance—
"only if you carefully obey the voice of the Lord
your God, to observe with care all these commandments
which I command you today.
For the Lord your God will bless you just as He promised
you; you shall lend to many nations, but you shall not borrow; you
shall reign over many nations, but they
shall not reign over you.
—Deuteronomy 15:1–6 NKJV*

*"For the poor will never cease from the land;
therefore I command you, saying, 'You shall open your hand
wide to your brother, to your poor and your needy, in your land.
—Deuteronomy 15:11 NKJV*

Who knew that that law came from the good book? Seven years, although it may be more today, we must realize that the Bible have been, is, and will always be the map by which our lives, our existence, is ordered. Although there are some who don't believe, they don't even realize that they live by the rule of the book, God rules. God rocks. Who's your Daddy? God, whether you recognize Him or not. Read the Old Testament books, lots of great references for living and how our ancestors did it, good and bad. Father God, thank You for Your teachings, for Your lessons, and for loving us so much that You show us how to love too. In Jesus's name. Amen.

Wisdom and Understanding
July 2

*Since God has so generously let us in on what
He is doing, we're not about to throw up
our hands and walk off the job just
because we run into occasional hard times.
We refuse to wear masks and play games.
We don't maneuver and manipulate behind the scenes.
And we don't twist God's Word to suit ourselves.
Rather, we keep everything we do and say out in
the open, the whole truth on display, so that those who want
to can see and judge for themselves in the presence of
God. If our Message is obscure to anyone, it's not because
we're holding back in any way. No, it's because
these other people are looking or going the wrong
way and refuse to give it serious attention. All
they have eyes for is the fashionable god
of darkness. They think he can give them
what they want, and that they won't have to
bother believing in a Truth they can't see.
They're stone-blind to the day-spring brightness of
the Message that shines with Christ, who
gives us the best picture of God we'll ever get.
—2 Corinthians 4:1–4 MSG*

*I will bless the Lord at all times;
His praise shall continually be
in my mouth. My soul shall
make its boast in the Lord; the humble
shall hear of it and be glad. Oh magnify the Lord with me, and
let us exalt His name together.
—Psalm 34:1–3 NKJV*

Christians, stand up, speak up, pray always, and study much. Let's make a difference, in Jesus's name. Amen.

Wisdom and Understanding
July 3

Rejoice in the Lord always. Again I will
say, rejoice!
Let your gentleness be known to all men.
The Lord is at hand.
Be anxious for nothing, but in everything
by prayer and supplication,
with thanksgiving, let your requests
be made know to God;
and the peace of God, which
surpasses all understanding, will guard your
hearts and minds through Christ Jesus.
Finally, brethren, whatever things
are true, whatever things are noble,
whatever things are just, whatever things
are pure, whatever things are lovely,
whatever things are of good report, if
there is any virtue and if there is anything
praiseworthy—meditate on these things.
—Philippians 4:4-8 NKJV

If you are a believer and you accepted Christ as your Lord and Savior, and you are going through some trials and tribulations, some sadness and financial challenges, some family issues, and some confusion, take heed to the Word of God. Don't give up. Faith is holding on to the biting edge. Sometimes that's how God tries you, and just when you thought He would allow you to lose all, right when you thought you would not have enough to make it, God steps in and makes a change, even a miracle. Thank You, Lord, for You are God Almighty. I know You will make everything all right. In Jesus's name. Amen.

Wisdom and Understanding
July 4

Dear friends, I've dropped everything to write you
about this life of salvation
That we have in common. I have to write insisting-begging!-that
you fight with
Everything you have in you for this faith entrusted to us as a gift
to guard and cherish. What has happened is that some people have
infiltrated our ranks (our Scriptures warned us
This would happen), who beneath their pious skin
are shameless scoundrels.
Their design is to replace the sheer grace of our God with sheer
License-which means doing away with Jesus Christ, our one and
Only Master.
—Jude 1:3-4 MSG

Doom to you who buy up all the houses and grab all the land
For yourselves-evicting the old owners, posting
NO TRESPASSING signs,
Taking over the country, leaving everyone homeless and landless.
I overheard God-of –the-Angel-Armies say; "Those
mighty houses will
End up empty. Those extravagant estates will be deserted. A ten-acre
Vineyard will produce a pint of wine, a fifty-pound sack
of seed, a quart of grain.
Doom to those who get up early and start drinking booze before
breakfast, who stay up all
Hours of the night drinking themselves into a stupor.
They make sure their
Banquets are well-furnished with harps and flutes
and plenty of wine,
But they'll have nothing to do with the work of God.
—Isaiah 5:8-11 MSG

Father God, in the year 2010, we are going through difficult times.
The number of poor and hungry people have increased tremendously.

Many have no jobs. Many people are losing their homes and all their life's investments. When rulers thought they would become richer while the people's needs were neglected, things has gotten so bad that every human on earth has to stop and consider their ways, not just the poor or the rich or the Democrat or the Republican, the free countries or the oppressed countries, but every human spirit is caused to consider his/her ways and look to You, God, who has all the answers. Show us how to love one another, to give charity and kindness without putting a price on our giving of self. In Jesus's name. Amen.

Wisdom and Understanding
July 5

*The Lord reigns; Let the
peoples tremble! He dwells between the
cherubim; let the earth be moved!
The Lord is great in Zion, and He is high above all
the peoples. Let them praise Your great and
awesome name—He is holy.
The King's strength also loves justice;
You have established equity; You have executed
justice and righteousness in Jacob.
Exalt the Lord our God, and worship at His
footstool—He is holy.
Moses and Aaron were among His priests, and
Samuel was among those who called upon His name;
They called upon the Lord, and He answered them.
He spoke to them in the cloudy pillar;
they kept His testimonies and the ordinance
He gave them. You answered them, O Lord our God;
You were to them God-Who-Forgives,
though You took vengeance on their deeds.
Exalt the Lord our God, and worship at
His holy hill; For the
Lord our God is Holy.
—Psalm 99 NKJV*

Father God, help us to believe in prayer. Hear us when we call on You that we may remember that prayer works. Give us the mind to come to You in prayer and fasting and supplication, on our knees, standing, sitting, together, or alone. Help us to pray more so we may hear from You more. In Jesus's name, we pray. Amen.

Wisdom and Understanding
July 6

Lord, You have been favorable to Your land;
You have brought back the captivity of Jacob.
You have forgiven the iniquity of Your people;
You have covered all their sin.
You have taken away all Your wrath;
You have turned from the fierceness of
Your anger. Restore us, O God of our salvation,
and cause Your anger toward us to cease.
Will You be angry with us forever? Will You
prolong Your anger to all generations?
Will You not revive us again, that Your people
may rejoice in You? Show us Your mercy, Lord,
and grant us Your salvation. I will hear what
God the Lord will speak, for He will speak
peace to His people and to His saints; but let them not
turn back to folly. Surely His salvation is near to those who
fear Him, that glory may dwell in our land.
Mercy and truth have met together;
righteousness and peace have kissed.
Truth shall spring out of the earth, and righteousness
shall look down from heaven.
Yes, the Lord will give what is good;
and our land will yield its increase.
Righteousness will go before Him,
and shall make His footsteps our pathway.
—Psalm 85 NKJV

My God, I thank You for being such a forgiving Father. Show us how to humble ourselves and seek Your face so that You may heal our land, so that you might bless us, and so we will bless others. Thank You for Your greatness, ever-forgiving ways, Your love, mercy, and grace. In Jesus's name. Amen.

Wisdom and Understanding
July 7

The Apostle Paul Speaks to Us

Brethren, I do not count myself to have
apprehended; but one thing I do,
forgetting those things which are behind and
reaching forward to those things which are ahead,
I press toward the goal for the prize of the upward
call of God in Christ Jesus.
Therefore let us, as many as are mature,
have this mind; and if in anything you think otherwise,
God will reveal even this to you.
Nevertheless, to the degree that we have already
attained, let us walk by the same rule, let us
be of the same mind. Brethren, join in following my
example, and note those who so walk,
as you have us for a pattern.
—Philippians 3:13–17 NKJV

Truly my soul silently waits for God;
from Him comes my salvation. He only
is my rock and my salvation; He is my defense;
I shall not be greatly moved.
—Psalm 62:1–2 NKJV

Wisdom and Understanding
July 8

Things that make you go hhhhmmmmm

These things also belong to the wise:
It is not good to show partiality in judgment.

He who says to the wicked, "You are righteous,"
Him the people will curse; Nations will abhor him.
But those who rebuke the wicked will have delight,
and a good blessing will come upon them.

He who gives a right answer kisses the lips.

Prepare your outside work,
make it fit for yourself in the field,
and afterward build your house.

Do not be a witness against your neighbor
without cause, for would you deceive with your lips?

Do not say, "I will do to him just as he has
done to me; I will render to the man according
to his work."

I went by the field of the lazy man, and by the vineyard
of the man devoid of understanding; and there it was,
all overgrown with thorns; its surface was covered with
nettles; its stone wall was broken down.
When I saw it, I considered it well;
I looked on it and received instruction;
A little sleep, a little slumber; a little folding
of the hands to rest; so shall your poverty come like a
prowler, and your need like an armed man.
—Proverbs 24:23–34 NKJV

Lord, give us the mind to pay attention and to listen and to obey what is good and righteous. In Jesus's name, we pray. Amen.

Wisdom and Understanding
July 9

Things That Make You Go *Hhhhmmmmm*

Better is the poor who walks in his/her integrity
than one who is perverse in his/her lips, and is a fool.

Also it is not good for a soul to be without knowledge,
and he/she sins who hastens with his/her feet.

The foolishness of a man/woman twists his/her way,
and his/her heart frets against the Lord.

Wealth makes many friends, but the poor is separated
from his/her friend.

A false witness will not go unpunished, and he/she
who speaks lies will not escape.

Many entreat the favor of the nobility, and every man/woman
is a friend to one who gives gifts.

All the brothers of the poor hate him; How much more
do his friends go far from him!

He/she who loves wisdom loves his/her own soul;
He/she who keeps understanding will find good.

A false witness will not go unpunished, and he/she
who speaks lies shall perish.
—Proverbs 19:1–9 NKJV

(If you don't understand it all, check it out in another version.)

How lovely is your tabernacle, O Lord of hosts!
My soul longs, yes, even faints for the courts of the Lord;
My heart and my flesh cry out for the living God.
—Psalm 84:1–2 NKJV

Wisdom and Understanding
July 10

Things That Make You Go *Hhhhmmmmm*

Every way of a man/woman is right in his/her own eyes,
but the Lord weights the hearts.

To do righteousness and justice is more acceptable
to the Lord than sacrifice.

A haughty look, a proud heart, and the plowing of the
wicked are sin.

The plans of the diligent lead surely to plenty, but
those of everyone who is hasty, surely to poverty.

Getting treasures by a lying tongue is the fleeting
fantasy of those who seek death.

The violence of the wicked will destroy them, because
they refuse to do justice.

The way of a guilty man is perverse; but
as for the pure, his work is right.

Better to dwell in a corner of a housetop, than
in a house shared with a contentious woman.

The soul of the wicked desires evil; His
neighbor finds no favor in his eyes.

When the scoffer is punished, the simple is made wise;
but when the wise is instructed, he receives knowledge.

The righteous God wisely considers the house of the wicked,
overthrowing the wicked for their wickedness.

—Proverbs 21:2–12 NKJV
(If you don't understand it all, pray and ask God
for understanding and discernment.)

Oh, clap your hands, all you peoples! Shout to God with the voice of
triumph! For the Lord Most High is awesome;
He is a great King over all the earth.
—Psalm 47:1–2 NKJV

Wisdom and Understanding
July 11

*So let no one judge you in food or
in drink, or regarding a festival or a new
moon or Sabbaths, which are a shadow
of things to come, but the substance is of
Christ.
Let no one cheat you of your reward,
taking delight in false humility and worship
of angels, intruding into those things which he
has not seen, vainly puffed up by his fleshly mind,
and not holding fast to the Head,
from whom all the body, nourished and knit
together by joints and ligaments, groans
with increase that is from God.
—Colossians 2:16–19 NKJV*

Our Father, who art in Heaven, we thank You for being the great judge and the only righteous judge. Help us to do the things You ask us to do, and help us to read the Bible to know those things. Help us to take our children to church and to read the Bible with them at home so that they may have a better understanding of life and things as our ancestors before us did, so they too will know right from wrong and behave accordingly. In Jesus's name, we pray. Amen.

Wisdom and Understanding
July 12

(Re: Jesus the Christ)

*Now this is the main point of the things
we are saying: We have such a High Priest, who is
seated at the right hand of the throne of the Majesty
in the heavens, a Minister of the sanctuary and of
the true tabernacle which the Lord erected,
and not man. For every high priest is appointed
to offer both gifts and sacrifices. Therefore it is necessary
that this One also have something to offer.
For if He were on earth, He would not be
a priest, since there are priests who offer the gifts
according to the law; who serve the copy and shadow of
the heavenly things, as Moses was divinely instructed
when he was about to make the
tabernacle. For He said, "see that you make all
things according to the pattern shown you on the mountain."
But now He has obtained a more excellent ministry, inasmuch
as He is also Mediator of a better covenant,
which was established on better promises.
—Hebrews 8:1–6 NKJV*

*Now to the King eternal, immortal, invisible,
to God who alone is wise, be honor, and glory,
for ever and ever.
Amen.
—1 Timothy 1:17 NKJV*

Wisdom and Understanding
July 13

Jesus went on to make these comments:
If you're honest in small things,
you'll be honest in big things;
if you're a crook in small things,
you'll be a crook in big things.
If you're not honest in small jobs,
who will put you in charge of the store?
No worker can serve two bosses:
He'll either hate the first and love the second
or adore the first and despise the second.
You can't serve both God and the Bank.
When the Pharisees, a money-obsessed bunch,
heard Him say these things, they rolled their eyes,
dismissing Him as hopelessly out of touch. So Jesus
spoke to them: "You are masters at making yourselves look
good in front of others, but God knows what's behind the
appearance.
What society sees and calls monumental,
God sees through and calls monstrous, God's law and the
prophets climaxed in John; now it's all kingdom of God—the glad
news and compelling invitation to every man and woman.
The sky will disintegrate and the earth dissolve
before a single letter of God's Law wears out.
—Luke 16:16:20 MSG

He's God, our God,
in charge of the whole earth. And He remembers,
His Covenant—for a thousand generations
He's been as good as His Word.
—Psalm 105:7–8 MSG

Father God, we pray for strength to trust Your ability to work things out for us as we lean on You and not on our own tricks and manipulations to get a good result. Father, we trust You, and we wait on You. In Jesus's name. Amen.

Wisdom and Understanding
July 14

Exhortation to the Church

*Now I urge you, brethren, note those
who cause divisions and offenses, contrary
to the doctrine which you learned, and avoid them.
For those who are such do not serve our
Lord Jesus Christ, but their own belly, and
by smooth words and flattering speech deceive the
hearts of the simple. For your obedience has become
known to all. Therefore I am glad on your
behalf; but I want you to be wise in what is good,
and simple concerning evil. And the God
of peace will crush Satan under your feet shortly. The
grace of our Lord Jesus Christ be with you.
Amen.
—Romans 16:17–20 NKJV*

*Preserve me, O God, for in You I put
my trust. O my soul, you have said to the Lord, "You
are my Lord, my goodness is nothing apart from You."
As for the saints who are on the earth, "they are the
excellent ones, in whom is all my delight."
—Psalm 16:1–3 NKJV*

Lord, teach us how to be of a united spirit in Your church. Help us to want the good of the whole body and not just spitting out our own stubborn opinions. But considering the good of the whole body, the church, help us to encourage one another. In Jesus's name, we pray. Amen.

Wisdom and Understanding
July 15

For as we have many members in one body,
but all the members do not have the same function,
so we, being many, are one body in Christ, and
individually members of one another.
Having then gifts differing according to the grace that
is given to us, let us use them: If prophecy, let us prophesy
in proportion to our faith;
Or ministry, let us use it in our ministering;
he who teaches, in teaching; he who exhorts, in exhortation;
he who gives, with liberality; he who leads, with diligence;
he who shows mercy, with cheerfulness.
Let love be without hypocrisy. Abhor what is evil.
Cling to what is good.
Be kindly affectionate to one another with brotherly love,
in honor giving preference to one another; not lagging
in diligence, fervent in spirit, serving the Lord;
rejoicing in hope, patient in tribulation,
continuing steadfastly in prayer; distributing to the needs of
the saints, given to hospitality.
—Romans 12:4–13 NKJV

Oh, how great is your goodness, which
You have laid up for those who fear you,
which You have prepared for those who trust
in You in the presence of the sons of men!
You shall hide them in the secret place of Your presence
from the plots of man; You shall keep them secretly
in a pavilion from the strife of tongues.
—Psalm 31:19–20 NKJV

Even encouraging someone today, saying something good to someone is an expression of brotherly love. Lord, show us how to love one another. In Jesus's name. Amen.

Wisdom and Understanding
July 16

Praise Him, Praise Him

Oh, that You would rend the heavens!
That You would come down! That the mountains
might shake at Your presence—as fire causes
water to boil—to make Your name know to Your
adversaries, that the nations may tremble at Your
presence! When You did awesome things for which
we did not look, You came down,
the mountains shook at your presence.
For since the beginning of the world Men have not heard
nor perceived by the ear, nor has the eye seen
any God besides You, Who acts for the
one who waits for Him.
—Isaiah 64:1–4 NKJV

But now, O Lord, You are our Father;
We are the clay, and You our potter; and all we are the
work of Your hand. Do not be furious, O Lord,
Nor remember iniquity forever; Indeed, please
look—we all are Your people!
—Isaiah 64:8–9 NKJV

Oh, sing to the Lord a new song! Sing to the Lord,
all the earth. Sing to the Lord, bless His name;
proclaim the good news of His salvation
from day to day. Declare His glory among the
nations, His wonders among all peoples.
—Psalm 96:1–3 NKJV

Wisdom and Understanding
July 17

Beloved, I pray that you may prosper
in all things and be in health, just as your
soul prospers. For I rejoice greatly when
brethren came and testified of the truth that is in you,
just as you walk in the truth. I have no
greater joy than to hear that my children walk in truth.
Beloved, you do faithfully whatever you do for the
brethren and for strangers, who have borne witness
of your love before the church.
—3 John 2–6a NKJV

I love the Lord, because He has heard
my voice and my supplications. Because He has
inclined His ear to me, therefore I will call upon Him
as long as I live. The pains of death surrounded me,
and the pangs of Sheol laid hold of me;
I found trouble and sorrow.
Then I called upon the name of the Lord;
"O Lord, I implore you, deliver my soul!"
Gracious is the lord, and righteous;
Yes, our God is merciful.
—Psalm 116:1–5 NKJV

Wisdom and Understanding
July 18

O Lord God, to whom vengeance belongs—
O God, to whom vengeance belongs, shine forth!
Rise up, O judge of the earth;
render punishment to the proud.
Lord, how long will the wicked,
How long will the wicked triumph?
They utter speech and speak insolent things;
all the workers of iniquity boast in themselves.
They break in pieces your people, O Lord,
and afflict Your heritage. They slay
the widow and the stranger, and murder the fatherless.
Yet they say, "The Lord does not see,
nor does the God of Jacob understand."
Understand, you senseless among the people;
and you fools, when will you be wise?
He who planted the ear, shall He not hear?
He who formed the eye, shall he not see?
He who instructs the nations, shall He not correct,
He who teaches man knowledge?
The Lord knows the thoughts of man,
that they are futile.
Blessed is the man/woman who you instruct,
O Lord, and teach out of Your law,
that You may give him/her rest from the
days of adversity, until the pit is dug for the wicked.
For the Lord will not cast off His people,
nor will He forsake His inheritance.
—Psalm 94:1–14 NKJV

Blessed is our Lord God Almighty. Although it takes fire and storm to refine us, suffering and pain, God restores us again and again. He lifts us high. He makes us look good among the people, and then He gives us wisdom and understanding. We thank You, Father, for Your greatness, Your unceasing love for us. In Jesus's name. Amen.

Wisdom and Understanding
July 19

Commit your way to the Lord,
trust also in Him, and He shall bring it to pass.
He shall bring forth your righteousness as the light,
and your justice as the noonday. Rest in the Lord,
and wait patiently for Him; do not fret
because of him who prospers in his way,
because of the man who bring wicked schemes to pass.
Cease from anger, and forsake wrath; do not fret—it
only causes harm. For evildoers shall be cut off;
but those who wait on the Lord,
they shall inherit the earth.
—Psalm 37:5–9 NKJV

Father God, give us Your protection. Shield us from harm seen and unseen. Protect us from those who seek to cause us harm. We know that You are an all-seeing Spirit, You know the heart of man. Bless Your people as we look to You to be our strong arm, our shield, and our protector. In Jesus's name. Amen.

I believe that God, in His amazing unselfish ways, created the ego so that we may have choice. We either choose the ways of our Maker, God Almighty and all-knowing, or we choose the ways of the ego. The ego is so limited and so empty and foolish when left on its own, when not coupled with God wisdom. Having the ego, we get to choose if we will love God and obey Him or we will choose to live only through our ego with all its limitations. See, the ego thinks it knows everything. The ego thinks it has all the answers, and its answers are not to be questioned, argued with, or challenged. I believe the ego, when it's the only mind we use, is the channel by which the Devil uses to deceive and destroy us while seeming right and righteous, smart and better than others. We have been duped by the ego, but for many of us, we realize we have been duped usually when we are older and tired, and by then, many good opportunities to make better choices have been missed, and it's too late to change things. We only have one opportunity in life to live each moment and each experience. Yes, we can do things better and smarter when we humble ourselves and include God's ordinances, laws, and rules in the next experience, in the next opportunity, but usually, when the ego gets away with its selfish ways, its selfish behavior, we will apply only ego to the next experience, the next opportunity. See, the ego is selfish, narrow-minded, cold-blooded, and among other negative things, it is all about its own gratification.

I find that some people calling themselves or portraying themselves as strong believers hide behind their ego. They use Christianity or pretense of deep belief in God to hide their big, gigantic, enormous, and humongous EGO. I recognize these people when I deal with them, when I converse with them. I recognize a sense of pretense, condemnation for all others, and a great sense of discomfort and defensiveness in them. When they speak about God and Christianity or whatever religious belief they have, they are desperate to convince, convert, impress, and show off that they know so much about it, and to show themselves extremely knowledgeable as they are eager to impress upon you that they are the ultimate authority on the subject of God and religion. A true believer does not have the need to convince, impress, or condemn others. A true believer shows mercy and understanding while calmly, even though at times excited, sharing the Word of God. Imagine countries ruled by individuals with pure ego personalities. Imagine countries ruled by individuals who recognize the ego in them but humble themselves to couple it with a true God and spiritual persona. Will you choose to get to know the spirit in you, the God in you, or are you living a pure ego existence, limited and unfulfilled? It's a choice, your choice. Choose life, eternal life. Choose God.

Wisdom and Understanding
July 20

We Cry Out to You, Oh, Lord!

By the rivers of Babylon,
there we sat down, yea, we wept
when we remembered Zion.
We hung our harps upon the willows
in the midst of it. For there are those who carried us
requested mirth, saying, "sing us one of the songs
of Zion!" How shall we sing the Lord's song
in a foreign land?
—Psalm 137:1–4 NKJV

Deliver me, O Lord, from evil men;
preserve me from violent men,
who plan evil things in their hearts;
They continually gather together for war.
They sharpen their tongues like a serpent;
The poison of asps is under their lips.
Keep me, O Lord, from the hands of
the wicked; preserve me from violent men
who have purposed to make my steps stumble.
The proud have hidden a snare for me
and cords; they have spread a net by the wayside;
they have set traps for me.
I said to the Lord: You are my God; hear
the voice of my supplications, O Lord.
O God the Lord, the strength of my salvation,
You have covered my head in the day of battle.
Do not grant, O Lord, the desires of the wicked;
Do not further his wicked scheme, lest they be exalted.
"As for the head of those who surround me, let the
evil of their lips cover them;
Let burning coals fall upon them; let them be
cast into the fire, into deep pits, that they rise not up again.

Let not a slanderer be established in the earth;
let evil hunt the violent man to overthrow him."
I know that the Lord will maintain the cause
of the afflicted, and justice for the poor.
Surely the righteous shall give thanks to Your name;
the upright shall dwell in Your presence
—Psalm 140 NKJV

Lord God, show Yourself mighty in the middle of our sorrows. Let the wicked power rulers know that You are God and You attend to Your people's needs. Lord, we need justice for our men and for our children, for every helpless human being. We need Your help to unify us, to show us how to allow love to prevail among us. Help us to stop harming one another and to make others respect us as Your children beloved. Show us how to seek peace to stop inflicting harm on one another. Stealing and killing and warring against one another benefits no one. Open our eyes, Lord. In Jesus's name, we pray. Amen.

Wisdom and Understanding
July 21

For we know that if our earthly house, this tent,
is destroyed, we have a building from God, a house
not made with hands, eternal in the heavens.
For in this we groan, earnestly desiring to be clothed
with our habitation which is from heaven,
if indeed, having been clothed, we shall not
be found naked. For we who are in this tent
groan, being burdened not because we want to be
unclothed, but further clothed, that
mortality may be swallowed up by life.
Now He who has prepared us for this very thing
is God, who also has given us the Spirit as a guarantee.
So we are always confident, knowing that
while we are at home in the body we are absent from the Lord.
For we walk by Faith, not by sight. We are confident,
yes, well pleased rather to be absent from the body
and to be present with the Lord.
Therefore we make it our aim, whether present or
absent, to be well pleasing to Him.
For we must all appear before the judgment
seat of Christ, that each one may receive the
things done in the body, according to what he has done,
whether good or bad.
—2 Corinthians 5:1–10 NKJV

Lord, we pray for a Spirit of discernment. We pray for wisdom and understanding. We pray for clarity. We pray for guidance from Your Holy Spirit. We pray for power, Your power. We pray for boldness in Your name that we may stand up to Caesar and tell him to let Your people go, let Your people live. Bless us again and again, O Lord, God Almighty. In Jesus's name. *Amen.*

Wisdom and Understanding
July 22

The Lord is my shepherd; I shall not want.
He makes me to lie down in green pastures;
He leads me beside the still waters.
He restores my soul; He leads me
in the paths of righteousness for His name's sake.
Yea, though I walk through the valley of the
shadow of death, I will fear no evil;
for You are with me; Your rod and Your staff,
they comfort me. You prepare a table before me
in the presence of my enemies; You anoint my head
with oil; my cup runs over.
Surely goodness and mercy shall follow me
all the days of my life; and I will dwell in the
house of the Lord forever.
—Psalm 23 NKJV

Lord, we thank You for this wonderful book called the Bible. We thank You for the different books in the Bible. We thank You for the words and their instructions and the parables and the history and Your promises therein and for Your Spirit that interprets the word to us. Blessed is Your name forever and ever. In Jesus's name, we praise and thank you. *Amen.*

Wisdom and Understanding
July 23

Walk prudently when you go to the house of God;
and draw near to hear rather than to give the sacrifice
of fools, for they do not know that they do evil.
Do not be rash with your mouth,
and let not your heart utter anything hastily
before God. For God is in heaven, and you on earth;
therefore let your words be few.
For a dream comes through much activity,
and a fool's voice is known by his many words.
When you make a vow to God, do not delay to pay it;
for He has no pleasure in fools.
Pay what you have vowed—better not to vow than to
vow and not pay.
Do not let your mouth cause your flesh to sin,
nor say before the messenger of God that it was an error.
Why should God be angry at your excuse and
destroy the work of your hands?
For in the multitude of dreams and many words
there is also vanity. But fear God.
—Ecclesiastes 5:1–7 NKJV

OH, sing to the Lord a new song! Sing to the Lord, all the earth.
Sing to the Lord, bless His name;
Proclaim the good news of His salvation from
day to day. Declare His glory among the nations,
His wonders among all peoples.
For the Lord is great and greatly to be praised;
He is to be feared above all gods.
For all the gods of the peoples are idols,
But the Lord made the heavens,
Honor and majesty are before Him;
Strength and beauty are in His sanctuary.
—Psalm 96:1–6 NKJV

Amen!

Wisdom and Understanding
July 24

Things That Make You Go *Hhhhmmmmm*

If you see the oppression of the poor,
and the violent perversion of justice and
righteousness in a province, do not marvel at the matter,
for high official watches over high official,
and higher officials are over them.

Moreover the profit of the land is for all;
even the king is served from the field.

He who loves silver will not be satisfied with silver;
Nor he who loves abundance, with increase.

This is all vanity.

When goods increase, they increase who eat them;
so what profit have the owners except to
see them with their eyes?

The sleep of a laboring man/woman is sweet,
whether he/she eats little or much;
but the abundance of the rich will not
permit him/her to sleep.

There is a severe evil which I have seen under the sun:
Riches kept for their owner to his hurt.
But those riches perish through misfortune;
when he begets a son, there is nothing in his hand.
As he came from his mother's womb, naked
shall he return, to go as he came;
and he shall take nothing from his labor
which he/she may carry away in his/her hand.
—Ecclesiastes 5:8–15 NKJV

Give to the Lord, O families of the peoples,
give to the Lord glory and strength.
Give to the Lord the glory due His name;
bring an offering, and come into His courts.
Oh, worship the Lord in the beauty of holiness!
Tremble before Him, all the earth.
Say among the nations, "The Lord reigns;
the world also is firmly established,
It shall not be moved;
He shall judge the peoples righteously."
—Psalm 96:7–10 NKJV

Father, help us to be still and consider what really matters in this earth. Although we like material things and money, we most love You, Lord, and we must love the poor and the needy. Help us to reach out to someone who has less than us, whether physically or spiritually. In Jesus's name. Amen.

Wisdom and Understanding
July 25

*Put on the whole armor of God, that
you may be able to stand against the wiles of the devil.
For we do not wrestle against flesh and blood,
but against principalities, against powers,
against the rulers of the darkness of this age, against
spiritual hosts of wickedness in the heavenly places.
Therefore take up the whole armor of God,
that you may be able to withstand in the evil day, and
having done all, to STAND.
Stand therefore, having girded your waist with truth,
having put on the breastplate of righteousness,
and having shod your feet with the preparation of
the gospel of peace; above all, taking the shield of faith
with which you will be able to quench all the fiery darts
of the wicked one. And take the helmet of salvation,
and the sword of the Spirit, which is the word of God;
praying always with all prayer and supplication in the Spirit,
being watchful to this end with all perseverance and
supplication for all the saints.
—Ephesians 6:11–18 NKJV*

*I love the lord, because He has heard
My voice and my supplications. Because
He has inclined His ear to me, therefore I will
call upon Him as long as I live.
—Psalm 116:1–2 NKJV*

I have everything I need, in Jesus's name. I have it all inside of me, in Jesus's name. I have His power, I have His love. I have everything I need, in Jesus's name. Amen.

Wisdom and Understanding
July 26

*Blessed be the God and Father of our
Lord Jesus Christ, who according to His
abundant mercy has begotten us again to a living hope
through the resurrection of Jesus Christ from the dead,
to an inheritance incorruptible and undefiled
and that does not fade away, reserved in
heaven for you, who are kept by the power of God
through faith for salvation ready to be revealed in the last time.
In this you greatly rejoice, though now for a little while,
if need be, you have been grieved by various trials,
that the genuineness of your faith,
being much more precious than gold that
perishes, though it is tested by fire, may be found to praise,
honor, and glory at the revelation of Jesus Christ,
whom having not seen,
you love. Though
now you do not see Him, yet believing, you rejoice with
joy inexpressible and full of glory,
receiving the end of your faith-the salvation of your souls.
—1 Peter 1:3–9 NKJV*

Lord, we want to have more faith. We want to lean on You and trust You more. Give us strength to walk in Your word. Teach us Your word as we read and study the Bible daily. In Jesus's name, we pray. Amen.

Wisdom and Understanding
July 27

Beloved, do not believe every spirit, but test the
spirits, whether they are of God; because
many false prophets have gone out into the world.
By this you know the Spirit of God;
Every spirit that confesses that Jesus Christ has come
in the flesh is of God, and every spirit that does not confess
that Jesus Christ has come in the flesh
is not of God. And this is the spirit of the
Antichrist, which you have heard was coming, and is
now already in the world.
You are of God, little children, and have overcome
them because He who is in you is greater than he who
is in the world. They are of the world. Therefore
they speak as of the world, and the
world hears them.
We are of God, He who knows God hears us; he
who is not of God does not hear us. By
this we know the spirit of truth and the spirit of error.
—1 John 4:1–6 NKJV

Father God, as Christians, we need to pray more. Heal our minds so that we may approach the throne of grace more often. Wherever we are, remind us to pray for this world and the people around us, remind us to pray for the poor and to help them, remind us to pray for evildoers that they may repent. We bless Your name, O Lord! For You and You alone are able to help us. In Jesus's name. Amen.

Wisdom and Understanding
July 28

Praise Him, Praise Him

To You, O Lord, I lift up my soul.
O my God, I trust in You;
Let me not be ashamed;
Let not my enemies triumph over me.
Indeed, let no one who waits on
You be ashamed;
Let those be ashamed who deal treacherously without cause.
Show me Your ways, O Lord;
teach me Your paths.
Lead me in Your truth and teach me,
For You are the God of my salvation;
On You I wait all the day.
—Psalm 25:1–5 NKJV

"When you go out to battle against
your enemies, and see horses and
chariots and people more numerous
than you, do not be afraid of them;
for the Lord your God is with you,
who brought you up from the land of Egypt.
—Deuteronomy 20:1 NKJV

I love this verse. It gives power to the people.
Read the whole chapter and the one before.
I wonder how this would read for God's people today.
When you go out to battle against your enemies
and face some crooked politicians,
and some very wealthy, crooked people with power,
and people more numerous than you,
do not be afraid of them;
for the Lord, your God is with you,
who brought you up from a state of bondage.

(Cynthia's version today.)

Lord, we praise You, and we adore You for You make the powers that be recognize that this is Your world and that all Your people will be included in all the benefits Your world renders. Thank you, Father, You include us, and You make us look good. In Jesus's name. Amen.

Wisdom and Understanding
July 29

Praise Him, Praise Him

*I said, "I will guard my ways, lest I sin
with my tongue; I will restrain my mouth with a
muzzle, while the wicked are before me."
I was mute with silence, I held my peace
even from good; and my sorrow was stirred up.
My heart was hot within me; while I was musing,
the fire burned. Then I spoke with my tongue:
"Lord, make me to know my end, and what is the measure of
my days, that I may know how frail I am.
Indeed, You have made my days as
an handbreadths, and my age is as nothing before You;
Certainly every man/woman at his/her best state
is but vapor. Surely every man walks about
like a shadow; surely they busy themselves in vain;
he heaps up riches, and does not know who will
gather them. "And now, Lord what do I wait for?
My hope is in You. Deliver me from all my
transgressions; do not make me the reproach of the foolish.
—Psalm 39:1–8 NKJV*

*Give unto the Lord, Oh you mighty ones,
give unto the Lord glory and strength.
Give unto the Lord the glory due to His name;
Worship the Lord in the beauty of holiness.
—Psalm 29:1–2 NKJV*

Father God, we are frail and weak without You. Father God, we are strong and great with You. Help us to seek Your face, to learn Your ways, and to be grateful. In Jesus's name, Amen!

Wisdom and Understanding
July 30

Jesus Shared This Parable

For the kingdom of heaven is like a
landowner who went out early in the morning
to hire laborers for his vineyard. Now when he had
agreed with the laborers for a denarius a day, he sent
them into his vineyard. And he went out about the third
hour and saw others standing idle in the marketplace,
and said to them, you also go into the vineyard, and
whatever is right I will give you. So they went.
Again he went out about the sixth and the ninth hour, and did
likewise. And about the eleventh hour he went out
and found others standing idle, and said to them,
why have you been standing here idle all day?
They said to him, because no one hired us. He said to them,
you also go into the vineyard, and whatever is right
you will receive. So when evening had come,
the owner of the vineyard said to his
steward, call the laborers and give them their wages,
beginning with the last to the first.
And when those came who were hired about the eleventh
hour, they each received a denarius.
But when the first came, they supposed that
they would receive more; and they likewise received
each a denarius. And when they had
received it, they complained against the landowner,
Saying, these last men have worked only one hour,
and you made them equal to us who have borne the
burden and the heat of the day.
But he answered one of them and said,
friend, I am doing you no wrong. Did you not agree
with me for a denarius? Take what is yours and go
your way. I wish to give to this last man the same as to you.
Is it not lawful for me to do what I wish with my own things?
Or is your eye evil because I am good?

So the last will be first, and the first last. For many
are called, but few chosen.
—Matthew 20:1–16 NKJV

(Let's read the Bible more. Do look up the
word *denarius*. Make it fun.)

Father God, give us a spirit of humility and love. We pray that You will teach us to see all men and women in need as brothers and sisters that we may help them and supply their needs according to the blessings given to us by You. Help us not to be envious when we see others' blessings. In the name of Jesus, we pray. Amen.

Wisdom and Understanding
July 31

Let not your heart be troubled; you believe in God,
believe also in Me.
In my Father's house are many mansions;
if it were not so, I would have told you. I go
to prepare a place for you. And if I go and prepare
a place for you, I will come again and receive you
to Myself; that where I am, there you may be also.
And where I go you know, and the way you know.
Thomas said to Him, Lord, we do not know
where You are going, and how can we know the way?
Jesus said to him, I am the way, the truth, and the life.
No one comes to the Father except through Me.
—John 14:1–6 NKJV

If you abide in Me, and My words abide in you, you
will ask what you desire, and it shall be done for you.
By this My Father is glorified, that you bear much
fruit; so you will be My disciples.
As the Father loved Me, I also have loved
you; abide in My love.
—John 15:7–9 NKJV

The earth is the Lord's, and all its fullness,
the world and those who dwell therein.
For He has founded it upon the seas,
and established it upon the waters.
—Psalm 24:1–2 NKJV

Father God, we pray for peace—peace in our hearts, peace in our relationships, peace at our jobs, peace with our family, and peace in our spirit. Give us Your joy and Your peace this day, in Jesus's name. Amen.

Wisdom and Understanding
August 1

Praise Him, Praise Him

The Lord thundered from heaven,
and the Most High uttered His voice,
hailstones and coals of fire.
He sent out His arrows and scattered the foe,
lightnings in abundance, and He
vanquished them. Then the channels of the sea
were seen, the foundations of the world were
uncovered at Your rebuke, O Lord,
at the blast of the breath of Your nostrils.
He sent from above, He took me;
He drew me out of many waters.
He delivered me from my strong enemy,
from those who hated me,
for they were too strong for me.
They confronted me in the day of
my calamity, but the Lord was my
support. He also brought me out into
a broad place; He delivered me because
He delighted in me.
The Lord rewarded me according
to my righteousness; According to the
cleanness of my hands He has recompensed me.
For I have kept the ways of the Lord, and
have not wickedly departed from my God.
—Psalm 18:13–21 NKJV

The psalmist David was so poetic in his exalting the Lord. He praised
God when he looked over his life and saw how his Lord took good care
of him. He was careful (I imagine) to do his best to worship and praise
God. Read the Psalms, they are awesome. When I look over my life,
I see so many miracles. I am praying for more, for my Father is great

and able. I worship and praise Him and try to obey His word, in Jesus's name. Amen!

Wisdom and Understanding
August 2

Praise Him, Praise Him

PRAISE the Lord!
Oh, give thanks to the Lord, for
He is good! For His mercy endures
forever. Who can utter the mighty acts of the Lord?
Who can declare all His praise? Blessed are
those who keep justice, and he who does
righteousness at all times!
—Psalm 106:1–3 NKJV

Make a joyful shout to the Lord, all you lands!
Serve the Lord with gladness; Come before His
presence with singing. Know that the Lord,
He is God; it is He who has made us, and not
we ourselves; we are His people and the sheep of
His pasture. Enter into His gates with thanksgiving,
and into His courts with praise. Be thankful
to Him, and bless His name. For the Lord is good;
His mercy is everlasting, and His
truth endures to all generations.
—Psalm 100 NKJV

Praise, the Lord. When things seem not to be going right, I dare you to praise the Lord. Smile when your heart is breaking and look upward to heaven and know that God sees and knows and He knows when to bring change. I am trusting in God. Say, "I am trusting in God." I am a Christian. I am a believer. I am trusting in God. Amen.

Wisdom and Understanding
August 3

*For God is not unjust to forget your work
and labor of love which you have shown
toward His name, in that you have ministered
to the saints, and do minister. And we desire that
each one of you show the same diligence to the full assurance
of hope until the end, that you do not become
sluggish, but imitate those who through faith and
patience inherit the promises. For when God made
a promise to Abraham, because He could swear by no one
greater, He swore by Himself, saying, "Surely blessing
I will bless you, and multiplying I will multiply
you." And so, after he had patiently endured, he
obtained the promise. For men indeed swear by the
greater, and an oath for confirmation is for them
an end of all dispute. Thus God, determining to show
more abundantly of His counsel, confirmed it by
an oath, that by two immutable things, in
which it is impossible for God to lie, we might have
strong consolation, who have fled for refuge to lay
hold of the hope set before us. This hope we have
as an anchor of the soul, both sure and steadfast, and
which enters the Presence behind the veil,
where the forerunner has entered for us, even
Jesus, having become High Priest forever according
to the order of Melchizedek.
—Hebrews 6:10–20 NKJV*

Oh, that we should trust You more. Father God, we pray for endurance, trust, and patience so that our faith will grow. We ask You to lift and sustain our spirit along the way so that our time waiting on Your answer will not feel in vain. Sometimes waiting seems fruitless, but we know that in due time, You will bless us in a way that we know the wait was worthwhile. You always come through. Give us patience to wait on You as we labor in Your name. In Jesus's name, we pray. Amen!

Wisdom and Understanding
August 4

Things That Make You Go *Hhhhmmmmm*

Do not boast about tomorrow
for you do not know what a day may bring forth.

Let another man praise you, and not your own mouth;
A stranger, and not your own lips.

A stone is heavy and sand is weighty, but a
fool's wrath is heavier than both of them.

Wrath is cruel and anger a torrent, but who is
able to stand before jealousy?

Open rebuke is better than love carefully concealed.

Faithful are the wounds of a friend, but the kisses
of an enemy are deceitful.

A satisfied soul loathes the honeycomb,
but to a hungry soul every bitter thing is sweet.

Like a bird that wanders from its nest
is a man/woman who wanders from his/her place.

Ointment and perfume delight the heart,
and the sweetness of a man's friend gives
delight by hearty counsel.

Do not forsake your own friend or your father's friend,
nor go to your brother's house in the day of your
calamity; better is a neighbor nearby than a
brother far away.
—Proverbs 27:1–10 NKJV
Behold, how good and how pleasant it is

for brethren to dwell together in unity!
It is like the precious oil upon the head,
running down on the bear, the beard of Aaron.
Running down on the edge of his garments.
It is like the dew of Hermon, descending upon
the mountains of Zion; For there the
Lord Commanded the blessing-Life forevermore.
—Psalm 133 NKJV

How sweet it is, the Word of God. Let us read the Bible for peace, for instruction, for guidance, for new ideas, for strength, for lessons, and for better living. Let us read the Bible to be better humans. Lord, we thank You for Your word. What peace we find in reading It. Thank You, in Jesus's name. Amen.

Wisdom and Understanding
August 5

Praise Him, Praise Him

*I will praise You, for I am fearfully and
wonderfully made; marvelous are
Your works, and that my soul knows very well.
My frame was not hidden from You,
when I was made in secret, and skillfully
wrought in the lowest parts of the earth. Your
eyes saw my substance, being yet unformed. And in
Your book they all were written, the days
fashioned for me, when as yet there
were none of them. How precious also are Your
thoughts to me, O God!
How great is the sum of them!
If I should count them, they would be more in
number than the sand; when I awake, I am
still with You.*
—Psalm 139:14–18 NKJV

*I will love You, O Lord, my strength.
The Lord is my rock and my fortress
and my deliverer; my God, my strength, in whom I
will trust; my shield and the horn of my
salvation, my stronghold. I will call upon
the Lord, who is worthy to be praised;
so shall I be saved from my enemies.*
—Psalm 18:1–3 NKJV

Wisdom and Understanding
August 6

Praise Him, Praise Him

Oh, give thanks to the Lord, for He is good!
For His mercy endures forever.
Oh, give thanks to the God of gods!
For His mercy endures forever.
Oh, give thanks to the Lord of lords!
For His mercy endures forever;
To Him who alone does great wonders,
for His mercy endures forever;
To Him who by wisdom made the heavens,
for His mercy endures forever;
To Him who laid out the earth above the waters,
For His mercy endures forever;
To Him who made great lights,
For His mercy endures forever—
The sun to rule by day,
For His mercy endures forever;
The moon and stars to rule by night,
For His mercy endures forever.
—Psalm 136:1–9 NKJV

What a mighty God we serve, worthy of all the praises. Father, we thank You for being on our side, those in the world who are not wealthy, those who have very little or nothing at all, those who are not able to amass lots and lots of money. We know You are God of all, great and might, and yet You consider the poor and the average, and You make a way for us too. Give us wisdom and understanding so that we too may rise up and help those less able, less capable, and less fortunate than us. We pray in the name of Jesus. Amen.

Wisdom and Understanding
August 7

Praise Him, Praise Him

I will praise You with my whole heart;
before the gods I will sing praises to You.
I will worship toward Your holy temple,
and praise Your name for Your loving-kindness
and Your truth; for You have magnified Your word
above all Your name. In the day when I cried
out, You answered me, and made me bold
with strength in my soul.
All the kings of the earth shall praise You, O Lord,
when they hear the words of Your mouth.
Yes, they shall sing of the ways of the Lord,
for great is the glory of the Lord. Though the Lord
is on high, yet He regards the lowly; but the
proud He knows from afar.
Though I walk in the midst of trouble, You
will revive me; You will stretch out Your
hand against the wrath of my enemies, and Your right
hand will save me. The Lord will perfect
that which concerns me;
Your mercy, O Lord, endures forever;
Do not forsake the works of Your hands.
—Psalm 138, NKJV

The psalmist David, the king David, the poet David—he inspires me with the way he wrote about the wonders of God. He was king and could do whatever he wanted, but he wanted to do the will of God. He realized how God was great in his life. Even as a king, he knew that God was and is and will be always the real King of kings. Oh, that we too will acknowledge God's greatness. I think we should write some psalms like David did but with our own praises on a piece of paper or a notebook. When our spirit is full, we should express it like King David did in those days. So one day somebody will know that we too were extremely in awe of the amazing ways God takes care of us. To God be the glory. Amen.

Wisdom and Understanding
August 8

And we know that all things work together
for good to those who love God, to those who
are the called according to His purpose.
For whom He foreknew, He also predestined
to be conformed to the image of His Son, that He
might be the firstborn among many brethren.
Moreover whom He predestined, these
He also called; whom He called, these He
also justified; and whom He justified,
these He also glorified. What then shall we say
to these things? If God is for us, who can be against us?
He who did not spare His own Son, but
delivered Him up for us all, how shall He
not with Him also freely give us all things?
Who shall bring a charge against God's elect?
It is God who justifies. Who is he who
condemns? It is Christ who died, and furthermore
is also risen, who is even at the right hand of God,
who also makes intercession for us.
—Romans 8:28–34 NKJV

Let the sea roar, and all its fullness,
the world and those who dwell in it;
let the rivers clap their hands;
let the hills be joyful together before the Lord,
for He is coming to judge the earth.
With righteousness He shall judge the world,
and the peoples with equity.
—Psalm 98:7–9 NKJV

What's your prayer today? Remember to pray! Praise, supplication, confession, expectation, thankfulness, and forgiveness, no matter what your prayer is about, God is waiting to hear from you. Pray today.

Wisdom and Understanding
August 9

Praise Him, Praise Him

Who shall separate us from the love of Christ?
Shall tribulation, or distress, or persecution, or
famine, or nakedness, or peril, or sword?
As it is written: "For Your sake we are killed
all the day long; we are accounted as sheep for the
slaughter." Yet in all these things we are
more than conquerors through Him who loved us.
For I am persuaded that neither death nor life,
nor angels nor principalities nor powers, nor things present
nor things to come, nor height nor depth, nor any other
created thing, shall be able to separate us from the
love of Christ Jesus our Lord.
—Romans 8:35–39 NKJV

Let God arise, let His enemies be scattered;
Let those also who hate Him flee before Him.
As smoke is driven away, so drive them away;
as wax melts before the fire,
so let the wicked perish at the presence of God.
But let the righteous be glad; let them rejoice exceedingly.
Sing to God, sing praises to His name;
extol Him who rides on the clouds, by His name YAH,
and rejoice before Him.
—Psalm 68:1–4 NKJV

To God be the glory for great things He is doing. Father, open our hearts and minds that we may receive Your blessings and share it with others. Let us be open and receptive to every great and new change You send our way. We thank You for protecting us. We need You every day and every night. We say thank You, in Jesus's name. Amen.

Wisdom and Understanding
August 10

*My brethren, count it all joy when you fall
into various trials, knowing that the
testing of your faith produces patience.
But let patience have its perfect work,
that you may be perfect and complete, lacking
nothing. If any of you lacks wisdom, let him
ask of God, who gives to all liberally and without
reproach, and it will be given to him.
But let him ask in faith, with no doubting, for he
who doubt is like a wave of the sea driven and
tossed by the wind. For let not that man/woman
suppose that he/she will receive anything from the Lord;
he/she is a double-minded man/woman, unstable in all
his/her ways. Let the lowly brother/sister
glory in his/her exaltation, but the rich in
his/her humiliation, because as a flower of the field
he will pass away. For no sooner has the
sun risen with a burning heat than it withers
the grass; its flower falls, and its beautiful appearance
perishes. So the rich man also will fade away
in his pursuits. Blessed is the man/woman who endures
temptation; for when he/she has been approved,
he/she will receive the crown of life which the
Lord has promised to those who love Him.*
—James 1:2–12 NKJV

*Praise the Lord!
Praise the name of the Lord;
Praise Him, O you servants of the Lord!
You who stand in the house of the Lord, in the courts
of the house of our God, praise the Lord, for the Lord
is good; Sing praises to His name, for
it is pleasant.*
—Psalm 135:1–3 NKJV

Father and God, we want to have more faith. We pray for great faith. We pray that after we have prayed and did our best, that we will stand in faith, knowing that You will bless us with what is good and pleasant for our lives as we grow in the power of the resurrected Christ, Jesus, Your Son, who abides with us in Spirit. Lord, bless us, Your people in a great way that our children might have trust again and they may rise up and call us blessed as we pave a better path for them and for generations to come. We want to be a better example for future generations.

Help us, show us, have mercy on us again. We pray. Amen!

Wisdom and Understanding
August 11

Something from Leviticus (read the book).

And the Lord spoke to Moses, saying,
"Speak to all the congregation of the children
of Israel, and say to them: 'You shall
be holy, for I the Lord your God am holy.
'Every one of you shall revere his mother and
his father, and keep My Sabbaths; I am the
Lord your God. 'Do not turn to idols, nor make for
yourselves molded gods: I am the Lord your God.
—Leviticus 19:1–4 NKJV

Therefore, holy brethren, partakers of the heavenly
calling, consider the Apostle and High Priest of
our confession, Christ Jesus,
who was faithful to Him who appointed Him,
as Moses also was faithful in all His house.
For this One has been counted worthy of more
glory than Moses, in as much as He who built the house
has more honor than the house.
For every house is built by someone,
but He who built all things is God.
—Hebrews 3:1–4 NKJV

Lord, we pray for families today. We pray that children may be raised in families again. We pray that families will remain together and that they would worship You again. We pray for fathers and mothers. We pray that people would look to God for better living. We pray for joy and happiness in households. Lord, we need to remember all Your laws and statutes. We need to be led by them again. Bless this generation, Lord. Help us to look to You. In Jesus's name. Amen.

Wisdom and Understanding
August 12

For every house is built by someone,
but He who built all things is God.
And Moses indeed was faithful in all His house as a
servant, for a testimony of those things which would
be spoken afterward, but Christ as a Son over His own
house, whose house we are if we hold fast the confidence and the
rejoicing of the hope firm to the end.
—Hebrews 3:4–6 NKJV

Beware, brethren, lest there be in any of you an evil heart of
unbelief in departing from the living God; but exhort
one another daily, while it is called "Today," lest
any of you be hardened through the deceitfulness of sin.
For we have become partakers of Christ if we hold the
beginning of our confidence steadfast to the end,
while it is said: "Today, if you will hear His voice,
do not harden your hearts as in the rebellion."
—Hebrews 3:12–15 NKJV

Blessed be the Lord, Who daily loads us
with benefits, the God of our salvation!
Our God is the God of salvation; and to God
the Lord belong escapes from death.
—Psalm 68:19–20 NKJV

Hear my voice, O God, in my meditation; preserve
my life from fear of the enemy. Hide me from the secret
plots of the wicked, from the rebellion of the
workers of iniquity, who sharpen their tongue like a sword,
and bend their bows to shoot their arrows—bitter words, that
they may shoot in secret at the blameless;
suddenly they shoot at him and do not fear.
—Psalm 64:1–4 NKJV

Lord, preserve us in Your glory. Help us to focus only on You and Your word so that we may see the good in one another and spit out the bad. You are the Maker of all things, and You know us well. We want to have more faith and trust in You. Bless Your name, O God. Amen.

Wisdom and Understanding
August 13

*Behold what manner of love the Father
has bestowed on us, that we should
be called children of God!
Therefore the world does not know us,
because it did not know Him.
Behold, now we are children of God;
and it has not yet been revealed what we
shall be, but we know that when He is revealed,
we shall be like Him, for we shall see Him as He is.
And everyone who has this hope in
Him purifies himself, just as He is pure.
—1 John 3:1–3 NKJV*

*Grace and peace be multiplied to you
in the knowledge of God and of Jesus our Lord.
As His divine power has given to us all things
that pertain to life and godliness, through the
knowledge of Him who called us by glory
and virtue, by which have been given to us exceedingly
great and precious promises, that through these
you may be partakers of the divine nature, having
escaped the corruption that is in the
world through lust. But also for this very
reason, giving all diligence, add to your faith
virtue, to virtue knowledge, to knowledge
self-control, to self-control perseverance, to
perseverance godliness, to godliness brotherly
kindness, and to brotherly kindness love.
—2 Peter 1:2–7 NKJV
Praise the Lord!
Praise the Lord, O my soul!
While I live I will praise the Lord; I will
sing praises to my God while I have
my being.*

—Psalm 146:1–2 NKJV
Wisdom and Understanding
August 14

Things That Make You Go *Hhhhmmmmm*

Wine is a mocker, strong drink is a brawler,
and whoever is led astray by it is not wise.

The wrath of a king is like the roaring of a lion;
whoever provokes him to anger
sins against his own life.

It is honorable for a man/woman to stop striving,
since any fool can start a quarrel.
—Proverbs 20:1–3 NKJV

He who walks with integrity walks securely,
but he who perverts his ways will become known.

He who winks with the eye causes trouble,
but a prating fool will fall.

The mouth of the righteous is a well of life,
but violence covers the mouth of the wicked.

Hatred stirs up strife, but love covers all sins.

Wisdom is found on the lips of him/her who
has understanding, but a rod is for the back
of him/her who is devoid of understanding.

Wise people store up knowledge, but
the mouth of the foolish is near destruction.

The rich man's wealth is his strong city;
The destruction of the poor is their poverty.

The labor of the righteous leads to life,
the wages of the wicked to sin.

He who keeps instruction is in the way of life.
—Proverbs 10:9–17 NKJV

O God, I know we need to humble ourselves more so that You will heal our land. O God, we need Your power, Your grace, and Your mercy every day. O God, I pray for those who don't know You and don't realize that they need You desperately. O God, help us in Jesus's name. Amen!

The Bible sometimes speaks in metaphors; knowing that too much wine or liquor (or any other mind-altering substance) can damage or destroy your life, why not practice self-control? Why not choose to be wise? Force yourself to leave it alone, or if it's not harmful to your body or mind, use it in moderation. Discipline your ego and be in control of it, not it in control of you. Do not provoke your boss or your leader unnecessarily since they can cause trouble for you. Break up a fight, stop arguing, anybody can create a problem, but can you prevent one? Can you stop one? If you always walk with truth and honesty, you will be known for those. It will show up in your character, but if you are sneaky, a liar, a thief, a jealous person, everything you hide will be exposed sooner or later, and you will be known for who you really are, and most everyone will turn away from you. People will start walking away and staying away from you. When you speak, we will know who you are. If you are an honest and respectful person, we will know. If you are a pretentious and dishonest person, we will know. Speak or not, we will know you from the spirit you exhibit.

Wisdom and Understanding
August 15

*Blessed is the man/woman
who walks not in the counsel of the ungodly,
nor stands in the path of sinners,
nor sits in the seat of the scornful;
but his delight is in the law of the Lord,
and in His law he meditates day and night.
he shall be like a tree planted by the rivers of water,
that brings forth its fruit in its season,
whose leaf also shall not wither;
and whatever he does shall prosper.
The ungodly are not so,
but are like the chaff which the wind drives away.
Therefore the ungodly shall not
stand in the judgment,
nor sinners in the congregation of the righteous.
For the Lord knows the way of the righteous,
but the way of the ungodly shall perish.
—Psalm 1 NKJV*

Lord, help us to choose good people as good friends. Help us to reject bad company. Help us to be good people ourselves that others might want to be our friends. Help us to make good choices and to reject wrongdoing. Bless our minds and our spirit in Jesus's name. Amen!

Wisdom and Understanding
August 16

Praise Him, Praise Him

Praise the Lord!
Praise the Lord from the heavens;
praise Him in the heights!
Praise Him, all His angels;
Praise Him, all His hosts!
Praise Him, sun and moon;
Praise Him, all you stars of light!
Praise Him, you heavens of heavens,
Let them praise the name of the Lord,
for He commanded and they were created,
He also established them forever and ever;
He made a decree which shall not pass away.
Praise the Lord from the earth, You great sea
creatures and all the depths;
Fire and hail, snow and clouds; stormy wind,
fulfilling His word; mountains and all hills;
fruitful trees and all cedars; beasts and all cattle;
Creeping things and flying fowl;
—Psalms 148:1–10 NKJV

What a mighty God we serve. God is able to do all things, anything and everything we ask and that He wants to do. Father, we pray for power and faith to do the things You will have us do that will make us strong and wise so that when all Your blessings are showered on us that we may be good stewards and spread Your word, Your gifts, and Your kindness on others not so fortunate, in Jesus's name. Amen!

Wisdom and Understanding
August 17

Praise Him, Praise Him

Arise, shine; for your light has come!
And the glory of the Lord is risen upon you.
For behold, the darkness shall cover the earth,
and deep darkness the people;
but the Lord will arise over you, and His glory
will be seen upon you. The Gentiles shall come
to your light, and kings to the brightness of your rising.
"Lift up your eyes all around, and see; they all gather
together, they come to you; your sons shall come from
afar, and your daughters shall be nursed
at your side. Then you shall see and become
radiant, and your heart shall swell with joy;
Because the abundance of the see shall be turned to you,
the wealth of the Gentiles shall come to you.
—Isaiah 60:1–5 NKJV

Preserve me, O God, for in You
I put my trust. O my soul, you have said to the Lord,
"You are my Lord, my goodness is nothing apart from You."
—Psalm 16:1–2 NKJV

O Lord, You are the portion of my inheritance
and my cup; You maintain my lot.
The lines have fallen to me in pleasant places;
yes, I have a good inheritance. I will bless the Lord
who has given me counsel; my heart also instructs
me in the night seasons. I have set the Lord always
before me; because He is at my right hand I
shall not be moved. Therefore my heart is glad, and my
glory rejoices; my flesh will not leave my soul in Sheol,
nor will You allow Your holy One to see corruption.
You will show me the path of life; In Your presence

is fullness of joy; at Your right hand are pleasures
forevermore.
—Psalm 16:5–11 NKJV

God, You are my God. You are all I need. You bless me so much that thank You is not enough. Thank You, Lord. I praise You, and I place my offering and my tithes, and then I try my best to do my best daily in honor of Your name. I try to love my brothers and my sisters, my fellow human beings. I try to help the needy. What else will you have me to do? I praise Your name in all the earth, in Jesus's name. Amen!

Have you ever wondered about your inheritance in this world or about what your children or family members may inherit from you? Have you ever considered how your path have been assigned to you and how wonderful it is, or do you not think it's a good path, and do you know that you can change it for yourself and for the generation after you by the choices you make? Your daughters, your sons, they come through you, or they come from your spirit as you raise them, and they tend to pattern after your teachings or lack thereof.

Wisdom and Understanding
August 18

Praise Him, Praise Him

Put in the sickle, for the harvest is ripe.
Come, go down; for the wine press is full,
the vats overflow—for their wickedness is great.
Multitudes, multitudes in the valley of decision!
For the day of the Lord is near in the valley of decision.
The sun and the moon will grow dark,
and the stars will diminish their brightness.
The Lord also will roar from Zion,
and utter His voice from Jerusalem;
The heavens and earth will shake; but the Lord
will be a shelter for His people.
"So you shall know that I am the Lord your God,
dwelling in Zion My holy mountain.
—Joel 3:13-17 NKJV

I will love You, O Lord my strength. The Lord
is my rock and my fortress and my deliverer;
My God, my strength, in whom I will trust;
my shield and the horn of my salvation, my stronghold.
I will call upon the Lord, who is worthy to be praised;
—Psalm 18:1-2 NKJV

Lord, I pray that more parents will sit with their children and read the Bible. I pray that more parents would sit with their children and help them with their homework. I pray we turn to You for the answers to all our questions, to all our needs. I pray every person on earth will look to the Bible for instruction, for guidance, for wisdom, and for understanding to learn the history of how it used to be and the revelation of how it should be in the future, and all this I pray in Jesus's holy name. Amen.

Wisdom and Understanding
August 19

"I, wisdom, dwell with prudence,
and find out knowledge and discretion.
The fear of the Lord is to hate evil;
pride and arrogance and the evil way and the
perverse mouth I hate.
Counsel is mine, and sound wisdom;
I am understanding, I have strength.
By me kings reign, and rulers decree justice.
By me princes rule, and nobles, all the
judges of the earth.
I love those who love me,
and those who seek me diligently will find me.
Riches and honor are with me,
enduring riches and righteousness.
My fruit is better than gold, yes, than fine gold,
and my revenue than choice silver.
I traverse the way of righteousness, in the midst of
justice, that I may cause those who love me to
inherit wealth, that I may fill their treasures
The Lord possessed me at the beginning of
His way, before His works of old. I have
been established from everlasting,
from the beginning, before there was ever an earth.
—Proverbs 8:12–23 NKJV

Praise the Lord!
Oh, give thanks to the Lord, for He is good!
For His mercy endures forever.
Who can utter the mighty acts of the Lord?
Who can declare all His praise?
Blessed are those who keep justice,
and he who does righteousness at all times!
—Psalm 106:1–3 NKJV

Lord, give us more wisdom; wisdom to be better at everything we do, wisdom to praise You more, wisdom to work better with others, wisdom to raise our children better, wisdom to love and understand others more; and with all that wisdom, please give us understanding, in Jesus's name. Amen!

Wisdom and Understanding
August 20

*Therefore David blessed the Lord
before all the assembly; and David said;
"Blessed are You, Lord God of Israel,
our Father, forever and ever. Yours, O Lord,
is the greatness, the power and the glory,
the victory and the majesty; for all that is in heaven
and in earth is Yours; Yours is the kingdom, O Lord,
and You are exalted as head over all.
Both riches and honor come from You,
and You reign over all. In Your hand is power
and might; in Your hand it is to make great and to
give strength to all.
"Now therefore, our God, we thank You and praise
Your glorious name. But who am I, and who are
my people, that we should be able to offer so
willingly as this? For all things come from You, and of
Your own we have given You.
—1 Chronicles 29:10–14 NKJV*

King David prayed this prayer after preparing rich offerings to the Lord: gold and silver and precious stones and lots more. It was right before he placed his son Solomon on the throne to be king instead of him. Read the rest; it is a very interesting history. Thank God today all we have to do is offer our heart and soul to God. We can be poor, rich, or in between. God is waiting and willing to accept us as we are. Say the prayer of salvation today. Father God, I accept You as my Lord and Savior. I believe that Jesus died on the cross for my sins, and I repent of my sins and call on Your name today. Please help me to walk in Your light. In Jesus's name, I pray. Amen. That's all it takes to be a Christian, then walk in the new light, and God will walk with you and make your life better as you study His word and learn of His ways.

Wisdom and Understanding
August 21

Receive one who is weak in the faith,
but not to disputes over doubtful things.
For one believes he may eat all
things, but he/she who is weak eats only vegetables.
Let not him/her who eats despise him who
does not eat, and let not him who does not
eat judge him who eats; for God has received him/her.
—Romans 14:1–3 NKJV

One person esteems one day above another;
another esteems every day alike. Let each be fully
convinced in his/her own mind.
He/she who observes the day, observes it
to the Lord; and he who does not observe the day,
to the Lord he/she does not observe it.
He who eats, eats to the Lord, for he gives
God thanks; and he who does not eat, to the
Lord he does not eat, and gives God thanks.
For none of us lives to himself/herself, and
no one dies to himself.
For if we live, we live to the Lord;
and if we die, we die to the Lord, therefore,
whether we live or die, we are the Lord's.
For to this end Christ died and rose and
lived again, that He might be Lord of both
the dead and the living.
—Romans 14:5–9 NKJV

Lord God, we are thankful that You are our God, that You love us unconditionally, and that you care about our comfort on this earth and You help us with your Spirit in our Spirit and give us peace and joy. We praise Your name forever and ever. Amen.

Wisdom and Understanding
August 22

And God spoke all these words, saying;
"I am the Lord your God, who brought you out
of the land of Egypt, out of the house of bondage.
"You shall have no other gods before me.
"You shall not make for yourself a carved image—any
likeness of anything that is in heaven above, or
that is in the earth beneath, or that is in the water
under the earth; you shall not bow down to them nor
serve them. For I, the Lord your God, am a jealous God,
visiting the iniquity of the fathers upon the children to the
third and fourth generations of those who hate Me,
but showing mercy to thousands, to those who love Me
and keep My commandments.
"You shall not take the name of the Lord your God
in vain, for the Lord will not hold him
guiltless who takes His name in vain.
"Remember the Sabbath day, to keep it holy.
—Exodus 20:1–8 NKJV

To be continued . . . !

Your kingdom is an everlasting kingdom,
and Your dominion endures throughout all
generations. The Lord upholds all who fall,
and raises up all who are bowed down.
The eyes of all look expectantly to You, and
You give them their food in due season.

You open Your hand and satisfy the desire
of every living thing. The Lord is righteous in all
His ways, Gracious in all His works.
—Psalm 145:13–17 NKJV

Precious and worthy of all glory is the Lord God Almighty, who cradles us in His great arms and keeps us from harm. Praise Your name, O Lord, my God. Amen!

Wisdom and Understanding
August 23

Continued . . .

Six days you shall labor and do all your work,
but the seventh day is the Sabbath of the Lord
your God. In it you shall do no work: You,
nor your son, nor your daughter, nor your male
servant, nor your female servant, nor your cattle,
nor your stranger who is within your gates.
For in six days the Lord made the heavens and
the earth, the sea, and all that is in them, and rested the
seventh day. Therefore the Lord blessed the
Sabbath day and hallowed it.
"Honor your father and your mother, that your days
may be long upon the land which the Lord your God
is giving you.
"You shall not murder.
"You shall not commit adultery.
"You shall not steal.
"You shall not bear false witness against your neighbor.
"You shall not covet your neighbor's house;
you shall not covet your neighbor's wife, nor his male
servant, nor his female servant, nor his ox,
nor his donkey, nor anything that is your neighbor's.
—Exodus 20:9–17 NKJV

The Lord is near to all who call upon Him,
to all who call upon Him in truth.
He will fulfill the desire of those who fear Him/
He also will hear their cry and save them.
The Lord preserves all who love Him,
but all the wicked He will destroy.
My mouth shall speak the praise of the Lord.
And all flesh shall bless His holy name.
Forever and ever.

—Psalm 145:18–21 NKJV

Those days, some envied others' ox, their servants, their donkey, etc. But today some envy others' cars, houses, jobs, others' man and others' woman, money, children. We don't appreciate what we already have, and some are not willing to work for what they want. Lord, help us to be thankful for what we have and to be patient until we get ours and always give thanks, tithes, and testimony, in Jesus's name. Amen.

Wisdom and Understanding
August 24

Jesus Spoke These Words

*"Most assuredly, I say to you, he who does
not enter the sheepfold by the door, but
climbs up some other way, the same is a thief and
a robber. "But he who enters by the door is the
shepherd of the sheep. "To him the doorkeeper
opens, and the sheep hear his voice; and he calls his own
sheep by name and leads them out. "And when he brings out
his own sheep, he goes before them; and the sheep follow
him, for they know his voice. "Yet they will by no
means follow a stranger, but will flee from him, for they
do not know the voice of strangers." Jesus used this
illustration, but they did not understand the things which
He spoke to them. Then Jesus said to them again,
"Most assuredly, I say to you, I am the door of the sheep.
"All who ever came before Me are thieves and robbers,
but the sheep did not hear them. "I am the door.
If anyone enters by Me, he will be saved, and will go
in and out and find pasture. "The thief does not come
except to steal, and to kill, and to destroy. I have come
that they may have life, and that they may have
it more abundantly. "I am the good shepherd. The good
shepherd gives His life for the sheep. "But a hireling,
he who is not the shepherd, one who does not own
the sheep, sees the wolf coming and leaves the sheep
and flees; and the wolf catches the sheep and scatters them.
"The hireling flees because he is a hireling and does not
care about the sheep. "I am the good shepherd; and I
know My sheep, and am known by My own.
—John 10:1–14 NKJV*

Father God, we thank You, we thank You because You do not bail out,
sneak out, and leave us when danger lurks around us. We thank You

because in all things, we can call on You, and You are there for us. We are grateful Lord that even when we feel like giving up, You are still there to be called on and to satisfy our yearning. We praise Your name, O Lord God Almighty. Amen.

Wisdom and Understanding
August 25

Jesus Spoke These Words

*"When the son of man comes in His glory,
all the holy angels with Him, then He will
sit on the throne of His glory. "All the nations will
be gathered before Him, and He will set the sheep
on His right hand, but the goats on the left. "Then the
King will say to those on His right hand, 'Come, you
blessed of My Father, inherit the kingdom prepared
for you from the foundation of the world; ' for I was
hungry and you gave Me food; I was thirsty and you gave Me
drink; I was a stranger and you took Me in;
'I was naked and you clothed Me; I was sick and you
visited Me; I was in prison and you came to Me.'
"Then the righteous will answer Him, saying, 'Lord when
did we see You hungry and feed You, or thirsty and give
You drink? 'When did we see You a stranger and take
You in, or naked and clothe You? 'Or when did
we see You sick, or in prison, and come to You?
"And the King will answer and say to them, 'Assuredly,
I say to you, inasmuch as you did it to one of the least
of these My brethren, you did it to Me.'
—Mathew 25:31–40 NKJV*

Lord, Father, my King, as much as it is possible in my power, please help me to help somebody else. Father, I want to always help others in need. Help me to open my eyes and see the needy around me. Open my ears and hear the cry of those who seek help. Open my mind that I may reach out and help whenever possible. For there is someone with less than I have, and I can help them along this life's journey. I thank You for Your gifts and all Your blessings toward me, in Jesus's name. Amen.

Wisdom and Understanding
August 26

Praise Him, Praise Him

Preserve me, O God, for in You I put my trust.
O my soul, you have said to the Lord,
"You are my Lord, My goodness is nothing apart from You."
—Psalm 16:1–2 NKJV

O Lord, You are the portion of my inheritance and my
cup; You maintain my lot. The lines have fallen to me
in pleasant places; Yes, I have a good inheritance.
I will bless the Lord who has given me counsel;
My heart also instructs me in the night seasons.
I have set the Lord always before me; because He
is at my right hand I shall not be moved. Therefore my
heart is glad, and my glory rejoices; my flesh also
will rest in hope. For You will not leave my soul
in Sheol, nor will You allow Your Holy One to see
corruption. you will show me the path of life;
In Your presence is fullness of joy;
At Your right hand are pleasures forevermore.
—Psalm 16:5–11 NKJV

The Lord lives! Blessed be my Rock!
Let the God of my salvation be exalted.
It is God who avenges me, and subdues
the peoples under me; He delivers me from my enemies.
You also lift me up above those who
rise against me; You have delivered me from the
violent man/woman. Therefore I will give thanks
to You, O Lord, among the gentiles, and sing
praises to Your name. Great deliverance He gives
to His king, and shows mercy to His anointed,
to David and his descendants forevermore.
—Psalm 18:46–50 NKJV

I wonder if I am a descendant of David the King. Either way, God is my defender, my sword, my shield; my rock, my deliverer, my restorer, my everything. What is God to you? Thank You, Lord! Amen.

Wisdom and Understanding
August 27

*But concerning brotherly love you have
no need that I should write to you, for you
yourselves are taught by God to love one another;
and indeed you do so toward all the brethren who
are in all Macedonia. But we urge you, brethren,
that you increase more and more; that you also aspire
to lead a quiet life, to mind your own business, and to
work with your own hands, as we commanded you,
that you may walk properly toward those who
are outside, and that you may lack nothing.
But I do not want you to be ignorant, brethren,
concerning those who have fallen asleep, lest you
sorrow as others who have no hope.
For if we believe that Jesus died and rose again,
even so God will bring with Him those who
sleep in Jesus. For this we say to you by the word of
the Lord, that we who are alive and remain until
the coming of the Lord will by no means precede
those who are asleep. For the Lord Himself will
descend from heaven with a shout, with the voice
of an archangel, and with the trumpet of God,
and the dead in Christ will rise first. Then we who are
alive and remain shall be caught up together with
them in the clouds to meet the Lord in the air.
And thus we shall always be with the Lord.
Therefore comfort one another with these words.
—Thessalonians 4:9–18 NKJV*

The Apostle Paul wrote a letter to the church of Macedonia. That very message is a word to us today, a reminder that death has no power with Christians. Those of us who believe in the Lord Jesus Christ, we know that we shall rise again and be with our Lord and God forever. Find peace in knowing that your loved ones are sleeping until that glorious day. And so will we one day rise again. Father, give us peace, power, and strength to know that whenever our loved ones pass away, that they are in resting in peace until You return for us. Thank You for eternal life with You. In Jesus's name, we pray. Amen. Mark 12:30–31 NKJV in the Bible, the Word of God, says, "And you shall love the Lord Your God with all your heart, and with all your soul, and with all your mind, and with all your strength"; this is the first commandment. The second is this: You shall love your neighbor as yourself. There is no commandment greater than these. It's very important to God that you love Him and next that you love all other human beings as you also love yourself. Learn to love yourself and who God sent you on this earth to be as you grow into that wonderful and amazing person, and as you grow, learn to love others. All other human beings are your neighbors. See them as you see yourself; lovingly and beautiful, worthy of kindness and consideration, worthy of love and a smile, worthy of pity and a hug, worthy of a second chance and mercy. See them through the eyes of God. Namaste. The divinity in me sees the divinity in you. I see only spirit and soul. The outer shell, the body does not speak for the spirit, the spirit speaks for the body and through the body. Treat everyone nicely. If they treat you badly, then step away if at all possible. Amen (let it be so).

Wisdom & Understanding
August 28

Praise Him, Praise Him

I will praise You,
for I am fearfully and wonderfully made;
Marvelous are Your works, and that my soul
knows very well. My form was not hidden from You,
when I was made in secret, and skillfully wrought in
the lowest parts of the earth. Your eyes saw my substance,
being yet unformed. And in Your book they all were
written, the days fashioned for me, when as yet there were
none of them. How precious also are Your thoughts
to me, O God! How great is the sum of them!
If I should count them, they would be more in number
than the sand; when I awake, I am still with You.
—Psalm 139:14–18 NKJV

I cry out to the Lord with my voice;
with my voice to the Lord I make my
supplication. I pour out my complain before Him;
I declare before Him my trouble.
When my spirit was overwhelmed within me,
Then You knew my path.
—Psalm 142:1–3 NKJV

When I think of how great You are, Lord, I realize how great Your creation of humans is. Lord, we thank You for creating us so special, and although we are a little lower than the angels, we are so very special to You. You made us in Your image, and You breathed glory and greatness in us. Help us to love ourselves and one another as You love us. Lord, we thank You for Your unceasing love forever and ever. Amen.

Wisdom and Understanding
August 29

*Oh, that men/women would give thanks to the
Lord for His goodness, and for His wonderful
works to the children of men!
Let them sacrifice the sacrifices of Thanksgiving,
and declare His works with rejoicing.
Those who go down to the sea in ships, who do business
in great waters, they see the works of the Lord,
and His wonders in the deep. For He commands and raises the
stormy wind, which lifts up the waves of the sea.
They mount up to the heavens, they go down again to
the depths; their soul melts because of trouble.
They reel to and fro and stagger like a drunken man/woman,
and are at their wits' end. Then they cry out to the Lord
in their trouble, and He brings them out of their distresses.
He calms the storm, so that its waves
are still. Then they are glad because they are quiet; So
He guides them to their desired haven.
Oh, that men/women would give thanks to the Lord for
His goodness, and for His wonderful works to the
children of men!
—Psalm 107:21–31 NKJV*

Wisdom and Understanding
August 30

Oh, that men would give thanks
to the Lord for His goodness, and for His
wonderful works to the children of men!
Let them exalt Him also in the assembly of the people,
and praise Him in the company of the elders.
He turns rivers into a wilderness, and the
watersprings into dry ground; a fruitful land into
barrenness, for the wickedness of those who
dwell in it. He turns a wilderness into pools of
water, and dry land into watersprings. There
He makes the hungry dwell, that they may establish
a city for a dwelling place, and sow fields and plant
vineyards that they may yield a fruitful harvest.
He also blesses them, and they multiply greatly;
and He does not let their castle decrease.
When they are diminished and brought low
through oppression, affliction and sorrow, He pours
contempt on princes, and causes them to wander in the
wilderness where there is no way; Yet He sets the
poor on high, far from affliction, and makes their
families like a flock. The righteous see it and rejoice,
and all iniquity stops its mouth. Whoever is wise will
observe these things, and they will understand the
loving kindness of the Lord.
—Psalm 107:31–43 NKJV

Imagine if God only cared about the rich and the very pretty and the very wealthy. The rest of us would be helpless, hopeless, and without a promise of a better tomorrow. O Lord, thank You for loving me. Thank You for opening Your arms to receive me. Thank You for loving the poor and powerless, making a way that we may rise up out of our poverty. Thank You for this world that You provided for all, that all might be partakers of its richness, its great rivers and beaches and oceans, its fruits and vegetables and trees and animals, and so much more. What an awesome God You are. You have included me, even me. Thank You, Father. Please teach me to include others that may have some need I can help them with. In Jesus's name, I pray. Amen.

Wisdom and Understanding
August 31

*Whatever your hand finds to do, do it with
your might; for there is no work or device or
knowledge or wisdom in the grave where you
are going.*
—Ecclesiastes 9:10 NKJV

*The race is not to the swift, nor the battle to the strong,
nor bread to the wise, nor riches to men of
understanding, nor favor to men of skill; but time
and chance happen to them all. For man/woman
also does not know his/her time: Like fish taken in
a cruel net, like birds caught in a snare, so the sons
of men are snared in an evil time, when it falls
suddenly upon them.*
—Ecclesiastes 9:11b–12 NKJV

*The days of our lives are seventy years; and if by
reason of strength they are eighty year, yet their
boast is only labor and sorrow; for it is soon cut
off, and we fly away. Who knows the power of
Your anger? For as the fear of You, so is Your wrath.
So teach us to number our days, that we may gain a heart
of wisdom. Return, O Lord! How Long?
And have compassion on Your servants. Oh, satisfy
us early with Your mercy, that we may rejoice and
be glad all our days! Make us glad according to the
days in which You have afflicted us, the years in
which we have seen evil. Let Your work appear to Your
servants, and Your glory to their children.
And let the beauty of the Lord our God be upon us,
and establish the work of our hands for us;
Yes, establish the work of our hands.*
—Psalm 90:10–17 NKJV

Father God, guide us and lead us, teach us how to live our lives in a way that it will glorify Your name. Help us to do more for others and to do it gladly. Give us the tools necessary to make our community a better place by helping those who don't have understanding, strength, and power. You give us all we need, Lord. Help us to use our hands, our minds, and our funds to help others. In Your name, I pray. Amen.

Wisdom and Understanding
September 1

Praise Him, Praise Him

Make a joyful shout to God, all the earth!
Sing out the honor of His name;
Make His praise glorious. Say to God,
"how awesome are Your works! Through
the greatness of Your power Your enemies
shall submit themselves to You. All the earth
shall worship You and sing praises to You;
They shall sing praises to Your name." Come and
see the works of God; He is awesome in His doing
toward the sons of men. He turned the sea into dry
land; they went through the river on foot.
There we will rejoice in Him. He rules by His
power forever; His eyes observe the nations;
Do not let the rebellious exalt themselves.
Oh, bless our God, you peoples!
and make the voice of His praise to be heard,
who keeps our soul among the living, and does
not allow our feet to be moved. For You,
O God, have tested us; You have refined us as silver
is refined. You brought us into the net;
You laid affliction on our backs. You have caused men
to ride over our heads; we went through fire
and through water; but You brought us out to
rich fulfillment.
—Psalm 66:1–12 NKJV

Blessed be our Lord God Almighty forever and ever. Amen.

Wisdom and Understanding
September 2

Wisdom, Understanding, and Love
(guess which one is the greatest)

*Though I speak with the tongues of men and of angels,
but have not love, I have become sounding brass or a clanging
cymbal. And though I have the gift of prophecy, and understand
all mysteries and all knowledge, and though I have all faith,
so that I could remove mountains, but have not love, I am
nothing. And though I bestow all my goods to feed the poor,
and though I give my body to be burned, but have not
love, it profits me nothing. Love suffers long and is kind; love
does not envy; love does not parade itself, is not puffed up;
does not behave rudely, does not seek its own, is not provoked,
thinks no evil; does not rejoice in iniquity, but rejoices
in the truth; bears all things, believes all things,
hopes all things, endures all things. Love never fails. But
whether there are prophecies, they will fail; whether
there are tongues, they will cease; whether there is
knowledge, it will vanish away.
For we know in part and we prophesy in part.
But when that which is perfect has come, then that which
is in part will be done away.
When I was a child, I spoke as a child, I understood as a child,
I thought as a child; but when I became a man/woman, I
put away childish things. for now we see in a mirror,
dimly, but then face to face. Now I know in part, but
then I shall know just as I also am known.
—1 Corinthians 13 NKJV*

What is your prayer today?

Amen.

Wisdom and Understanding
September 3

The Lord Speaks, If We Would Only Listen

"Behold! My Servant whom I uphold,
My Elect One in whom My soul delights!
I have put My Spirit upon Him;
He will bring forth justice to the Gentiles.
He will not cry out, nor raise his voice,
Nor cause His voice to be heard in the street.
A bruised reed He will not break,
and smoking flax He will not quench;
He will bring forth justice for truth.
He will not fail nor be discouraged,
till He has established justice in the earth;
and the coast lands shall wait for His law."
Thus says God the Lord,
who created the heavens and stretched them out,
Who spread forth the earth and that
which comes from it, Who gives breath
to the people on it, and spirit to those who walk
on it: "I, the Lord, have called You in righteousness,
and will hold Your hand; I will keep You
and give You as a covenant to the people, as a
light to the Gentiles, to open blind eyes,
to bring out prisoners from the prison, those
who sit in darkness from the prison house.
I am the Lord, that is My name; and My glory
I will not give to another, nor My praise to carved
images. Behold, the former things have come
to pass, and new things I declare; before they spring
forth I tell you of them."
—Isaiah 42:1–9 NKJV
Oh, sing to the Lord a new song!
Sing to the Lord, all the earth.
Sing to the Lord, bless His name;

318

Proclaim the good news of His salvation
from day to day.
Declare His Glory among the nations,
his wonders among all peoples.
—Psalm 96:1–3 NKJV

What is your prayer today?

Amen.

Do you live your life so busy, so consumed with things to do that you do not make time for quiet time, for meditation, for inspiration, for quiet thoughts, for silence, for quiet consideration of others, of flowers, of the ocean, of the trees? Really? You have not sat quietly in a very long time or at all? You must try it. What a discipline, what a humbling time it is. Sunshine, rain, snow, freezing weather, thunderbolts, lightnings, storms—O Lord, I hear you, I see you. Tell me what to do, how to think. Fix me, I want to be the best me ever. Break me and fix me and put me back together again. I want to be a light for others on this earth. I want to make a difference. I want to do my part, and my part is good and helpful. Help me, Father, great Spirit. I am not comfortable being regular or being unhelpful, not doing nothing. I want to inspire others, bless others' lives. I want to grow and laugh and encourage and bless others. Show me how. I am willing to accept my call, the call on my life. Thank you, Lord, for speaking to me. I hear you, and I accept. Amen!

Wisdom and Understanding
September 4

Praise Him, Praise Him

O God, my heart is steadfast; I will
sing and give praise, even with my glory.
Awake, lute and harp! I will awaken the dawn.
I will praise You, O Lord, among the peoples,
and I will sing praises to You among the nations.
For Your mercy is great above the heavens,
and Your truth reaches to the clouds.
Be exalted, O God, above the heavens,
and Your glory above all the earth; T
hat Your beloved may be delivered,
save with Your right hand, and hear me.
—Psalm 108:1–6 NKJV

Praise the Lord!
I will praise the Lord with my whole heart,
in the assembly of the upright and in the
congregation. The works of the Lord are great,
studied by all who have pleasure in them.
His work is honorable and glorious, and His
righteousness endures forever. He has made His
wonderful works to be remembered; the Lord
is gracious and full of compassion. He has given
food to those who fear Him; He will ever be mindful
of His covenant. He has declared to His
people the power of His works, in giving them
the heritage of the nations.
—Psalm 111:1–6 NKJV

What is your prayer today?

Amen!

Wisdom and Understanding
September 5

Praise Him, Praise Him

PRAISE the Lord!
I will praise the Lord with my whole heart,
in the assembly of the upright and in the congregation.
The works of the Lord are great, studied by all
who have pleasure in them.
—Psalm 111:1–2 NKJV

The works of His hands are verity and justice;
all His precepts are sure. They stand fast forever
and ever, and are done in truth and uprightness.
He has sent redemption to His people;
He has commanded His covenant forever;
Holy and awesome is His name.
The fear of the Lord is the beginning of wisdom;
a good understanding have all those who do His
commandments.
His praise endures forever.
—Psalm 111:7–10 NKJV

I will bless the Lord at all times;
His praise shall continually be in my mouth.
My soul shall make its boast in the Lord;
The humble shall hear o fit and be glad.
Oh, magnify the Lord with me, and let us
exalt His name together.
—Psalm 34 NKJV

Are you plotting and planning every day, all day, in your head how to scheme and trick your way with relationships, family, friends, stranger in every situation in your life? How silently stressful that must be. You yourself don't know you are living a fully stressful life. You become frosted when your schemes don't work out, and you set out to plan a new scheme. When your schemes work out, you think that is the way to go, and so you continue your life in that manner. One day your realize you are exhausted—body, mind, soul, and spirit—and you have nothing to show for all the schemes you did in your life. Schemes have no root, no permanent benefit, no substance. Now you are older and empty. You should have lived an honest life, a life with soul and spirit. What do you do now? Since you are still breathing, it's not too late to get it right. It's going to be hard, though, but you can do it. It's a choice.

Wisdom and Understanding
September 6

Praise Him, Praise Him

Praise the Lord!
Blessed is the man who fears the Lord,
who delights greatly in His commandments.
His descendants will be mighty on earth;
The generation of the upright will be blessed.
Wealth and riches will be in his house, and his
righteousness endures forever.
Unto the upright there arises light in the darkness;
He is gracious, and full of compassion, and righteous.
A good man deals graciously and lends;
He will guide his affairs with discretion.
Surely he will never be shaken; The righteous
will be in everlasting remembrance.
He will not be afraid of evil tidings;
his heart is steadfast, trusting in the Lord.
His heart is established;
He/she will not be afraid, until he/she sees his/her
desire upon his/her enemies.
He has disperse abroad, he has given to the poor;
His righteousness endures forever;
His horn will be exalted with honor.
The wicked will see it and be grieved;
He will gnash his teeth and melt away;
The desire of the wicked shall perish.
—Psalm 112 NKJV

Bless the Lord, O my soul!
O Lord my God, You are very great:
You are clothed with honor and majesty,
Who cover Yourself with light as with a garment,
Who stretch out the heavens like a curtain.
He lays the beams of His upper chambers

in the waters, Who makes the clouds His chariot,
Who walks on the wings to the wind, Who makes His angels spirits,
His ministers a flame of fire.
—Psalm 104:1–4 NKJV

What is your prayer today?

Wisdom and Understanding
September 7

Praise Him, Praise Him

PRAISE the Lord!
Praise, O servants of the Lord,
praise the name of the Lord!
Blessed be the name of the Lord from this
time forth and forevermore!
From the rising of the sun to its going down
The Lord's name is to be praised.
The Lord is high above all nations,
His glory above the heavens.
Who humbles Himself to behold the things that are
in the heavens and in the earth?
He raises the poor out of the dust,
and lifts the needy out of the ash heap,
That He may seat him with princes—with the princes
of His people, He grants the barren woman a home,
like a joyful mother of the children.
Praise the Lord!
—Psalm 113 NKJV

Give ear, O Shepherd of Israel,
You who lead Joseph like a flock;
You who dwell between the cherubim, shine forth!
Before Ephraim, Benjamin, and Manasseh,
stir up Your strength, and come and save us!
Restore us, O God; cause Your face to shine,
and we shall be saved!
—Psalm 80:1–2 NKJV

This is your challenge today or tomorrow, but as soon as you have time, or make time soon, Google (or search the web) for the three names in the above scripture and then read their stories in the Bible. They are really very interesting characters that we can learn from. To God be the glory. Amen.

Wisdom and Understanding
September 8

*On the twenty-third day of the seventh
month he sent the people away to their
tents, joyful and glad of heart for the good
that the Lord had done for David, for Solomon, and
for His people Israel.
Thus Solomon finished the house of the Lord
and the king's house; and Solomon successfully
accomplished all that came into his heart
to make in the house of the Lord and in his own house.
Then the Lord appeared to Solomon by night, and
said to him: "I have heard your prayer, and have
chosen this place for Myself as a house of sacrifice.
"When I shut up heaven and there is no rain,
or command the locusts to devour the land, or send
pestilence among My people,
"IF MY PEOPLE WHO ARE CALLED BY MY NAME
WILL HUMBLE THEMSELVES, AND PRAY
AND SEEK MY FACE, AND TURN FROM THEIR
WICKED WAYS, THEN I WILL HEAR FROM
HEAVEN, AND WILL FORGIVE THEIR SIN
AND HEAL THEIR LAND.
"Now my eyes will be open and My ears attentive to prayer
made in this place. "For now I have chosen and sanctified
this house, that My name may be there forever; and My
eyes and My heart will be there perpetually.
—2 Chronicles 7:10–16 NKJV*

O Lord, show me how to be humble and when to be humble. Teach me Your ways in every situation. Teach me how to discern what my actions, my words, my attitude should be in every occasion. Help me to trust You so that I don't feel I need tricks and dishonesty to get the things I need. Help me to trust You more. In Jesus's name. Amen.

Wisdom and Understanding
September 9

Jesus Spoke These Words

*Verily I say unto you, Except ye be converted,
and become as little children, ye shall not enter into
the kingdom of heaven.
Whosoever therefore shall humble himself/herself
as this little child, the same is greatest in the
kingdom of heaven. And whoso shall receive
one such little child in my name receiveth me.
But whoso shall offend one of these little ones
which believe in me, it were better for him/her that a
millstone were hanged about his neck, and that he/she
were drowned in the depth of the sea.
Woe unto the world because of offenses! For
it must needs be that offenses come; but woe to the
man/woman by whom the offense cometh!
—Matthew 18:3–7 KJV*

Lord, I pray for the children of the world, so innocent, children abused and mistreated by evil adults. Father, protect the children, we pray. Send them someone who cares and can help against the abuse they suffer. So many vulnerable and innocent little ones are suffering great harm from people possessed with evil. Help us to speak up against violence to children all over the world. We pray, in Jesus's name. Amen.

Wisdom and Understanding
September 10

Praise Him, Praise Him

Blessed are the undefiled in the way,
who walk in the law of the Lord!
Blessed are those who keep His testimonies,
who seek Him with the whole heart!
They also do no iniquity;
they walk in His ways.
You have commanded us to keep your precepts
diligently. Oh, that my ways were directed
to keep Your statutes!
Then I would not be ashamed, when I look
into all Your commandments.
I will praise you with uprightness of heart, when
I learn your righteous judgments.
—Psalm 119:1–7 NKJV

PRAISE the Lord!
Praise God in His sanctuary;
Praise Him in His mighty firmament!
Praise Him for His mighty acts;
Praise Him according to His excellent greatness!
Praise Him with the sound of the trumpet;
Praise Him with the lute and harp!
Praise Him with the timbrel and dance;
Praise Him with stringed instruments and flutes!
Praise Him with loud cymbals;
Praise Him with clashing cymbals!
Let everything that has breath
praise the Lord!
Praise the Lord!
—Psalm 150 NKJV

What is your prayer today?

Blessed be the Lord God Almighty. Amen!

Wisdom and Understanding
September 11

Things That Make You Go *Hhhhmmmmm*

*Surely oppression destroys a wise man's reason,
and a bribe debases the heart.*

The end of a thing is better than its beginning;

The patient in spirit is better than the proud in spirit.

*Do not hasten in your spirit to be angry, for anger
rests in the bosom of fools.*

*Do not say, "why were the former days better than these?"
For you do not inquire wisely concerning this.*

*Wisdom is good with an inheritance, and profitable
to those who see the sun. For wisdom is a defense as
money is a defense, but the excellence of
knowledge is that wisdom gives life to those who have it.*

*Consider the work of God; for who can make
straight what He has made crooked?*

*In the day of prosperity be joyful, but in the day
of adversity consider; surely God has appointed
the one as well as the other, so that man can
find out nothing that will come after him.
(I have seen everything in my days of vanity:)*

*There is a just man/woman who perishes in his/her
righteousness, and there is a wicked man/woman who
prolongs life in his/her wickedness.
Do not be overly righteous, nor be overly wise:
Why should you destroy yourself? Do not be overly
wicked, nor be foolish: Why should you die before your time?*

*It is good that you grasp this, and also not remove
your hand from the other; for he who fears God will escape them all.*

*Wisdom strengthens the wise more than ten rulers
of the city. For there is not a just man/woman on
earth who does good and does not sin.*

*Also do not take to heart everything people say,
lest you hear your servant cursing you. For many
times, also, your own heart has known
that even you have cursed others.*
—Ecclesiastes 7:7–22 NKJV

*The Lord opens the eyes of the blind;
The Lord raises those who are bowed down;
the Lord loves the righteous.*
—Psalm 146:8 NKJV

What is your prayer today?

Amen.

Wisdom and Understanding
September 12

*These are the things I want you to teach and
preach. If you have leaders there who teach otherwise,
who refuse the solid words of our Master Jesus
and this godly instruction, tag them for what they are:
Ignorant windbags who infect the air with germs
of envy, controversy, bad-mouthing, suspicious
rumors. Eventually there's an epidemic of backstabbing,
and truth is but a distant memory. They think
religion is a way to make a fast buck.
A devout life does bring wealth, but it's the
rich simplicity of being yourself before God.
Since we entered the world penniless and will leave it
penniless, if we have bread on the table and shoes
on our feet, that's enough. But if it's only money these
leaders are after, they'll self-destruct in no time.
Lust for money brings trouble and nothing but trouble.
Going down that path, some lose their footing in the
faith completely and live to regret it bitterly
ever after.
—1 Timothy 6:2–10 MSG*

O God, help us to rely on money only as a tool to get things done, as a tool to provide for our needs and some wants. Let us not become so greedy for money that we steal, we lie, we covet others' assets and things, so much so that we lose our way. Help us to work for and earn what we want. Help us not to make money our god and to remember that as long as we do our part that our God, You Lord, is able to provide for us. In Jesus's name, we pray. Amen.

Wisdom and Understanding
September 13

*Nevertheless He did not leave himself without
witness, in that He did good, gave us rain
from heaven and fruitful seasons, filling our
hearts with good and gladness.*
—Acts 14:17 NKJV

*Is anyone among you Sick? Let him/her
call for the elders of the church, and let them
pray over him, anointing him/her with oil
in the name of the Lord. And the prayer of faith will
save the sick, and the Lord will raise him/her up.
And if he has committed sins, he will be forgiven.
Confess your trespasses to one another, and
pray for one another, that you may be healed.
The effective, fervent prayer of a righteous man/woman
avails much. Elijah was a man with a nature like
ours, and he prayed earnestly that it would
not rain; and it did not rain on the land for three
years and six months. And he prayed again,
and the heaven gave rain, and the earth produced its
fruit. Brethren, If anyone among you wanders from
the truth, and someone turns him/her back, let him know
that he/she who turns a sinner from the
error of his/her way will save a soul from death
and cover a multitude of sins.*
—James 5:14–20 NKJV

*It is good to give thanks to the Lord,
and to sing praises to Your name, O Most High;
To declare Your loving kindness in the morning,
and Your faithfulness every night.*
—Psalm 92:1–2 NKJV

Oh, Father, we thank You for the rain. Let it rain. We thank You for the rain. If it does not rain on the planet, we will not have food to eat. So we thank You for the rain. The streets become quiet and the families get together when it rains. We thank You for the rain. We say "sorry" for cursing the rain when it rains because we need the rain. Lord, You are all-wise and all- knowing, and thank You for giving us rain. Thank You. Amen.

Wisdom and Understanding
September 14

I Look to You

Be merciful to me, O God, be merciful to me!
For my soul trusts in You;
and in the shadow of Your wings I will make
my refuge, until these calamities have passed by.
He shall send from heaven and save me;
He reproaches the one who would swallow me up.
God shall send forth His mercy and His truth.
My soul is among lions; I lie among
the sons of men who are set on fire,
whose teeth are spears and arrows, and
their tongue a sharp sword.
Be exalted, O God, above the heavens;
Let Your glory be above all the earth.
They have prepared a net for my steps;
my soul is bowed down; they have dug a pit
before me; into the midst of it they themselves
have fallen. My heart is steadfast,
O God, my heart is steadfast; I will sing and
give praise. Awake, my glory!
Awake, lute and harp! I will awaken the dawn.
I will praise You, O Lord, among the peoples;
I will sing to You among the nations. For Your
mercy reaches unto The heavens, and
Your truth onto the clouds. Be exalted, O God,
above the heavens; let Your glory be above
all the earth.
—Psalm 57 NKJV

O God, how magnificent is all Your creation: the sun at dusk, the full moon in the night sky, and everything in between; Your love for me and Your love for Your world. Thank You for being the great I *Am.* Amen.

Wisdom and Understanding
September 15

Things That Make You Go *Hhhhmmmmm*

*The discretion of a man/woman makes him/her
slow to anger, and his glory is to overlook a
transgression.*

*The King's wrath is like the roaring of a lion,
but his favor is like dew on the grass.*

*A foolish son is the ruin of his father,
and the contentions of a wife are a
continual dripping.*

*Houses and riches are an inheritance from parents,
but a prudent wife is from the Lord.*

*Laziness casts one into a deep sleep,
and an idle person will suffer hunger.*

*He who keeps the commandments keeps his soul,
but he who is careless of his ways will die.*

*He who has pity on the poor lends
to the Lord, and He will pay back what he has given.*

*Chasten your son/daughter while there is hope,
and do not set your heart on his/her destruction.*

*A man of great wrath will suffer punishment;
for if you rescue him, you will have to do it again.*

*Listen to counsel and receive instruction,
that you may be wise in your latter days.*

There are many plans in a man's heart,
nevertheless the Lord's counsel—that will stand.

What is desired in a man is kindness,
and a poor man is better than a liar.

The fear of the Lord leads to life, and he who has
it will abide in satisfaction;
he will not be visited with evil.
—Proverbs 19:11–23 NKJV

The Lord reigns, He is clothed with majesty;
the Lord is clothed, He has girded Himself
with strength. Surely the world is established,
so that it cannot be moved. Your throne is established
from old; you are from everlasting.
—Psalm 93:1–2 NKJV

Father, teach me to make the right decisions in this life experience. Help me to make right choices and to trust You as I stay on the right path. Forgive me for bad choices made and evil acts done. I pray You guide me along the right way, in Jesus's name. Amen.

Wisdom and Understanding
September 16

*For thus saith the Lord of hosts; Yet
once, it is a little while, and I will shake the
heavens, and the earth, and the sea, and the dry land;
and I will shake all nations, and the desire of all nations shall
come: and I will fill this house with glory, saith
the Lord of hosts.
The silver is mine, and the gold is mine, saith the Lord of
hosts. The glory of this latter house shall be greater
than of the former, saith the Lord of hosts: and in this
place will I give peace, saith the Lord of hosts.
—Haggai 2:6–9 KJV*

Read it again and think of your life. During all the hard times you've been through, you kept the faith, you stayed in the race, you endured grave hardship, and now your Father is telling you, "The silver is mine, and the gold is mine." The glory of your future, the glory of my future will be greater than the glory of your past. In this new future, I will give you peace. Lord, give me strength to endure.

Help me to see Your light shining before me and guiding me into a better time. In Jesus's name, we pray. Amen.

Wisdom and Understanding
September 17

Praise Him, Praise Him

God is our refuge and strength,
a very present help in trouble.
Therefore we will not fear,
even though the earth be removed,
and though the mountains be carried into
the midst of the sea; though its waters roar
and be troubled, though the mountains
shake with its swelling. There is a river whose
streams shall make glad the city of God,
the holy place of the tabernacle of the Most High.
God is in the midst of her, she shall not be moved;
God shall help her, just at the break of dawn.
The nations raged, the kingdoms were moved;
He uttered His voice, the earth melted.
The Lord of hosts is with us;
the God of Jacob is our refuge.
—Psalm 46:1–7 NKJV

O God, I trust You. If I did not know You, I don't know who I would turn to for those questions that man cannot answer, those questions that the soul and the spirit ask. O God, You are the only Spirit that can answer those questions. Thank You for hearing my cry, in Jesus's name. Amen.

Wisdom and Understanding
September 18

Paul Reminds Us

Therefore I exhort first of all that supplications,
prayers, intercessions, and giving of thanks be
made for all men/women, for kings and all
who are in authority, that we may lead a quiet
and peaceable life in all godliness and reverence.
For this is good and acceptable in the sight of
God our Savior, who desires all men/women to be
saved and to come to the knowledge of the truth.
For there is one God and one Mediator between God
and men, the Man Christ Jesus,
who gave Himself as ransom for all, to be testified
in due time, for which I was appointed a
preacher and an apostle—I am speaking the truth
in Christ and not lying—a teacher of the Gentiles in
faith and truth. I desire therefore that the men
pray everywhere, lifting up holy hands, without
wrath and doubting; in like manner also, that the
women adorn themselves in modest apparel,
with propriety and moderation.
—1 Timothy 2:1–9 NKJV

Restore us, O God of hosts; Cause Your face to shine,
and we shall be saved! You have brought
a vine out of Egypt; You have cast out the
nations, and planted it. You prepared room for it,
and caused it to take deep root, and it filled the land.
The hills were covered with its shadow, and the
mighty cedars with its boughs. She sent out her
boughs to the sea, and her branches to the River.
—Psalm 80:7–11 NKJV
Restore us, O Lord God of hosts;
cause Your face to shine, and we shall be saved.
—Psalm 80:19 NKJV

Father God, we need guidance and direction. Help us to open our eyes and receive from You, we pray. Amen.

Sometimes family and friends are suffering, are in need of a job, are in need of a kinder and gentler spirit and character. Sometimes they are in need of money, but you know that you giving them help will not fix the problem. Offer them prayer, "I can't help you with that, but I am going to pray for you and your situation." Know that that is a valid and great help. To offer prayer is a wonderful effort to help but only if you mean it. If you are going to take the time, just a few minutes or a long time, whatever you chose, say a word about that person in your moment of prayer to the Almighty and capable God that knows exactly what is happening with that person. So many times a person in our lives will tell us one part of the problem while there is so much more to the problem. Probably, something's steaming from their childhood that is still affecting them in a negative way or something they experienced at work

Wisdom and Understanding
September 19

This I say, therefore, and testify in the Lord,
that you should no longer walk as the rest of
the gentiles walk, in the futility of their mind,
having their understanding darkened, being alienated
from the life of God, because of the ignorance that
is in them, because of the blindness of their heart;
who, being past feeling, have given themselves
over to lewdness, to work all uncleanness
with greediness. But you have not so learned
Christ, if indeed you have heard Him and have been
taught by Him, as the truth is in Jesus:
That you put off, concerning your former conduct,
the old man/woman which grows corrupt according
to the deceitful lusts, and be renewed in the
spirit of your mind, and that you put on the new
man/woman which was created according to God,
in true righteousness and holiness, therefore putting
away lying, "Let each one of you speak truth
with his neighbor," for we are members of one another.
"Be angry, and do not sin." Do not let the sun
go down on your wrath, nor give place to the
devil, let him who stole steal no longer, but rather
let him labor, working with his hands what is good,
that he/she may have something to give him who has need.
—Ephesians 4:17–28 NKJV

Make me understand the way of your precepts;
so shall I meditate on Your wonderful works.
My soul melts from heaviness; strengthen me
according to Your word. Remove from me the way
of lying, and grant me Your law graciously.
I have chosen the way of truth, Your judgments
I have laid before me.
—Psalm 119:27–30 NKJV

Father God, we need more of your grace and mercy. Help us to be still when angry, that we may not strike a blow or pick up a weapon or hurt someone in anger. Help us to learn to reach out to You when we are upset, that we may not say or do regrettable things in the midst of our anger; lest the devil wins and we end up in jail here on earth and be punished forever. Help us to think of tomorrow and the consequences when we allow anger to get the better of us. I pray for more of Your power and wisdom, in Jesus's name. Amen.

Wisdom and Understanding
September 20

We Cry Out to You Lord

Hear a just cause, O Lord,
attend to my cry;
Give ear to my prayer which is not from
deceitful lips. Let my vindication
come from your presence;
Let Your eyes look on the things
that are upright. You have tested my heart;
You have visited me in the night;
You have tried me and have found nothing;
I have purposed that my mouth
shall not transgress. Concerning the
works of men, by the word of Your lips,
I have kept away from the paths of the
destroyer. Uphold my steps in Your paths,
that my footsteps may not slip.
I have called upon You, for You will hear
me O God; Incline Your ear to me,
and hear my speech. Show Your marvelous
loving kindness by Your right hand,
O You who save those who trust in You
from those who rise up against them.
Keep me as the apple of Your eye;
Hide me under the shadow of Your wings,
from the wicked who oppress me,
from my deadly enemies who surround me.
—Psalm 17:1–9 NKJV
As for me, I will see Your face in
righteousness; I shall be satisfied
when I awake in Your likeness.
—Psalm 17:15 NKJV

Lord, please protect us with Your loving spirit. Send Your angels to shelter us from harm and wrong decisions. We need Your protection from evil spirits. We need Your protection always. We say, thank You, Lord, in Jesus's name. Amen.

Wisdom and Understanding
September 21

Go ahead and be angry. You do well to be angry
but don't use your anger as fuel for revenge.
And don't stay angry. Don't go to bed angry.
Don't give the devil that kind of foothold in your life.
Did you use to make ends meet by stealing? Well, no more!
Get an honest job so that you can help others who
can't work. Watch the way you talk. Let nothing f
oul or dirty come out of your mouth. Say only what
helps, each word a gift. Don't grieve God. Don't break
His heart. His Holy Spirit, moving and breathing in you,
is the most intimate part of your life, making you fit
for Himself. Don't take such a gift for granted.
Make a clean break with all cutting, backbiting,
profane talk. Be gentle with one another, sensitive.
Forgive one another as quickly and thoroughly as
God in Christ forgave you.
—Ephesians 4:26–32 MSG

Blessed are the people who know the
joyful sound! They walk, O Lord, in the light of
Your countenance. In Your name they rejoice
all day long, and in Your righteousness they are
exalted. For You are the glory of their
strength, and in Your favor our horn is exalted.
For our shield belong to the Lord, and
our king to the Holy One of Israel.
—Psalm 89:15–18 NKJV

Lord, we know Your laws are righteous. We were made to obey Your laws; to love You, to love one another, to not to kill, to not to steal, to not to offend our brother or sister, but in all good things, to encourage one another. Teach us Your laws again and show us how to abide by them that our soul will be at peace always, in Jesus's name. Amen.

Wisdom and Understanding
September 22

*Now the Spirit expressly says that in latter
times some will depart from the faith,
giving heed to deceiving spirits and doctrines
of demons. Speaking lies in hypocrisy, having
their own conscience seared with a hot iron, forbidding
to marry, and commanding to abstain from foods which
God created to be received with thanksgiving
by those who believe and know the truth.
For every creature of God is good, and nothing
is to be refused if it is received with thanksgiving;
for it is sanctified by the word of God and prayer.
If you instruct the brethren in these things, you
will be a good minister of Jesus Christ, nourished
in the words of faith and of the good doctrine which you
have carefully followed. But reject profane and old
wives' fables, and exercise yourself toward godliness.
For bodily exercise profits a little, but godliness
is profitable for all things, having promise of the life that
now is and of that which is to come. This is a faithful saying
and worthy of all acceptance. For to this end we both
labor and suffer reproach, because we trust in the
living God, who is the Savior of all men,
especially of those who believe.
These things command and teach.
—1 Timothy 4:1-11 NKJV*

*The Lord is my light and my salvation;
Whom shall I fear? The Lord is the
strength of my life; of whom shall I be afraid?
When the wicked came against me to eat up my flesh,
my enemies and foes, they stumbled and fell.
Though an army may encamp against me,
my heart shall not fear; though war may arise
against me, in this I will be confident.*

One thing I have desired of the Lord that I will seek:
That I may dwell in the house of the Lord all the days
of my life, to behold the beauty of the Lord, and to
inquire in His temple.
Psalm 27:1–4 NKJV

Amen.

(Remember to pray today)

Wisdom and Understanding
September 23

*God proves to be good to
the man who passionately waits, to the woman who
diligently seeks. It's a good thing to quietly hope,
quietly hope for help from God. It's a good thing when
you're young to stick it out through the
hard times. When life is heavy and hard to take,
go off by yourself. Enter the silence. Bow in prayer.
Don't ask questions: Wait for hope to appear.
Don't run from trouble. Take it full-face. The "worst"
is never the worst. Why? Because the Master won't
ever walk out and fail to return.
If he works severely, he also works tenderly.
His stockpiles of loyal love are immense.
He takes no pleasure in making life hard, in throwing
roadblocks in the way: Stomping down hard
on luckless prisoners, refusing justice to victims
in the court of High God, tampering with evidence—
the Master does not approve of such things.*
—Lamentations 3:25–36 The Message/Remix Version

*The Heavens declare the glory of God;
and the firmament shows His handiwork.
Day unto day utters speech, and night unto night
reveals knowledge. There is no speech nor language
where their voice is not heard. Their line has gone
out through all the earth, and their words to the end
of the world. In them He has set a tabernacle for the sun,
which is like a bridegroom coming out of his chamber,*

*and rejoices like a strong man to run its race.
Its rising is from one end of heaven, and its circuit to
the other end; and there is nothing hidden from its heat.*
—Psalm 19:1–6 NKJV

Lord, we thank You for everything you have made and given to us for our enjoyment. We thank You for loving us and protecting us. Help us to say thank You more often, in Jesus's name. Amen.

Wisdom and Understanding
September 24

*Let no one despise your youth, but
be an example to the believers in word, in conduct,
in love, in spirit, in faith, in purity.
—1 Timothy 4:12 NKJV*

*The law of the Lord is perfect,
converting the soul;
The testimony of the Lord is sure,
making wise the simple; the statutes of the Lord
are right, rejoicing the heart; the commandment
of the Lord is pure, enlightening the eyes;
the fear of the Lord is clean, enduring forever;
the judgments of the Lord are true and righteous
altogether. More to be desired are they
then gold, Yea, than much fine gold;
Sweeter also than honey and the honeycomb.
—Psalm 19:7–10 NKJV*

*Let the words of my mouth and the
meditation of my heart, be acceptable
in Your sight, O Lord, my strength and
my redeemer.
—Psalm 19:14 NKJV*

What is your prayer today?

Amen.

Wisdom and Understanding
September 25

Praise Him, Praise Him

*Forever, O Lord, Your word is
settled in heaven. Your faithfulness endures
to all generations; You established the earth,
and it abides. They continue this day according to
Your ordinances, for all are Your servants.
Unless Your law had been my delight, I would
then have perished in my affliction. I will never
forget Your precepts. For by them You have
given me life. I am Yours, save me;
for I have sought Your precepts. The wicked wait for me
to destroy me, but I will consider Your testimonies.
I have seen the consummation of all perfection,
but Your commandment is exceedingly broad.
Oh, how I love Your law!
it is my meditation all the day. You, through Your
commandments, make me wiser than my enemies;
for they are ever with me. I have more
understanding than all my teachers, for Your testimonies
are my meditation. I understand more than the
ancients, because I keep Your precepts.
I have restrained my feet from every evil way,
that I may keep Your word.
—Psalm 119:89–101 NKJV*

Like King David, sing your own psalm to the Lord today.

Wisdom and Understanding
September 26

Things That Make You Go *Hhhhmmmmm*

He who is often rebuked, and hardens his/her neck,
will suddenly be destroyed, and that without
remedy.

When the righteous are in authority, the people
rejoice; but when a wicked man/woman rules, the people
groan.

Whoever loves wisdom makes his/her father/mother rejoice,
but a companion of harlots wastes his/her wealth.

The king/president establishes the land by justice,
but he who receives bribes overthrows it.

A man/woman who flatters his/her neighbor
spreads a net for his feet.

By transgression an evil man/woman is snared,
but the righteous sings and rejoices.

The righteous considers the cause of the poor,
but the wicked does not understand such knowledge.

Scoffers set a city aflame, but wise men turn away wrath.

If a wise man/woman contends with a foolish person,
whether the fool rages or laughs there is no peace.

The bloodthirsty hate the blameless, but
the upright seek his well-being.

A fool vents all his feelings, but a wise man/woman
holds them back.

*If a ruler pays attention to lies, all his/her servants
become wicked.*

*The poor man/woman and the oppressor have this in common:
The Lord gives light to the eyes of both.*

*The King/President/leader who judges the poor
with truth, his/her throne will be established
forever.*

*The rod and rebuke give wisdom. but a child left to
himself brings shame to his mother.
—Proverbs 29:1–15 NKJV*

*Praise the Lord!
Praise the Lord, O my soul!
While I live I will praise the Lord;
I will sing praises to my God while I have my being.
—Psalm 146:1–2 NKJV*

Remember to pray today.

Wisdom and Understanding
September 27

Beloved, let us love one another, for
love is of God; and everyone who loves is born
of God and knows God.
He who does not love does not know God, for
God is Love.
In this the love of God was manifested toward
us, that God has sent His only begotten Son into
the world, that we might live through Him.
In this is love, not that we loved God,
but that He loves us and sent His Son to be
the propitiation for our sins.
Beloved, if God so loved us, we also ought
to love one another. No one has seen God
at any time. If we love one another, God abides in us,
and His love has been perfected in us.
By this we know that we abide in Him,
and He in us, because He has given us of His Spirit.
And we have seen and testify that the Father
has sent the Son as Savior of the world.
—1 John 4:7–14 NKJV

I believe in God as sovereign, the one and only God; God Almighty, all powerful, magnificent, and wonderful. I believe in His Son, Jesus Christ, my Savior and my Redeemer. Father God, thank You for Your awesome power, grace, and mercy, in Jesus's name. Amen.

Wisdom and Understanding
September 28

Things That Make You Go *Hhhhmmmmm*

*The rod and rebuke give wisdom, but a
child left to himself brings shame to his mother.*

*When the wicked are multiplied, transgression
increases; but the righteous will see their fall.*

*Correct your son/daughter and he/she will give
you rest; Yes, he/she will give delight to your soul.*

*Where there is no revelation, the people cast off restraint;
but happy is he who keeps the law.*

*A servant will not be corrected by mere words; for though he/she
understands, he/she will not respond.*

*Do you see a man/woman hasty in his words?
there is more hope for a fool than for him.*
—Proverbs 29:15–20 NKJV

*An angry man/woman stirs up strife, and a furious
man/woman abounds in transgression.*

*A man/woman's pride will bring him low,
but the humble in spirit will retain honor.*

*Whoever is a partner with a thief hates his own life;
he swears to tell the truth, but reveals nothing.*

*The fear of man brings a snare, but whoever trusts
in the Lord shall be safe.
Many seek the ruler's favor, but justice for man
comes from the Lord.*

An unjust man is an abomination to the righteous
and he who is upright in the way is an abomination to the wicked.
—Proverbs 29:22–27 NKJV

I have not departed from Your judgments,
for You Yourself have taught me.
How sweet are Your words to my taste,
sweeter than honey to the mouth!
Through Your precepts I get understanding;
Therefore I hate every false way.
—Psalm 119:102–104 NKJV

How can I make the world a better place? I can be a better person. I can use better judgment in every situation. I can be just, kind, and nice. I can choose to do the right thing instead of the devious, tricky, wrong thing. I chose to trust God and love my neighbors, in Jesus's name. Amen.

Wisdom and Understanding
September 29

Praise Him, Praise Him

Your word is a lamp to my feet and a light to my path.
I have sworn and confirmed that I will keep Your righteous
judgments. I am afflicted very much; revive me, O Lord,
according to Your word. Accept, I pray, the freewill
offerings of my mouth, O Lord, and teach me Your
judgments. My life is continually in my hand,
yet I do not forget Your law. The wicked have laid
a snare for me, yet I have not strayed from Your
precepts. Your testimonies I have taken as a heritage
forever, for they are the rejoicing of my heart.
I have inclined my heart to perform Your statues
forever, to the very end.
—*Psalm 119:105–112 NKJV*

How rich and wonderful is Your word, O Lord. Even as King David prayed to You and sang Psalms to You, he uttered words that live in my heart today. Sometimes his Psalms have the very word I need to cry out to You, Lord, and so I thank You for Your precious Bible, the guide for better, happier, and richer life on earth, until we meet face-to- face. Thank You, Lord God, in Jesus's name. Amen.

Sit and meditate today, even if you are in trouble. If you are having a hard life, if you are sad, today take a minute or two, an hour or two, and just be still and let your thoughts consider good things of life, like the moon, the sun, the flowers, the rain, whatever else that's good and wonderful. Close your eyes, take a break, and let that be your moment to slow down, and after you are done, see how you feel. Maybe new hope, new insights, newness and great expectations will mobilize you to action that will bring joy and happiness to your life. Slow down and see.

Wisdom and Understanding
September 30

You realize, don't you, that you are the
temple of God, and God himself is present in you?
No one will get by with vandalizing God's temple,
you can be sure of that. God's temple is sacred—
and you, remember, are the temple.
Don't fool yourself. Don't think that you can be
wise merely by being up-to-date with the times.
Be God's fool—that's the path to true wisdom.
What the world calls smart, God calls stupid.
It's written in the Scripture, He exposes the
chicanery of the chic. The Master sees through the
smoke screens of the know-it-alls.
I don't want to hear any of you bragging about yourself
or anyone else. Everything is already yours as a
gift-all of it is yours, and you are privileged to be
in union with Christ, who is in union with God.
—1 Corinthians 3:16–23 The Message/Remix Version

Do not keep silent, O God of my praise!
—Psalm 109:1 NKJV

O God, You are the great Creator. You made us humans so special and so unique. We cannot yet understand how wonderfully and awesomely we are made. Our parts are complex and intricate and amazing. You made our eyes, our ears, and our amazing brains. Every part of our body is amazing and works amazingly. Our spirit is not yet fully known. You keep us busy, learning more and more about Your awesome work in us. We praise You, and we adore You. We love You, God, in Jesus's name. Amen.

Wisdom and Understanding
October 1

I hate the double-minded,
but I love Your law.
You are my hiding place and my shield;
I hope in Your word.
Depart from me, you evildoers,
for I will keep the commandments of my God!
Uphold me according to Your word, that I may live;
and do not let me be ashamed of my hope.
Hold me up, and I shall be safe, and I shall
observe Your statutes continually.
—Psalm 119:113–117 NKJV

Oh, give thanks to the Lord, for He is good!
For His mercy endures forever.
Let Israel now say, "His mercy endures forever."
Let the house of Aaron now say, "His mercy endures
forever." Let those who fear the Lord now say,
"His mercy endures forever."
—Psalm 118:1–4 NKJV

Lord God, all wisdom belong to You. I pray You impart some of Your wisdom to me that I may walk the hard, narrow, but correct path in Your name. I know the road will get easier if I endure. Give me Your Spirit that I may do the right thing, O Lord, in Jesus's name. Amen.

Wisdom and Understanding
October 2

Jesus Spoke These Words

*Now it came to pass, as He was praying
in a certain place, when He ceased, that
one of His disciples said to Him, "Lord teach
us to pray, as John also taught his disciples."
So He said to them, "When you pray, say:
Our Father in heaven, Hallowed be Your Name.
Your kingdom come. Your will be done
on earth as it is in heaven. Give us day by day
our daily bread. And forgive us our sins.
For we also forgive everyone who is indebted
to us. And do not lead us into temptation,
but deliver us from the evil one.*
—Luke 11:1-4 NKJV

*Then He said, "Imagine what would happen if you went to a friend
in the middle of the night and said, 'Friend, lend me
three loaves of bread. An old friend traveling through
just showed up, and I don't have a thing on hand.'
"The friend answers from his bed, 'Don't bother me. The door is
locked, my children are all down for the night; I can't get up
to give you anything.' "But let me tell you, even if he
won't get up because he's a friend, if you stand your ground,
knocking and waking all the neighbors, he'll finally get
up and get you whatever you need. Here's what I'm saying:
Ask and you'll get;
Seek and you'll find;
Knock and the door will open.*
—Luke 11:5-9 The Message/Remix Version

Lord God, all my hope is in You. I know that my struggles will change into blessings. I know that as long as I do my best, You will do the rest. Thank You for Your grace and mercy showered on me every day. I need

Your blessings because I am just not that good without You. In Jesus's name, I pray. Amen.

Wisdom and Understanding
October 3

How many are the days of Your servant?
When will You execute judgment on those
who persecute me? The proud have dug pits
for me, which is not according to Your law.
All Your commandments are faithful; they
persecute me wrongfully; Help me!
they almost made an end of me on earth, but
I did not forsake Your precepts. Revive me according
to Your loving-kindness, so that I may keep the testimony
of Your mouth. Forever, O Lord, Your word is
settled in heaven. Your faithfulness endures to all
generations; You established the earth, and it abides.
They continue this day according to Your ordinances,
for all are Your servants. Unless Your law had been my
delight, I would then have perished in my affliction.
I will never forget Your precepts, for by them You have
given me life.
—Psalm 119:84–93 NKJV

O Lord, my soul feeds on Your word. My body feeds on physical food, but my soul needs Your word. Oh, it is so good for me, and such wisdom and understanding is rich and tasty to my soul. Thank You, Lord. Amen.

Wisdom and Understanding
October 4

Now the purpose of the commandment
is LOVE from a pure heart, from a
good conscience, and from sincere faith,
from which some, having strayed, have turned
aside to idle talk, desiring to be teachers of
the law, understanding neither what they say
nor the things which they affirm.
But we know that the law is good if one uses
it lawfully, knowing this: that the law is not
made for a righteous person, but for the lawless
and insubordinate, for the ungodly and the sinners,
for the unholy and profane, for murderers of fathers
and murderers of mothers, for manslayers, for fornicators,
for sodomites, for kidnappers, for liars, for perjurers,
and if there is any other thing that is contrary to
sound doctrine, according to the glorious gospel of
the blessed God which was committed to my trust.
And I thank Christ Jesus our Lord who has
enabled me, because He counted me faithful,
putting me into the ministry, although I was
formerly a blasphemer, a persecutor, and an insolent
man; but I obtained mercy because I did it
ignorantly in unbelief. And the grace of our Lord
was exceedingly abundant, with faith and love which are in
Christ Jesus.
—1 Timothy 1:5–14 NKJV

(Read and study the Bible. No one is perfect, but God can change souls
that want to change. Even Paul was transformed.)

I will love You, O Lord, my strength.
The Lord is my rock and my fortress and
my deliverer; My God, my strength, in whom
I will trust; my shield and the horn of my

salvation, my stronghold.
—Psalm 18:1–2 NKJV

O Lord, righteousness and goodness is what You want from us. Help us to consider our ways and correct our ways that they may be pleasant and pleasing in Your sight, in Jesus's name. Amen.

Wisdom and Understanding
October 5

*If you confess with your mouth the Lord
Jesus and believe in your heart that God has raised
Him from the dead, you will be saved.
For with the heart one believes unto
righteousness, and with the mouth confession is
made unto salvation. For the Scripture says,
"whoever believes on Him will not be put to shame."
For there is no distinction between Jew and
Greek, for the same Lord over all is rich to all who
call upon Him. For "whoever calls on the name of
the Lord shall be saved." How then shall they call
on Him in whom they have not believed? And how shall
they believe in Him of whom they have not heard?
And how shall they hear without a preacher?
And how shall they preach unless they are sent?
As it is written: "How beautiful are the feet of
those who preach the gospel of peace, who bring
glad tidings of good things!"
—Romans 10:9–15 NKJV*

*The Lord lives! Blessed be my Rock!
Let the God of my salvation be exalted.
It is God who avenges me, and subdues
the peoples under me; He delivers me from my
enemies, You also lift me up above those who
rise up against me; You have delivered me from the
violent man. Therefore I will give thanks to You,
O Lord, among the Gentiles, and sing
praises to Your name. Great deliverance He
gives to His king, and shows mercy to His anointed,
to David and his descendants forevermore.
—Psalm 18:46–50 NKJV*

Pray every day and read a scripture from the Bible. Blessed be the name of the Lord God Almighty. He did it for David the king, and He will do it for the simplest, most unpopular, and quietest one of us. All we have to do is ask Him, and He will satisfy our every need. In Jesus's name. Amen.

Wisdom and Understanding
October 6

*And let the peace of God rule in your
hearts, to which also you were called
in one body; and be thankful.
Let the word of Christ dwell in you richly in all
wisdom, teaching and admonishing one another
in psalms and hymns and spiritual songs, singing
with grace in your hearts to the Lord.
And whatever you do in word or deed,
do all in the name of the Lord Jesus, giving
thanks to God the Father through Him.
Wives, submit to your own husbands,
as is fitting in the Lord.
Husbands, love your wives and do not be
bitter toward them. Children, obey your
parents in all things, for this is well pleasing
to the Lord. Fathers, do not provoke your children
lest they become discouraged.
—Colossians 3:15–21 NKJV*

*And whatever you do, do it heartily,
as to the Lord and not to men, knowing that from
the Lord you will receive the reward of the
inheritance; for you serve the Lord Christ.
But he who does wrong will be repaid for
what he/she has done, and there is no partiality.
—Colossians 3:23–25 NKJV*

*Make a joyful shout to the Lord, all you lands!
Serve the Lord with gladness; come before His
presence with singing. Know that the Lord, He
is good; it is He who has made us and not we ourselves;
We are His people and the sheep of His pasture.
Enter into His gates with thanksgiving, and into
His courts with praise. Be thankful to Him, and
bless His name. For the Lord is good; His*

mercy is everlasting, and His truth endures
to all generations.
—Psalm 100 NKJV

Pray for someone or for a family that is less fortunate than you today; someone who needs a job or a place to live, someone who lacks wisdom and understanding. Remember to pray today.

Wisdom and Understanding
October 7

*Grace and peace be multiplied to you
in the knowledge of God and of Jesus our Lord,
as His divine power has given to us all things
that pertain to life and godliness, through the
knowledge of Him who called us by glory and virtue,
by which have been given to us exceedingly great
and precious promises, that through these you may
be partakers of the divine nature, having escaped the
corruption that is in the world through lust.
But also for this very reason, giving all diligence, add to
your faith virtue, to virtue knowledge, to knowledge
self-control, to self control perseverance,
to perseverance godliness, to godliness brotherly
kindness, and to brotherly kindness* **love.**
*For if these things are yours and abound, you will be
neither barren nor unfruitful in the knowledge
of our Lord, Jesus Christ.
For he/she who lacks these things is shortsighted, even
to blindness, and has forgotten that he/she was
cleansed from his/her old sins.
—2 Peter 1:2–9 NKJV*

*There is a river whose streams shall make
glad the city of God, the holy place of the
tabernacle of the Most High. God is in the
midst of her, she shall not be moved; God shall
help her, just at the break of dawn.
—Psalm 46:4–5 NKJV*

Remember to say a prayer today. Pray for the world, the country, the city, the town, and your neighborhood. Amen.

Wisdom and Understanding
October 8

Praise Him, Praise Him

The Mighty One, God the Lord,
has spoken and called the earth from the
rising of the sun to its going down.
Out of Zion, the perfection of beauty,
God will shine forth. Our God shall come,
and shall not keep silent; a fire shall devour before Him,
and it shall be very tempestuous
all around Him. He shall call to the heavens from above,
and to the earth, that He may judge His people:
"Gather My saints together to Me, those who
have made a covenant with Me by sacrifice."
Let the heavens declare His righteousness, for
God Himself is judge. "Hear, O My people, and I will
speak, O Israel, and I will testify against you;
I am God, your God!
—Psalm 50:1–7 NKJV

In You, O Lord, I put my trust;
let me never be put to shame.
Deliver me in Your righteousness,
and cause me to escape; incline Your ear to
me, and save me. Be my strong refuge, to which I may
resort continually; You have given
the commandment to save me, for You are my rock
and my fortress. Deliver me, O my God, out of the hand
of the wicked, out of the hand of the unrighteous
and cruel man. for You are my hope, O Lord
God; You are He who took me out of my
mother's womb. My praise shall be continually of you.
—Psalm 71:1–6 NKJV

Praise the Lord today. Just think of something that you are thankful for, something that you did not think you would have accomplished by today, something that makes you happy, and something you know you have more than someone else who is happy with less.

Wisdom and Understanding
October 9

*So don't put up with anyone pressuring you
in details of diet, worship services/ or holy days.
All those things are mere shadows cast before what
was to come; the substance is Christ.
don't tolerate people who try to run your life,
ordering you to bow and scrape, insisting that you
join their obsession with angels and that you seek out
visions. They're a lot of hot air, that's all they are. They're
completely out of touch with the source of life, Christ,
who puts us together in one piece, whose very breath
and blood flow through us. He is the Head and we are the
body. We can grow up healthy in God only as he nourishes us.
So, then, if with Christ you've put all that pretentious and
infantile religion behind you, why do you let yourselves
be bullied by it? "Don't touch this! Don't taste that!
Don't go near this!" Do you think things that are here today
and gone tomorrow are worth that kind of attention?
Such things sound impressive if said in a deep enough
voice. They even give the illusion of being pious and humble
and ascetic. But they're just another way of showing
off, making yourselves look important.
—Colossians 2:16–23 The Message/Remix Version*

Lord, Your word is the Bible. The Bible is Your word. You inspired the writers to write, to teach us. Help us to accept Your word as a guide for study and growth to be better human beings. We thank You for Your word, in Jesus's name. Amen.

Wisdom and Understanding
October 10

My son, keep your father's command,
and do not forsake the law of your mother.
Bind them continually upon your heart;
tie them around your neck.
When you roam, they will lead you; and when
you awake, they will speak with you.
For the commandment is a lamp, and the
law a light; reproofs of instruction are the way of life,
to keep you from the evil woman, from the flattering tongue of a
seductress. Do not lust after her beauty in your heart,
nor let her allure you with her eyelids. For by means
of a harlot a man is reduced to a crust of bread; and
an adulterous will prey upon his precious life.
Can a man take fire to his bosom, and his clothes not be
burned? Can one walk on hot coals, and his feet not be seared?
So is he who goes in to his neighbor's wife;
whoever touches her shall not be innocent.
—Proverbs 6:20–29 NKJV

Oh boy! A word to the men!

The heavens declare the glory of God;
and the firmament shows His handiwork.
Day unto day utters speech, and night unto
night reveals knowledge. There is no speech nor
language where their voice is not heard. Their
line has gone out through all the earth, and their
words to the end of the world. In them He has set a
tabernacle for the sun, which is like a bridegroom
coming out of his chamber, and rejoices like a strong
man to run its race. Its rising is from one end of the heaven,
and its circuit to the other end; and there is nothing hidden
from its heat. The law of the Lord is perfect,
converting the soul; the testimony of the Lord is sure,

making wise the simple.
—Psalm 19:1–7 NKJV

Bless the Lord, oh, my soul. Amen.

Wisdom and Understanding
October 11

*Remember now your Creator in the days
of your youth, before the difficult days come,
and the years draw near when you say,
"I have no pleasure in them":
While the sun and the light, the moon and the stars,
are not darkened, and the clouds do not
return after the rain; in the day when the keepers of the
house tremble, and the strong men bow down;
when the grinders cease because they are few,
and those that look through the windows grow dim;
when the doors are shut in the streets, and the sound
of grinding is low; when one rises up
at the sound of a bird, and all the daughters of music are
brought low. Also they are afraid of height,
and of terrors in the way; when the almond tree
blossoms, the grasshopper is a burden
and desire fails. For man goes to his eternal
home, and the mourners go about the streets.
—Ecclesiastes 12:1–5 NKJV*

*Bless the Lord, O my soul; and all that is
within me, bless His holy name! Bless the
Lord, O my soul, and forget not all His benefits:
Who forgives all your iniquities, who heals all your diseases,
Who redeems your life from
destruction, Who crowns you with
loving-kindness and tender mercies, Who
satisfies your mouth with good things, so that your
youth is renewed like the eagle's.
—Psalm 103:1–5 NKJV*

Father, we pray that parents will teach their children about You, like our grandparents did teach us. We pray parents and families will remember that we must dedicate our children to You and teach them Your ways so that their lives will be better and their future brighter. Give us the sense to be sensible and to make better choices. In Jesus's name. Amen.

Wisdom and Understanding
October 12

Praise Him, Praise Him

Your mercy, O Lord, is in the heavens;
Your faithfulness reaches to the clouds.
Your righteousness is like the great mountains;
Your judgments are a great deep; O Lord,
You preserve man and beast. How precious
is Your loving kindness, O God! Therefore the children
of men put their trust under the shadow of Your wings.
They are abundantly satisfied with the fullness
of Your house, and You give them drink from the
river of Your pleasures. For with You is the
fountain of life; in Your light we see light. Oh,
continue Your loving kindness to those who know You,
and Your righteousness to the upright in heart.
Let not the foot of pride come against me,
and let not the hand of the wicked drive me away.
There the workers of iniquity have fallen; they have
been cast down and are not able to rise.
—Psalm 36:5–12 NKJV

Write your own psalm today. Write how God is great in your life and be grateful. Amen.

Wisdom and Understanding
October 13

*Now the Spirit expressly says that in
latter times some will depart from the faith,
giving heed to deceiving spirits and doctrines
of demons, speaking lies in hypocrisy,
having their own conscience seared with a hot iron,
forbidding to marry, and commanding to abstain from
foods which God created to be received with
thanksgiving by those who believe and know the truth.
For every creature of God is good, and
nothing is to be refused if it is received with thanksgiving;
for it is sanctified by the word of God and prayer.
If you instruct the brethren in these things,
you will be a good minister of Jesus Christ, nourished
in the words of faith and of the good doctrine
which you have carefully followed. But reject
profane and old wives' fables, and exercise
yourself toward godliness. For bodily exercise profits
a little, but godliness is profitable for all things,
having promise of the life that now is and of that
which is to come. This is a faithful saying and worthy
of all acceptance. For to this end we both labor and
suffer reproach, because we trust in the living God, who
is the Savior of all men, especially of those who believe.
—1 Timothy 4:1–10 NKJV*

*Now to the King Eternal, Immortal, invisible,
to God who alone is wise, be honor and glory forever
and ever, Amen.
—1 Timothy 1:17 NKJV*

Pray for someone who is in need of a specific blessing today.

Wisdom and Understanding
October 14

"Comfort, yes, comfort My people!"
Says your God.
"Speak comfort to Jerusalem, and
cry out to her, that her warfare is ended, that
her iniquity is pardoned; or she has received
from the Lord's hand double for all her sins."
The voice of one crying in the wilderness:
"Prepare the way of the Lord; Make straight in
the desert a highway for our God.
Every valley shall be exalted and every mountain
and hill brought low; the crooked places smooth;
the glory of the Lord shall be revealed, and all
flesh shall see it together; for the mouth of the Lord
has spoken." The voice said, "Cry out!"
and he said, "What shall I cry?" "all flesh is grass,
and all its loveliness is like the flower of the field.
The grass withers, the flower fades, because
the breath of the Lord blows upon it;
surely the people are grass. The grass withers,
the flower fades, but the word of our God
stands forever."
—Isaiah 40:1–8 NKJV

The Bible can be so poetic. It is so easy to read, makes me want to write my praises, my prayers, and my thoughts. Put your gratefulness to God on paper, your anxieties, your sadness, your joy, your testimonies, your hopes, your faith, your prayers, your sadness. Intangible yet so tangible. Hhhhmmmmm. Try it today. One line, two lines, forty lines. Your words will live.

Wisdom and Understanding
October 15

Confession and Adoration

I acknowledged my sin to You,
and my iniquity I have not hidden, I said,
"I will confess my transgressions to the Lord,"
and You forgave the iniquity of my sin. for this cause
everyone who is godly shall pray to You in a time
when You may be found; surely in a flood of great
waters they shall not come near him. You are my
hiding place; You shall preserve me from trouble;
You shall surround me with songs of deliverance.
I will instruct you and teach you in the way
you should go; I will guide you with my eye.
Do not be like the horse or like the mule, which have
no understanding, which must be harnessed with
bit and bridle, else they will not come near you.
Many sorrows shall be to the wicked; but he who
trusts in the Lord, mercy shall surround him/her.
Be glad in the Lord and rejoice, you righteous;
and shout for joy, all you upright in heart!
—Psalm 32 NKJV

O Lord God Almighty, give us faith to trust in You, give us heart to dare to trust in You, give us patience to wait on You, and please give us joy to sustain us in the meantime, in Jesus's name. Amen.

Wisdom and Understanding
October 16

Praise Him, Praise Him

Therefore be imitators of God as dear children.
And walk in love, as Christ also has loved us
and given Himself for us, an offering and a
sacrifice to God for a sweet-smelling aroma.
—Ephesians 5:1–2 NKJV

Therefore, holy brethren, partakers of the
heavenly calling, consider the Apostle and
High Priest of our confession, Christ Jesus,
who was faithful to Him who appointed Him,
as Moses also was faithful in all his house.
For this One has been counted worthy of more
glory than Moses, inasmuch as He who built
the house has more honor than the house.
For every house is built by someone, but
He who built all things is God.
And Moses indeed was faithful in all His house as
a servant, for a testimony of those things which
would be spoken afterward, but Christ
as a Son over His own house, whose house
we are if we hold fast the confidence and the
rejoicing of the hope firm to the end.
—Hebrews 3:1–6 NKJV

Oh, love the Lord, all you His saints!
For the Lord preserves the faithful, and fully
repays the proud person. Be of good courage,
and He shall strengthen your heart, all you who
hope in the Lord.
—Psalm 31:23–24 NKJV

Say a prayer of thanksgiving today.

Amen.

Wisdom and Understanding
October 17

Praise Him, Praise Him

Give unto the Lord, O you mighty ones,
give unto the Lord glory and strength.
Give unto the Lord the glory due to His name;
worship the Lord in the beauty of holiness.
The voice of the Lord is over the waters;
The God of glory thunders;
The Lord is over many waters.
The voice of the Lord is powerful;
The voice of the Lord is full of majesty.
The voice of the Lord brakes the cedars,
Yes, the Lord splinters the cedars of Lebanon.
He makes them also skip like a calf,
Lebanon and Sirion like a young wild ox.
The voice of the Lord divides the flames of fire.
The voice of the Lord shakes the wilderness;
The Lord shakes the wilderness of Kadesh.
The voice of the Lord makes the deer give birth,
and strips the forests bare; and in His temple
everyone says, "Glory!"
The Lord sat enthroned at the flood, and the
Lord sits as King forever.
The Lord will give strength to His people;
The Lord will bless His people with peace.
—Psalm 29 NKJV

Whatever is wrong could be worse and have been worse at one point, so even in the midst of problems and troubles, let us rejoice and give thanks unto our Lord, our God Almighty. Let us be thankful and bless His name. Change will come. Thank You, Lord. Amen.

Wisdom and Understanding
October 18

Praise Him, Praise Him

May the Lord answer you in the day of trouble;
May the name of the God of Jacob defend you;
May He send you help from the sanctuary,
and strengthen you out of Zion;
May He remember all your offerings, and accept
your burnt sacrifice. May he grant you according to
your heart's desire. And fulfill all your purpose.
We will rejoice in your salvation, and in the
name of our God we will set up our banners!
May the Lord fulfill all your petitions.
Now I know that the Lord saves His anointed;
He will answer him from His holy heaven
with the saving strength of His right hand.
Some trust in chariots, and some in horses;
but we will remember the name of the Lord
our God. They have bowed down and fallen;
but we have risen and stand upright.
Save, Lord!
May the King answer us when we call.
—Psalm 20 NKJV

May you take time to sing praises to the Lord. May you take time to think and meditate when you are angry. May you take time to tell someone you love them. May you take time to go to church and hear a sermon. May you take time to help someone. May you take time to pray. Amen.

Wisdom and Understanding
October 19

Trust the Lord Today

Truly my soul silently waits for God;
from Him comes my salvation.
He only is my rock and my salvation; He is my
defense; I shall not be greatly moved. How long will
you attack a man/woman? You shall be slain, all of you,
like a leaning wall and a tottering fence. They only
consult to cast him down from his high position;
they delight in lies; they bless with their mouth, but
they curse inwardly.
My soul, wait silently for God alone, for my
expectation is from Him. He only is my rock
and my salvation; He is my defense; I shall not be moved.
In god is my salvation and my glory; the rock of my
strength, and my refuge, is in God.
Trust in Him at all times, you people; pour out your
heart before Him; God is a refuge for us.
—Psalm 62 NKJV

Trust the Lord for something that is good but difficult to attain. Trust the Lord for the humanly impossible. Trust the Lord for what you hope for but cannot see. Trust the Lord for what you want but cannot touch. Trust the Lord for greater and higher things. Trust the Lord for He is able. Do your part and trust the Lord to do the other part. In Jesus's name. Amen.

Wisdom and Understanding
October 20

Praise Him, Praise Him

O Zion,
You who bring good tidings,
get up into the high mountain;
O Jerusalem,
You who bring good tidings,
lift up your voice with strength,
lift it up, be not afraid; say to the cities
of Judah, "behold your God shall come
with a strong hand, and His arm shall rule for Him;
behold, His reward is with Him, and His
work before Him. He will feed His flock
like a shepherd; He will gather the lambs with
His arm, and carry them in His bosom, and
gently lead those who are with young. Who
has measured the waters in the hollow of
His hand, measured heaven with a span
and calculated the dust of the earth
in a measure?
Weighed the mountains in scales and the
hills in a balance?
Who has directed the Spirit of the Lord,
or as His counselor has taught Him?
With whom did He take counsel, and who
instructed Him, and taught Him in the path of
justice? Who taught Him knowledge, and
showed Him the way of understanding?
—Isaiah 40:9–14 NKJV
To whom then will you liken God?
Or what likeness will you compare to Him?
—Isaiah 40:18 NKJV

Father God, You made us, and You know us. Help us to trust in You and to abide by Your Holy Bible, Your holy word; the Old Testament, how it was; the New Testament, a new guide for us. Icons and superstitions will never compare to Your greatness. Teach us not to live in the flesh only, but to abide in Your Spirit also. We love You, and we thank You for Your greatness imparted to us daily, in Jesus's name. Amen.

Wisdom and Understanding
October 21

*Bear one another's burdens, and so
fulfill the law of Christ. For if anyone
thinks himself/herself to be something,
when he/she is nothing, he/she deceives himself.
But let each one examine his/her own work,
and then he/she will have rejoicing in
himself/herself alone, and not in another.
For each one shall bear his own load.
Let him/her who is taught the word share in
all good things with him who teaches.
Do not be deceived, God is not mocked; for
whatever a man/woman sows, that he/she will
also reap. For he/she who sows to his/her flesh
will of the flesh reap corruption, but he/she who sows
to the Spirit will of the Spirit reap everlasting life.
And let us not grow weary while doing good,
for in due season we shall reap if we do not
lose heart. Therefore, as we have opportunity,
let us do good to all, especially to those who are
of the household of faith.
—Galatians 6:2–10 NKJV*

*Those who sow in tears,
shall reap in joy. He who continually
goes forth weeping, bearing seed for
sowing, shall doubtless come again with
rejoicing, bringing his/her sheaves with him/her.
—Psalm 126:5–6 NKJV*

Blessed is the Word of God. I believe it, and according to my belief in it, I see God blessing me every day. He blesses in short term and in long term. He plants a seed in me, and He grows the tree in me, and He brings great fruit from this tree. I see God in my life. Do you see God in your life, or do you have to try to make things happen on your own? I always go with God. In the name of Jesus. Amen.

Wisdom and Understanding
October 22

Praise Him, Praise Him

*Lord, You have been our dwelling place
in all generations. Before the mountains were
brought forth, or ever You had formed the
earth and the world, even from everlasting to
everlasting, You are God.*
—Psalm 90:1–2 NKJV

*I will sing of the mercies of the Lord forever;
with my mouth will I make known Your
faithfulness to all generations. For I have said,
"Mercy shall be built up forever; Your
faithfulness You shall establish in the very heavens."*
—Psalm 89:1–2 NKJV

*Lord, You have been favorable to Your land;
You have brought back the captivity of Jacob.
You have forgiven the iniquity of your people;
You have covered all their sin.
You have taken away all Your wrath;
You have turned from the fierceness of Your anger.
Restore us, O God of our salvation, and cause Your
anger toward us to cease. Will You be angry with us
forever? Will You prolong Your anger to all generations?
Will You not revive us again, that Your people may
rejoice in You? Show us Your mercy, Lord, and
grant us Your salvation. I will hear what God the Lord will
speak, for He will speak peace to His people and to His saints;
but let them not run back to folly. Sure His salvation
is near to those who fear Him, that glory may
dwell in our land.*
—Psalm 85:1–9 NKJV

Remember to say a prayer today.

Wisdom and Understanding
October 23

Jesus Spoke These Words

*"Listen. What do you make of this? A farmer
planted seed. As he scattered the seed, some
of it fell on the road and birds ate it. Some fell in
the gravel; it sprouted quickly but didn't put down
roots, so when the sun came up it withered just as
quickly. Some fell in the weeds; as it came up, it was s
trangled among the weeds and nothing came of it.
Some fell on good earth and came up with a flourish,
producing a harvest exceeding his/her wildest dreams.*
—Mark 4:3–8 MSG

*He continued, "Do you see how this story works?
All my stories work this way. "The farmer plants the
Word. Some people are like the seed that falls
on the hardened soil of the road. No sooner do they
hear the Word than Satan snatches away what
has been planted in them. "And some are like
the seed that lands in the gravel. When they first hear
the Word, they respond with great enthusiasm. But
there is such shallow soil of character that when the emotions
wear off and some difficulty arrives, there is nothing
to show for it. "The seed cast in the weeds represents the ones
who hear the kingdom news but are overwhelmed with worries
about all the things they have to do and all the things
they want to get. The stress strangles what they heard,
and nothing comes of it. "But the seed planted in the good
earth represents those who hear the Word, embrace it,
and produce a harvest beyond their wildest dreams."*
—Mark 4:13–20, The Message/Remix Version Yeah! MSG

Read a scripture from the Bible today. Pray today. Smile to a stranger
today. Give love, get love. Amen.

Wisdom and Understanding
October 24

Praise Him, Praise Him

Praise the Lord!
Oh, give thanks to the Lord, for He is good!
For His mercy endures forever.
Who can utter the mighty acts of the Lord?
Who can declare His praise?
Blessed are those who keep justice, and he
who does righteousness at all times!
—Psalm 106:1–3 NKJV

Blessed is every one who fears the Lord,
who walks in His ways.
When you eat the labor of your hands,
you shall be happy, and it shall be well with you.
Your wife shall be like a fruitful vine
in the very heart of your house, your children
like olive plants all around your table.
Behold, thus shall the man be blessed who
fears the Lord. The Lord bless you out
of Zion, and may you see the good of Jerusalem
all the days of your life. Yes, may you see your
children's children.
Peace be upon Israel!
—Psalm 28 NKJV

Consider writing your psalm of thanksgiving unto the Lord God Almighty. Your words, your testimony. Amen.

Wisdom and Understanding
October 25

Do not withhold good from those
to whom it is due, when it is in the power
or your hand to do so. Do not say to your
neighbor, "go, and come back, and tomorrow
I will give it," when you have it with you.
Do not devise evil against your neighbor,
for he dwells by you for safety's sake.
Do not strive with a man/woman without cause,
if he/she had done you no harm.
Do not envy the oppressor, and choose none
of his/her ways; for the perverse person
is an abomination to the Lord, but His secret
counsel is with the upright. The curse of the
Lord is on the house of the wicked, but He
blesses the home of the just. Surely He scorns
the scornful, but gives grace to the humble.
The wise shall inherit glory, but shame
shall be the legacy of fools.
—Proverbs 3:27–35 NKJV

Oh, give thanks to the Lord, for He is good!
For His mercy endures forever.
Let the redeemed of the Lord say so, whom He
has redeemed from the hand of the enemy,
and gathered out of the lands, from the east and from the west,
from the north and from the south.
—Psalm 107:1–3 NKJV

Blessed be the name of Jesus, our Lord forever. Amen.

Wisdom and Understanding
October 26

Praise Him, Praise Him

I will praise you with my whole heart;
before the gods I will sing praises to You.
I will worship toward Your holy temple,
and praise Your name for Your loving kindness
and Your truth; for You have magnified Your
word above all Your name.
In the day when I cried out, You answered me,
and made me bold with strength in my soul.
All the kings of the earth shall praise You, O Lord,
when they hear the words of Your mouth.
Yes, they shall sing of the ways of the Lord,
for great is the glory of the Lord. Though
the Lord is on high, Yet He regards the lowly;
but the proud He knows from afar.
Though I walk in the midst of trouble,
You will revive me; You will stretch Your
hand against the wrath of my enemies,
and Your right hand will save me. The Lord
will perfect that which concerns me;
Your mercy, O Lord, endures forever;
Do not forsake the works of Your hands.
—Psalm 138 NKJV

Lord, I lean firmly on Your word. Please help us, Your people, to trust and obey You more and to love one other with a spirit of tenderness and forgiveness. Help us to humble ourselves and say "I am sorry" or "Forgive me" when we offend our brother or sister, mother or father, aunt or uncle, or anyone else. Help us to see others as seeing ourselves in a clean mirror. Give us more of Your spirit, in Jesus's name. Amen.

Wisdom and Understanding
October 27

The Word of God, The Bible

*Now when the queen of Sheba heard
of the fame of Solomon, she came to Jerusalem
to test Solomon with hard questions,
having a very great retinue, camels that
bore spices, gold in abundance, and precious stones;
and when she came to Solomon, she spoke with him
about all that was in her heart. So Solomon
answered all her questions; there was nothing so
difficult for Solomon that he could not explain
it to her. And when the queen of Sheba had seen
the wisdom of Solomon, the house that he had built,
the food on his table, the seating of his
servants, the service of his waiters and their
apparel, and his entryway by which he went up
to the house of the Lord, there was no more
spirit in her. Then she said to the king: "It was a
true report which I heard in my own land about
your words and your wisdom."
—2 Chronicles 9:1–5 NKJV*

*My mouth shall speak wisdom, and
the meditation of my heart shall give understanding.
I will incline my ear to a proverb;
Psalm 49:3–4a NKJV*

The history and the stories in the Bible are rich and very captivating. Read a story in the Old Testament today. Read about David and Solomon and the kings and the prophets, stories to share and to be intrigued by. What a word, the Word of God, the Bible. Read and get wisdom and understanding.

Wisdom and Understanding
October 28

Praise Him, Praise Him

I waited patiently for the Lord;
and He inclined to me, and heard my cry.
He also brought me up out of a horrible pit,
out of the miry clay, and set my feet upon a rock,
and established my steps. He has put a new
song in my mouth—Praise to our God;
Many will see it and fear, and will trust in the Lord.
Blessed is that man/woman who makes the
Lord his trust, and does not respect the proud,
nor such as turn aside to lies. Many, O Lord
my God, are Your wonderful works which
You have done; and Your thoughts toward us
cannot be recounted to You in order;
If I would declare and speak of them,
they are more than can be numbered.
Sacrifice and offering You did not desire;
My ears You have opened. Burnt offering and
sin offering You did not require. Then I said,
"Behold, I come; in the scroll of the book it is
written of me. I delight to do Your will, O my
God, and Your law is within my heart."
I have proclaimed the good news of righteousness
in the great assembly; indeed, I do not
restrain my lips, O Lord, You Yourself know.
I have not hidden Your righteousness
within my heart; I have declared Your faithfulness
and Your salvation; I have not concealed Your
loving kindness and Your truth from the great

assembly. Do not withhold Your tender mercies
from me, O Lord; Let Your loving kindness and Your
truth continually preserve me.
Psalm 40:1–11 NKJV

A Psalm of King David, there is a rich man that worshipped his God! Count your blessings and be thankful. There is more goodness to come.

Wisdom and Understanding
October 29

*I beseech you therefore, brethren,
by the mercies of God, that you present
your bodies a living sacrifice, holy, acceptable
to God, which is your reasonable service.
And do not be conformed to this world but be
transformed by the renewing of your mind, that you
may prove what is that good and acceptable
and perfect will of God. For I say, through
the grace given to me, to everyone who is among
you, not to think of himself/herself more highly
than he/she ought to think, but to think
soberly, as God has dealt to each one a measure
of faith. For as we have many members
in one body, but all the members do not have
the same function, so we, being many, are one
body in Christ, and individually members of one
another. Having then gifts differing according
to the grace that is given to us, let us use them:
if prophecy, let us prophesy in proportion to our faith;
or ministry, let us use it in our ministering; he who teaches,
in teaching; he who exhorts, in exhortation; he who gives,
with liberality; he who leads, with diligence; he who show
mercy, with cheerfulness.
—Romans 12:1–8 NKJV*

*My heart is steadfast, O God, my heart is steadfast;
I will sing and give praise.
Awake, my glory! Awake, lute and harp!
I will awaken the dawn. I will praise You, O Lord,
among the peoples; I will sing to You among the nations.
For Your mercy reaches unto the heavens, and Your
truth unto the clouds. Be exalted, O God, above the heavens;
Let Your glory be above all the earth.
—Psalm 57:7–11 NKJV*

I need oceans and rivers and vast greenery and butterflies and hills and mountains and clouds and rain and snow and nature and those things that remind me of God's greatness. It's all in me. God's greatness. Amen.

Wisdom and Understanding
October 30

Let love be without hypocrisy.
Abhor what is evil. Cling to what is good.
Be kindly affectionate to one another with
brotherly love, in honor giving preference
to one another; not lagging in diligence, fervent
in spirit, serving the Lord; rejoicing in
hope, patient in tribulation, continuing
steadfastly in prayer; distributing to the needs
of the saints, given to hospitality. Bless those
who persecute you; bless and do not curse.
Rejoice with those who rejoice and weep with
those who weep. Be of the same mind
toward one another. Do not set your mind
on high things, but associate with the humble.
Do not be wise in your own opinion.
Repay no one evil for evil. Have regard for
good things in the sight of all men.
If it is possible, as much as depends on you,
live peaceably with all men. Beloved, do not
avenge yourselves, but rather give place to wrath;
for it is written, "vengeance is Mine, I will repay,"
says the Lord. Therefore "if your enemy is
hungry, feed him; if he is thirsty, give him a drink;
for in so doing you will heap coals of fire on his head."
Do not be overcome by evil, but
overcome evil with good.
—Romans 12:9–21 NKJV
Deep calls unto deep at the noise
of Your waterfalls; all Your waves and
billows have gone over me. The Lord will
command His loving kindness in the daytime.
And in the night His song shall be with me—A prayer
to the God of my life.
—Psalm 42:7–8 NKJV

What will you meditate on today?

Wisdom and Understanding
October 31

Apocalypses/Revelation

Now I saw a new heaven and a new earth,
for the first heaven and the first earth had
passed away. Also there was no more sea.
Then I, John, saw the holy city, New Jerusalem,
coming down out of heaven from God, prepared
as a bride adorned for her husband.
And I heard a loud voice from heaven saying,
"Behold, the tabernacle of God is with men,
and He will dwell with them, and they shall be
His people. God Himself will be with them and
be their God. "And God will wipe away every
tear from their eyes; there shall be no more
death, nor sorrow, nor crying. There shall be
no more pain, for the former things have
passed away." Then He who sat on the
throne said, "Behold, I make all things new." And
He said to me, "Write, for these words are true
and faithful." And He said to me, "it is done! I am the
Alpha and the Omega, the Beginning and the End. I will
give of the fountain of the water of life freely
to him who thirsts. He who overcomes shall
inherit all things, and I will be his God and he shall
be My son.
—Revelation 21:1-7 NKJV

Because you have made the Lord,
who is my refuge, even the Most High, your
dwelling place, no evil shall befall you,
nor shall any plague come near your dwelling;
for He shall give His angels charge over you,
to keep you in all your ways.
—Psalm 91:9-11 NKJV

Lord, help us to live a good and decent life today. Show us how to live each day in honor of Your name, remembering that You give eternal life to those who chose to acknowledge their Maker and His sacrifice for us, Jesus Christ, our Lord and Savior. It's a better life when we live through Your spirit. Amen.

The Bible is such a fantastic, amazing, thought-provoking, and unusual book, not to mention ancient and modern at the same time, very relevant, story-telling, history-telling that not to find time often to read even one line in it is missing out on your own potential to be a greater you. So many answers and questions and revelations and mysteries lie therein. The usual sixty-six books in the Bible are enough to give you something good to start with, fuel for your journey in this life. Reading it will eventually show you how to fix the engine, to change the different oils, the direction to take to solve a problem. It can make you look at yourself before you look at someone else's shortcomings. That is probably the reason many people don't want to take the time to read the Bible. It makes us look within before we look without, and so when we have to be our own worse critic and take stock in fixing ourselves, many times we just don't want to do it. Choice. We make that choice, but then we blame others when things don't to go our way.

Wisdom and Understanding
November 1

Praise Him, Praise Him

The Lord has been mindful of us;
He will bless us;
He will bless the house of Israel;
He will bless the house of Aaron.
He will bless those who fear the Lord,
Both small and great. May the Lord give
you increase more and more,
You and your children. May you be
blessed by the Lord, who made heaven
and earth. The heaven, even the heavens,
are the Lord's; but the earth He has given
to the children of men. The dead do not praise
the Lord, nor any who go down into silence.
But we will bless the Lord from this time
forth and forevermore.
Praise the Lord!
—Psalm 116:12–18 NKJV

I love the Lord because He has heard
my voice and my supplications. Because He has
inclined His ear to me, therefore I will
call upon Him as long as I live.
—Psalm 116:1–2 NKJV

Wisdom and Understanding
November 2

Praise Him, Praise Him

The Lord is my light and my salvation;
Whom shall I fear? The Lord is the
strength of my life; of whom shall I be afraid?
When the wicked came against me to eat
up my flesh, my enemies and foes, they
stumbled and fell. Though an army may encamp
against me, my heart shall not fear; though war may rise
against me, in this I will be confident. One thing
I have desired of the Lord that will I seek: That I
may dwell in the house of the Lord all the days
of my life, to behold the beauty of the Lord, and to
inquire in His temple. For in the time of trouble
He shall hide me in His pavilion; in the secret place
of His tabernacle He shall hide me; He shall
set me high upon a rock. And now my head shall
be lifted up above my enemies all around me;
Therefore I will offer sacrifices of joy in His
tabernacle; I will sing, yes, I will sing praises
to the Lord. Hear, O Lord, when I cry with my voice!
Have mercy also upon me, and answer me. When You said,
"Seek My face," my heart said to you, "Your face, Lord,
I will seek." Do not hide Your face from me; Do not
turn Your servant away in anger; You have been my help;
do not leave me nor forsake me, O God of my
salvation. When my father and mother forsake me,
Then the Lord will take care of me. Teach me Your
way, O Lord, and lead me in a smooth path,
because of my enemies. Do not deliver me to the
will of my adversaries; for false witnesses have risen
against me, and such as breathe out violence.
I would have lost heart, unless I had believed
that I would see the goodness of the Lord in the land

of the living. Wait on the Lord; be of good courage,
and He shall strengthen your heart;
Wait, I say, on the Lord!
—Psalm 27 NKJV

Pray for yourself today.

Wisdom and Understanding
November 3

Praise Him, Praise Him

Mercy and truth have met together;
Righteousness and peace have kissed.
Truth shall spring out of the earth,
and righteousness shall look down from heaven.
Yes, the Lord will give what is good;
and our land will yield its increase.
Righteousness will go before him, and shall
make His footsteps our pathway.
—Psalm 85:10–13 NKJV

O Lord God of hosts, hear my prayer;
give ear, O God of Jacob! O God,
behold our shield, and look upon the face
of Your anointed. For a day in Your court
is better than a thousand. I would rather
be a doorkeeper in the house of my God
than dwell in the tents of wickedness. For the Lord
is a sun and shield; the Lord will give grace
and glory; no good thing will He withhold
from those who walk uprightly. O Lord of hosts,
blessed is the man who trusts in You!
—Psalm 84:8–12

Father God, we thank You for Your greatness over and above all powers on earth, in the universe, and in existence. We thank You because we can talk to the one and only God Almighty. Bless us with Your spirit daily, show us Your will, and guide us as we rise up and do Your bidding on this earth. In the name of Jesus, we pray. Amen.

Wisdom and Understanding
November 4

*Woe to you who plunder, though
you have not been plundered; and you who
deal treacherously, though they have not
dealt treacherously with you! When you cease
plundering, you will be plundered; when you make
an end of dealing treacherously, they will deal
treacherously with you.
O Lord, be gracious to us; we have waited
for You. Be thou their arm every morning, our
salvation also in the time of trouble. At the noise of
the tumult the people shall flee;
When You lift Yourself up, the nations shall
be scattered; and Your plunder shall be gathered
like the gathering of the caterpillar; as the running
to and fro of locusts, He shall run upon them.
The Lord is exalted, for He dwells on high;
He has filled Zion with justice and
righteousness. Wisdom and Knowledge
will be the stability of your times, and the strength
of salvation; the fear of the Lord is His treasure.
—Isaiah 33:1–6 NKJV*

*Praise the Lord!
Sing to the Lord a new song,
and His praise in the assembly of saints.
Let Israel rejoice in their Maker;
Let the children of Zion be joyful in
their King. Let them praise His name with
the dance; let them sing praises to Him with
the timbrel and harp. For the Lord takes
pleasure in His people; He will beautify
the humble with salvation. Let the saints
be joyful in glory; Let them sing aloud
on their beds. Let the high praises of God be*

in their mouth, and a two-edged sword in their hand,
—Psalm 149:1–6 NKJV

Praise the Lord from Whom all blessings flow. Meditate on the goodness, the greatness of our God today. Amen.

Wisdom and Understanding
November 5

*There shall come forth a Rod from the
stem of Jesse, and a branch shall grow
out of his roots. The Spirit of the Lord
shall rest upon Him, the Spirit of wisdom
and understanding, the Spirit of counsel and
might, the Spirit of knowledge and of the fear
of the Lord. His delight is in the fear of the
Lord, and He shall not judge by the sight
of His eyes, nor decide by the hearing
of His ears; but with righteousness He shall
judge the poor, and decide with equity
for the meek of the earth; He shall strike the
earth with the rod of His mouth, and with the
breath of His lips He shall slay the wicked.
Righteousness shall be the belt of His loins,
and faithfulness the belt of His waist.
"The wolf also shall dwell with the lamb, the
leopard shall lie down with the young goat,
the calf and the young lion and the fatling
together; and a little child shall lead them.
—Isaiah 11:1–6 KJV*

*By You I have been upheld from
birth; You are He who took me out of
my mother's womb. My praise shall be continually
of You. I have become as a wonder to many,
but You are my strong refuge. Let my
mouth be filled with your praise and with Your
glory all the day.
—Psalm 71:6–8*

Jesus is the answer to all your troubles. Trust in Him, read the Bible, pray, go to church, and meditate among those who are trying to better their lives and their behavior in life. Ask God to help you and walk in His light until your change comes and beyond. Then bless someone else with a kind word or a dollar in their cup or with an encouraging word. Thank You, Lord, for wisdom and understanding. Amen.

Wisdom and Understanding
November 6

Praise Him, Praise Him

*The Lord rewarded me according
to my righteousness; according to the
cleanness of my hands He has recompensed
me. For I have kept the ways of the Lord,
and have not wickedly departed from my God.
For all His judgments were before me. And I did
not put away His statutes from me. I was also
blameless before Him, and I kept myself from my
iniquity. Therefore the Lord has recompensed me
according to my righteousness, according to the
cleanness of my hands in His sight. With the merciful
You will show Yourself merciful; with a
blameless man You will show Yourself blameless; with
the pure You will show yourself pure; and with
the devious You will show Yourself shrewd.
For You will save the humble people, but will
bring down haughty looks. For You will light
my lamp; the Lord my God will enlighten my darkness.
For by You I can run against a troop, by my God
I can leap over a wall. As for God, His way is perfect;
The word of the Lord is proven; He is a shield to all who
trust in Him. For who is God, except the Lord?
and who is a rock, except out God?*
—Psalm 18:20–31 KJV

Lord God, come into my heart and make me more like You. Help me to be helpful and encouraging to others. Help me to see the good in others even as I am not so good myself. Help me to do better by your standards each day and show me the path to righteousness. In Jesus's name, I pray. Amen.

Wisdom and Understanding
November 7

*We then who are strong ought to bear with
the scruples of the weak, and not to please
ourselves. Let each of us please his neighbor
for his good, leading to edification. For even
Christ did not please Himself; but as it is
written, "The reproaches of those who
reproached You fell on Me."
For whatever things were written before were
written for our learning, that we through the
patience and comfort of the Scriptures might have hope.
Now may the God of patience and comfort grant you
to be like-minded toward one another, according
to Christ Jesus, that you may with one mind and one
mouth glorify the God and Father of our
Lord Jesus Christ.
Therefore receive one another, just as Christ also
received us, to the glory of God.
Now I say that Jesus Christ has become a servant
to the circumcision for the truth of God, to
confirm the promises made to the fathers, and
that the Gentiles might glorify God for His mercy,
as it is written: "For this reason I will confess to You
among the Gentiles, and sing to Your name.
—Romans 15:1–9 NKJV*

*Praise the Lord!
For it is good to sing praises to our God;
For it is pleasant, and praise is beautiful.
The Lord builds up Jerusalem; He gathers
together the outcasts of Israel. He heals the
broken hearted and binds up their wounds.
He counts the number of the stars; He calls them
all by name. Great is our Lord, and mighty in power;
His understanding is infinite. The Lord lifts up the humble;*

He casts the wicked down to the ground. Sing to the
Lord with thanksgiving; sing praises on the harp to our
God, Who covers the heavens with clouds.
—Psalm 147:1–8 NKJV

When I feel as though I am losing hope, I think of things like the words in this portion of Psalm 147. What can't a God Who calls each star by its name and a God Whose understanding is infinite not do? I know He knows all my needs, so I will wait. I will regain hope and wait. Lord, thank You for a word that encourages us and helps us to be patient and wait on You, in Jesus's name. Amen.

Finally, brethren, whatever things are true,
whatever things are noble,
whatever things are just
whatever things are pure,
whatever things are lovely,
whatever things are of good report,
if there is any virtue and
if there is anything praiseworthy-
meditate on these things.
—Philippians 4:8 NKJV

Wisdom and Understanding
November 8

Praise Him, Praise Him

God be merciful to us and bless us,
and cause His face to shine upon us,
That Your way may be known on earth,
Your salvation among all nations.
Let the peoples praise You, O God;
Let all the peoples praise Your.
Oh, let the nations be glad and sing for joy!
For You shall judge the people righteously,
and govern the nations on earth.
Let the peoples praise You, O God;
let all the peoples praise You. Then the
earth shall yield her increase; God, our
own God, shall bless us. God shall bless
us, and all the ends of the earth shall fear Him.
—Psalm 67 NKJV

If it were not for God Who reigns over everything, the poor and the powerless would simply be forgotten, abandoned, ignored. So thank God that in His Bible, He teaches us to look out for one another, to reach out to someone who does not have as much as we have. Thank God that He instructs us to care, to help, and to do our best according to all the blessings He has freely given us. Thank You, Lord, because You teach us how we must behave as Your children. In Jesus's name. Amen.

Wisdom and Understanding
November 9

Then Job answered the Lord and said:
"I know that You can do everything, and
that no purpose of Yours can be withheld from You.
You asked, "Who is this who hides counsel without
knowledge?" Therefore I have uttered what
I did not understand, things too wonderful for me,
which I did not know. Listen, please, and let me
speak; You said, 'I will question you, and you shall
answer Me.' "I have heard of You by the hearing
of the ear, but now my eye sees You. Therefore
I abhor myself, and repent in dust and ashes.
—Job 42:1–6 NKJV

And the Lord restored Job's losses when he
prayed for his friends. Indeed the Lord
gave Job twice as much as he had before.
—Job 42:10 NKJV

Now the Lord blessed the latter days of Job
more than his beginning; for he had fourteen
thousand sheep, six thousand camels, one
thousand yoke of oxen, and one thousand female
donkeys.
—Job 42:12 NKJV

Job was blessed tremendously in the latter part of his life. Please read the book of Job and see the crazy things he went through, but he remained steadfast in his love for God and righteousness. If we do good, if we do our best, we will still go through trials and tribulations, but God promises that He will make things better in due time. The book of Job is such a wonderful example of how God is in control of everything good and bad that happens to those of us who love Him, trust Him, and depend on Him in every aspect of our lives. Father, we thank You for having full control when we give our lives over to You. In the name of Jesus. Amen.

Wisdom and Understanding
November 10

Wisdom and Understanding and Knowledge

Your hands have made me and fashioned me;
Give me understanding, that I may learn Your
commandments. Those who fear You will be
glad when they see me, because I have hoped
in Your word. I know, O Lord, that Your
judgments are right, and that in faithfulness You
have afflicted me. Let, I pray, Your merciful
kindness be for my comfort, according to Your
word to Your servant. Let Your tender mercies
come to me, that I may live; for Your law is
my delight. Let the proud be ashamed, for they
treated me wrongfully with falsehood; but I will
meditate on Your precepts. Let those who
fear You turn to me, those who know Your
testimonies. Let my heart be blameless
regarding Your statutes, that I may not be ashamed.
—Psalm 119:73–88 NKJV

The fear of the Lord leads to life, and he who
has it will abide in satisfaction; he will not be
visited with evil. A lazy man/woman buries
his hands in the bowl, and will not so much as
bring it to his mouth again.
Strike a scoffer, and the simple will become
wary; rebuke one who has understanding,
and he/she will discern knowledge.
—Proverbs 19:23–25 NKJV

What a sweet book. The Bible is full of W and
U. So get K and be the greatest you ever.
(W=wisdom, U=understanding and K=knowledge)

Wisdom and Understanding
November 11

Prayer and Supplication

*Give ear, O Shepherd of Israel, You
who lead Joseph like a flock; You who dwell
between the cherubim, shine forth!
Before Ephraim, Benjamin and Manasseh,
stir up Your strength, and come and save us!
Restore us, O God; cause Your face
to shine, and we shall be saved!
O Lord God of hosts, how long will
You be angry against the prayer of
Your people? You have fed them with the bread
of tears, and given them tears to drink in great
measure. You have made us a strife to our
neighbors, and our enemies laugh among themselves.
Restore us, O God of hosts; cause
Your face to shine, and we shall be saved!
You have brought a vine out of Egypt;
You have cast out the nations, and planted it.
You prepared room for it, and caused it to
take deep root, and it filled the land. The hills
were covered with its shadow, and the mighty
cedars with its boughs. She sent out her boughs to
the sea, and her branches to the River. Why have
You broken down her hedges, so that all who pass
by the way pluck her fruit? The boar out of the
woods uproots it, and the wild beast of the field
devours it. Return, we beseech You, O God of
hosts; look down from heaven and see, and visit
this vine and the vineyard which Your right hand
planted, and the branch that You made strong for
Yourself. It is burned with fire, it is cut down; they perish
at the rebuke of Your countenance. Let Your hand be
upon the man of Your right hand, upon the son of*

man whom You made strong for Yourself. Then
we will not turn back from You; revive us, and we
will call upon Your name. Restore us, O Lord
God of hosts; cause Your face to shine, and
we shall be saved!
—Psalm 80 NKJV

The Bible, all of it, is the Word of God of past days for a testimony and for future days, for a road as a path that guides. Read and be the best you ever. In Jesus's name, Amen.

Wisdom and Understanding
November 12

Praise Him, Praise Him

Your name, O Lord, endures forever,
Your fame, O Lord, throughout all
generations. For the Lord will judge His
people, and He will have compassion on His
servants. The idols of the nations are silver and gold,
the work of men's hands. They have mouths,
but they do not speak; eyes they have, but they do not
see; they have ears, but they do not hear; nor is there
any breath in their mouths. Those who make them are like them;
So is everyone who trusts in them.
Bless the Lord, O house of Israel! Bless the Lord, O house
of Aaron! Bless the Lord, O house of Levi! You who fear
the Lord, bless the Lord! Blessed be the Lord out of Zion,
Who dwells in Jerusalem!
Praise the Lord!
—Psalm 135:13–21 NKJV

Dare any of you, having a matter
against another, go to law before the
unrighteous, and not before the saints?
Do you not know that the saints will judge
the world? And if the world will be judged
by you, are you unworthy to judge the
smallest matters? Do you not know that we
shall judge angels? How much more, things that
pertain to this life? If then you have
judgments concerning things pertaining to this life
do you appoint those who are least esteemed
by the church to judge? I say this to your shame.
Is it so, that there is not a wise man among you,
not even one, who will be able to judge
between his brethren? But brother goes to law

against brother, and that before unbelievers!
—1 Corinthians 6:1–6 NKJV

Read the Bible and know the stories of Israel and Aaron and Levi. Put their names in the Internet and find the scriptures that tell their stories, stories to learn great lessons for living this life. To God be the glory always. Amen.

Wisdom and Understanding
November 13

Praise and Supplication

*HELP, Lord, for the godly
man/woman ceases! For the faithful
disappear from among the sons of men.
They speak idly everyone with his/her
neighbor; with flattering lips and a double
heart they speak. May the Lord cut off all
flattering lips, and the tongue that speaks proud
things, who have said, "With our tongue we will
prevail; our lips are our own; who is lord over us?"
"For the oppression of the poor, for the sighing
of the needy, now I will arise," says the Lord;
"I will set him in the safety for which he yearns."
The words of the Lord are pure words, like silver
tried in a furnace of earth, purified seven times.
You shall keep them, O Lord, You shall preserve them
from this generation forever. The wicked prowl on every
side, when vileness is exalted among the sons of men.
—Psalm 12 NKJV*

*Preserve me, O God, for in You I
put my trust.
—Psalm 16:1 NKJV*

That's my prayer today: Preserve me, O God, for in You, I put my trust. In the name of Jesus. Amen.

Wisdom and Understanding
November 14

God's Kingdom Is Like . . .

A man going off on an extended trip. He called his servants together and delegated responsibilities. To one he gave five thousand dollars, to another two thousand, to a third one thousand depending on their abilities. Then he left. Right off, the first servant went to work and doubled his master's investment. The second did the
same. But the man with the single thousand dug a hole and carefully buried his master's money. "After a long absence, the master of those three servants came back and settled up with them. The one given five thousand dollars showed him how he had doubled his investment. His master commended him: 'Good work! You did your job well. From now on be my partner.' "The servant with the two thousand
showed how he also had doubled his master's investment. His master commended him: Good Work! You did your job well. From now on be my partner.' "The servant given one thousand said, ' Master,
I know you have high standards and hate careless ways, that you demand the best and make no allowances for error. I was afraid I might disappoint you, so I found a good hiding place and secured your
money. Here it is, safe and sound down to the last cent.' "The master was furious. 'That's a terrible way to live! It's criminal to live cautiously like that! If you knew I was after the best, why did you do less than the least? The least you could have done would have been to invest the sum with the bankers, where at least I would have gotten a little interest. "'Take the thousand and give it to the one who risked the most. And get rid of this "play-it-safe" who won't go out on a limb. Throw him out into utter darkness.'
—*Mathew 25:14–18, the Message/Remix Version, Huh*

The mighty One, God the Lord, has
spoken and called the earth from the rising of the sun
to its going down. Out of Zion, the perfection of beauty,
God will shine forth.
—Psalm 50:1–2 NKJV

Amen.

Wisdom and Understanding
November 15

The Apostle Paul Says . . .

*So let's not allow ourselves to get fatigued doing good.
At the right time we will harvest a good crop if we
don't give up, or quit. Right now, therefore, every
time we get the chance, let us work for the benefit
of all, starting with the people closest to us in the
community of faith.*

—Galatians 6:9–10 The Message/Remix Version

*For my part, I am going to boast about nothing
but the Cross of our Master, Jesus Christ. Because
of the Cross, I have been crucified in relation to the
world, set free from the stifling atmosphere of
pleasing others and fitting into the little patterns that
they dictate. Can't you see the central issue in all
this? It is not what you and I do—submit to
circumcision, reject circumcision. It is what God
is doing, and he is creating something totally new, a free life!
All who walk by this standard are the true Israel
of God—his chosen people. Peace and mercy on them!
Quite frankly, I don't want to be bothered anymore by
these disputes. I have far more important things to do—the
serious living of this faith. I bear in my body scars
from my service to Jesus. May what our Master
Jesus Christ gives freely be deeply and
personally yours, my friends. Oh, yes!
—Galatians 6:14–18 The Message/Remix Version*

*Blessed is the man/woman who walks
not in the counsel of the ungodly, nor stands in the
path of sinners, nor sits in the seat of the scornful;
But his/her delight is in the law of the Lord,*

and in His law he meditates day and night.
—Psalm 1:1–2 NKJV

O God, all we have is You. You are the center and the whole reason for my joy. If I genuinely love You, then I can sincerely love my neighbors and my family. Teach me how to love You, Lord, and to do Your will every day, to make a difference in this world. In Jesus's name. Amen.

By disciplining ourselves while we are young, unknowingly, we invest in our future as we work hard and we play or relax very little. Some have figured out how to do both, work hard and still enjoy the pleasant and fun things of life while still young. When we grow older, fifties and beyond, we will look back and see just what it is we did with our youth. The lives of those who played more than they worked, living scared to take advantage of great opportunities, those who chose to live small and safe, their lives have not changed, it's monotonous and boring. When they compare their lives with the chance-takers, the hard-workers, those who sincerely trusted in God, they see a big difference. The hard workers are relaxing, enjoying life, and reaping the benefits of their sacrifice and effort from their younger days. Oh, what sorrow comes over the lazy, scared, cheap, dishonest, and sad person who lived their whole life through that ego personality. Regret, regret, regret. One thing I hate to have in my life is regret. I rather do the hard work than to have regret for something I should have done to make a difference. You have to put in to get out. Don't bother hating your family, friends, and neighbors who are doing well. Instead, learn from them and teach your children better habits, better ways to make their future more comfortable and happy. Teach them good habits and teach them well so they have good character as they grow into adulthood, reap from the hope that lay in them, and that will be your second chance for a better legacy.

Wisdom and Understanding
November 16

Praise Him, Praise Him

Oh come, let us sing to the Lord!
Let us shout joyfully to the Rock of our
salvation. Let us come before His presence
with thanksgiving; let us shout joyfully to Him
with psalms. For the Lord is the great God.
And the great King above all gods.
In His hand are the deep places of the earth;
The heights of the hills are His also. The sea is
His, for He made it; and His hands formed the dry
land. Oh come, let us worship and bow down;
Let us kneel before the lord our Maker. For He is
our God, and we are the people of His pasture,
and the sheep of sheep of His hand.
Today, if you will hear His voice: "Do not harden
your hearts, as in the rebellion, as in the day of trial in the
wilderness, when your fathers tested Me; they tried Me,
though they saw My work. For forty years I was grieved
with the generation. And said, 'It is a people who go
astray in their hearts, and they do not know My
ways.' so I swore in My wrath, 'they shall not enter My rest.'"
—Psalm 95 NKJV

OH, Sing to the Lord a new song!
Sin to the Lord, all the earth. Sing to the Lord,
bless His name; proclaim the good news of His
salvation from day to day. Declare His glory among
the nations, His wonders among all people.
—Psalm 96:1–3 NKJV

Even in hard times, Lord, You guide us if we seek You. As Your people, we know that trouble will come, but when we pray and call on Your wonderful name, You will walk with us and bring us to a better place in our lives. A joyful place, a peaceful place, a better place. Thank you, Lord Jesus. Amen.

Wisdom and Understanding
November 17

*But when all is said and done,
GOD's Temple on the mountain, firmly fixed, will
dominate all mountains, towering above
surrounding hills. People will stream to it and many
nations set out for it, saying, "Come, let's climb God's
mountain. Let's go to the Temple of Jacob's God.
He will teach us how to live. We'll know how to live
God's way." True teaching will issue from Zion,
GOD's revelation from Jerusalem. He'll establish
justice in the rabble of nations and settle disputes in
faraway places. They'll trade in their swords for shovels,
their spears for rakes and hoes. Nations will quit
fighting each other, quit learning how to kill
one another. Each man will sit under his own shade tree,
each woman in safety will tend her own garden. GOD-of-the-
Angel-Armies say so, and he means what he says.
Meanwhile, all the other people live however they wish,
picking and choosing their gods. But we live honoring
GOD, and we're loyal to our God forever and ever.
—Micah 4:1–5 The Message/Remix Version*

*Forever, O Lord, Your word is
settled in heaven. Your faithfulness endures
to all generations; You established the earth,
and it abides. They continue this day according
to Your ordinances, for all are Your servants.
Unless Your law had been my delight, I would
then have perished in my affliction. I will never forget
Your precepts, for by them You have given me life.
I am Yours, save me; for I have sought Your
precepts.
—Psalm 119:89–94 NKJV*

I thank God for the sunshine. I thank God for the rain. I thank God
for His Spirit. I thank God for making me. Amen.

Wisdom and Understanding
November 18

When God made his promise to Abraham,
He backed it to the hilt, putting his own reputation
on the line. He said, "I promise that I'll bless you
with everything I have—bless and bless and bless!"
Abraham stuck it out and got everything that had
been promised to him. When people make promises,
they guarantee them by appeal to some authority above
them so that if there is any question that they'll make good
on the promise, the authority will back them up. When God
wanted to guarantee his promises, He gave His word, a rock-solid
guarantee—God can't break his word. And because his
word cannot change, the promise is likewise unchangeable.
We who have run for our very lives to God have every
reason to grab the promised hope with both hands and never
let go. It's an unbreakable spiritual lifeline, reaching past all
appearances right to the very presence of God where Jesus/
running on ahead of us, has taken up His permanent
post as high priest for us, in the order of Melchizedek.
—Hebrews 6:13–20, the Message/Remix Version

The eyes of the Lord are on the righteous,
and His ears are open to their cry.
The face of the Lord is against those who do evil,
to cut off the remembrance of them from the earth.
The righteous cry out, and the Lord hears, and
delivers them out of all their troubles. The Lord is
near to those who have a broken heart, and saves
such as have a contrite Spirit.
—Psalm 34:15–18 NKJV

Lord, I am Yours, and I know You will always take care of me. Teach me Your ways and guide me daily in everything I do. In Jesus's name, I pray. Amen.

What's your prayer today?

Wisdom and Understanding
November 19

Praise Him, Praise Him

Open to me the gates of righteousness;
I will go through them. And I will
praise the Lord. This is the gate of the Lord,
through which the righteous shall enter.
I will praise You, for You have answered me,
and have become my salvation.
The stone which the builders rejected has become
the chief cornerstone. This was the Lord's doing;
It is marvelous in our eyes.
This is the day the Lord has made;
we will rejoice and be glad in it.
Save now, I pray, O Lord; O Lord, I pray,
send now prosperity. Blessed is he who comes in
the house of the Lord. God is the Lord, and He
has given us light; bind the sacrifice with cords
to the horns of the altar. You are my God,
and I will praise You; You are my God, I will exalt You.
Oh, give thanks to the Lord, for He is good!
For His mercy endures forever.
—Psalm 118:19-29 NKJV

Make up your own Psalm of thanksgiving, of praise, of supplication, of forgiveness to the Lord. Write down a sentence or two of where you are today and make it a prayer to God. Sad, lonely, struggling with something, regretful, grateful, greedy, angry, mean, happy, thankful—talk to God and tell Him, and He will bring change in you. You have to tell Him though. Yeah, He knows, but when you tell Him, you heal. In Jesus's name. Amen.

Wisdom and Understanding
November 20

Praise Him, Praise Him

Blessed are the undefiled in the way,
who walk in the law of the Lord!
Blessed are those who keep His testimonies, who
seek Him with the whole heart! They also
do no iniquity; they walk in His ways. You have
commanded us to keep Your precepts diligently.
Oh, that my ways were directed to keep Your statutes!
Then I would not be ashamed, when I look into all
Your commandments. I will praise You with
uprightness of heart, when I learn Your righteous
judgments. I will keep Your statutes; Oh, do not
forsake me utterly! How can a young man/woman
cleanse his/her way? By taking heed according to
Your word. With my whole heart I have sought You;
Oh, let me not wander from Your commandments!
Your word I have hidden in my heart, that I might not
sin against You. Blessed are You, Lord!
Teach me Your statutes. With my lips I have declared
all the judgments of Your mouth. I have rejoiced in
the way of Your testimonies, as much as in all riches.
I will meditate on Your precepts, and
contemplate Your ways. I will delight myself in
Your statutes;
I will not forget Your word.
—Psalm 119:1–16 NKJV

Each human being is so amazingly and wonderfully made, so meticulously and purposefully put together by our Creator that many of us believe that because we are unique and awesome, no one else is unique and awesome, so we look down, we sneer, we abuse, we disrespect others. We see the greatness in how our minds and our bodies are made, and we think the other person is not as great, not as wonderful; but that's how great a God He is. He gave us choice. We are able to choose how to think and how to behave. He did say in the good book we are to love our brothers and sisters. Our brothers and sisters are all the other human beings. We are to see the beauty in them as in us. We are to bless and appreciate them. So what is it when a person thinks too highly of themselves and see others as less than or as not deserving of a good and peaceful life as he or she thinks of themselves to be deserving? That person lives through their ego, their undisciplined "do what I want to do" ego, an ego that has been allowed to bully, lie, cheat, mistreat others. By the time this person is a mature adult and have no discipline in this area, have not learned to control and manage their ego, then that person will eventually exhibit bad character, a difficult citizen of the world. Sometimes the psalmist David, sounds so repetitious. But when I think of God's greatness, His mercy and grace showered on me: the way He still blesses me despite my shortcomings or my not- so-good thoughts toward other people who offend me, the way He still provides for me although I have fallen short of His glory, the way He makes me look good while in this life experience even when things are not so good in my life in my limited estimation. When I think of those things, then I can be repetitious like King David and just thank God for His "loving kindness" over and over and over again. If God doesn't get tired looking out for me, then I know I should not get tired praising Him. Hallelujah! Amen.

Wisdom and Understanding
November 21

*Grace to you and peace from God
our Father and the Lord Jesus Christ.
Blessed be the God and Father of our Lord
Jesus Christ, who has blessed us with every
spiritual blessing in the heavenly places in Christ,
just as He chose us in Him before the
foundation of the world, that we should be holy
and without blame before Him in love,
having predestined us to adoption as sons by
Jesus Christ to Himself, according to the good
pleasure of His will, to the praise of the glory
of His grace, by which He made us accepted
in the Beloved. In Him we have redemption
through His blood, the forgiveness of sins,
according to the riches of His grace which
He made to abound toward us in all wisdom
and prudence, having made known to us the
mystery of His will, according to His good
pleasure which He purposed in Himself, that
in the dispensation of the fullness of the times He
might gather together in one all things in
Christ, both which are in heaven and which
are on earth—in Him.
—Ephesians 1:2–10 NKJV*

*Praise the Lord! I will praise the Lord
with my whole heart, in the assembly of the
upright and in the congregation.
—Psalm 111:1 NKJV
He has sent redemption to His people; He has
commanded His covenant forever: Holy and
awesome is His name.
The fear of the Lord is the beginning of wisdom;
a good understanding have all those who*

do His commandments.
His praise endures forever.
—Psalm 111:9–10 NKJV

Praise the Lord. Take time to hug somebody. Walk away if somebody has harsh words for you, most of all if you don't deserve it. Bring peace and harmony to a situation and know that if you aggravate things, there is a word of condemnation for you in the good book. If provoked, walk away. Sticks and stones may break my bones, but words will roll right off my back. Don't worry about what others may think. You may help save your life or the life of another. Pray in your mind and ask God to guide your every move. "Be angry and don't sin." Let's make a difference. In Jesus's name. Amen.

Wisdom and Understanding
November 22

Praise Him, Praise Him

The Lord is my shepherd; I shall not want.
He makes me to lie down in green pastures;
He leads me to lie down in green pastures;
He leads me beside the still waters.
He restores my soul;
He leads me in the paths of righteousness
for His name sake. Yea, though I walk through
the valley of the shadow of death, I will
fear no evil; for You are with me; Your rod
and Your staff, they comfort me.
You prepare a table before me in the presence
of my enemies; You anoint my head with oil;
My cup runs over. Surely goodness and mercy
shall follow me all the days of my life;
and I will dwell in the house of the
Lord forever.
—Psalm 23 NKJV

Oh, that more people would seek the Lord and rest in the fact that You God will guide us if we discipline ourselves and obey Your word. So much trouble in the inner city, so much trouble in the world. Just listening to the news daily can be traumatic to the spirit. Lord, I pray for the urban communities in particular. Help us to seek your face and to love our neighbors. I pray that the crime will cease and that people will think before they act, that they will not allow passion of the flesh to overcome their minds and their spirits, that they would call on Your Son Jesus to redeem them from wrongdoing. Help us, Lord. We need help. In Jesus's name. Amen.

Wisdom and Understanding
November 23

Praise Him, Praise Him

Wait on the Lord, and keep His way,
and He shall exalt you to inherit the land;
When the wicked are cut off, you shall see it.
I have seen the wicked in great power, and
spreading himself like a native green tree.
Yet he passed away, and behold, he was no more;
Indeed I sought him, but he could not be found.
Mark the blameless man, and observe the upright;
for the future of that man is peace. But the
transgressors shall be destroyed together;
the future of the wicked shall be cut off.
But the salvation of the righteous is from the
LORD;
He is their strength in the time of trouble.
And the Lord shall help them and deliver them;
He shall deliver them from the wicked, and save them.
Because they trust in Him.
—Psalm 37:34–40 NKJV

The Lord will command His loving kindness
in the daytime, and in the night His song
shall be with me—a prayer to the God of my life.
I will say to God my Rock, "Why have
You forgotten me? Why do I go mourning
because of the oppression of the enemy?"
As with a breaking of my bones, my enemies
reproach me, while they say to me all day long,
"Where is Your God?" Why are you cast down,
O my soul? Hope in God; For I shall yet praise Him,
The help of my countenance and my God.
—Psalm 42:8–11 NKJV

O God, I am relieved when I come to You in prayer and I tell You just what is bothering me. O God, I am so glad I can always come to You directly and kneel and bow and sit and pray. O God, You gave us free will so we may choose to do the right thing. O God, give us wisdom and understanding so we will do good and not harm one another. O God, bless us again, I pray. You are always sending blessings. You give us grace and mercy. We need more and more and more of Your love. We are so limited without You. At our best, we are just not complete without You. We thank You for Your Spirit that abides with us and in us. You gave us choice. Help us to choose right. In Jesus's name. Amen.

Wisdom and Understanding
November 24

The Rules Still Apply Today

*God spoke to Moses: "Speak to the congregation
of Israel. Tell them: Be holy because I, God, your
God, am holy. "Every one of you must respect his
mother and father. "Keep my Sabbaths. I am God,
your God. "Don't take up with no—God idols. Don't
make gods of cast metal. I am God, your God.
—Leviticus 19:1–4 The Message/Remix Version*

Yeah

*"Don't steal. Don't lie. Don't deceive anyone. Don't
sear falsely using my name, violating the name of your God.
I am God. Don't exploit your friend or rob him. Don't hold
back the wages of a hired hand overnight. don't curse the
dear; don't put a stumbling block in front of the blind;
fear your God. I am God. Don't pervert justice. Don't
show favoritism to either the poor or the great. Judge
on the basis of what is right. Don't spread gossip
and rumors. Don't just stand by when your neighbor's life
is in danger. I am God. Don't secretly hate your neighbor.
If you have something against him, get it out into the open;
otherwise you are an accomplice in his guilt. Don't seek
revenge or carry a grudge against any of your people.
Love your neighbor as yourself. I am God.
Keep my decrees.
—Leviticus 19:11–19 The Message/Remix Version, Huh*

*The law of the Lord is perfect, converting
the soul; the testimony of the Lord is sure,
making wise the simple; the statures of the Lord
are right, rejoicing the heart; the commandment
of the Lord is pure, enlightening the eyes; the fear of the*

*Lord is clean, enduring forever; the judgments of the
Lord are true and righteous altogether. More to be
desired are they than gold, yea, than much fine gold;
sweeter also than honey and the honeycomb.*
—Psalm 19:7–10 NKJV

That's why there is so much crime today. Lord, we have turned away from Your laws. You made us, You know us, and You laid down the laws for us. We have lost our way, and we kill, steal, lie, etc., without considering Your laws.

Because we fool one another, we forget that we act against our God—Spirit nature. Bring us back, Lord. Forgive us and bring us back to Your loving arms. In Jesus's name, we pray. Amen.

Wisdom and Understanding
November 25

Praise Him, Praise Him

*In Him also we have obtained an inheritance,
being predestined according to the purpose
of Him who works all things according to the
counsel of His will, that we who first trusted in Christ
should be to the praise of His glory. In Him you also
trusted, after you heard the word of truth, the gospel of
your salvation; in whom also, having believed, you were
sealed with the Holy Spirit of Promise, who is the guarantee
of our inheritance until the redemption of the purchased
possession, to the praise of His glory.
—Ephesians 1:11–14 NKJV*

*And you He made alive, who were dead in trespasses and sins,
in which you once walked according to the course of this
world, according to the prince of the power of the air, the spirit who
now works in the sons of disobedience, among whom also we all
once conducted ourselves in the lusts of our flesh, fulfilling
the desires of the flesh and of the mind, and were by
nature children of wrath, just as the others.
But God, who is rich in mercy, because of His great love
with which He loved us, even when we were dead in
trespasses, made us alive together with Christ (by grace
you have been saved), and raised us up together
and made us sit together in the heavenly places in
Christ Jesus, that in the ages to come He might show the
exceeding riches of His grace in His kindness toward us in
Christ Jesus. For by grace you have been saved
through faith, and that not of yourselves;
It is the gift of God, not of works, lest anyone should boast.
—Ephesians 2:1–9 NKJV
How precious also are Your thoughts
to me, O God! How great is the sum*

of them! If I should count them, they would
be more in number than the sand: when I awake, I am
still with You.
—*Psalm 139:17–18 NKJV*

I have not yet come to understand how precious I am to God, my Maker; how special and dear I am to Him, you are to Him, we are to Him. He made us, and He loves us. If we understood how dear and precious and unique we are to Him, we would love ourselves more and our neighbors too. Lord, we thank You for Your unusual love for us. We love You because You loved us first. Thank You, Lord, in the name of Jesus. Amen.

Wisdom and Understanding
November 26

Thanksgiving

For all things are for your sakes,
that grace, having spread through the
many, may cause thanksgiving to abound
to the glory of God.
—2 Corinthians 4:15 NKJV

As you therefore have received
Christ Jesus the Lord, so walk in Him,
rooted and built up in Him and established
in the faith, as you have been taught, abounding
in it with thanksgiving.
—Colossians 2:6–7 NKJV

For the Lord will comfort Zion, He will comfort
all her waste places; He will make her wilderness
like Eden, and her desert like the garden of
the Lord; joy and gladness will be found in it,
Thanksgiving and the voice of melody.
—Isaiah 51:3 NKJV

Be anxious for nothing, but in everything
by prayer and supplication, with
Thanksgiving, let your requests be made
known to God; and the peace of God, which
surpasses all understanding, will guard your
hearts and minds through Christ Jesus.
—Philippians 4:6–7 NKJV
Now may He who supplies seed to the sower,
and bread for food, supply and multiply the
seed you have sown and increase the fruits of your
righteousness, while you are enriched in everything
for all liberality, which causes thanksgiving

through us to God.
—2 Corinthians 9:10–12 NKJV

I am sure that if it had not been for my relationship with Jesus Christ, my Savior, with God, my Father, I would not be joyful and peaceful today. I am blessed more than I had imagined I would be today at my age in life. Without great wealth of money and material things, God has made my spirit, my mind rich. I would love to have those other riches, and I may yet have them, but I am sure that if I have them and I don't have my Jesus, that I would not want those other riches. Give me Jesus, then give me the other riches. Despite some trouble and some loneliness and some discomforts in my life, I am extremely thankful in this season of thanksgiving. God has been exceedingly good to me. In Jesus's name. Amen.

Wisdom and Understanding
November 27

Praise Him, Praise Him

O Lord, how manifold are Your works!
In Wisdom you have made them all.
The earth is full of Your possessions—this
great and wide sea, in which are innumerable
teeming things, living things both small and great.
There the ships sail about; there is that leviathan which
You have made to play there. These all wait for You, that You may
give them their food in due season. What You give them they gather in;
You open Your hand, they are filled with good. You hide
Your face, they are troubled; You take away their breath,
they die and return to their dust. You send forth Your
Spirit, they are created; and You renew the face of the earth.
May the glory of the Lord endure forever; May the
Lord rejoice in His works. He looks on the earth, and it
trembles; He touches the hills, and they smoke. I will sing
to the Lord as long as I live; I will sing praise to my God
while I have my being. May my meditation be sweet to Him;
I will be glad in the Lord. May sinners be consumed from
the earth, and the wicked be no more.
Bless the Lord, O my soul!
Praise the Lord!
—Psalm 104:24–35 NKJV

Do we stop being thankful after Thanksgiving Day? O Lord, I realize that my day of thanksgiving is every day. O Lord, You bless me every single day, and I am grateful. O Lord, I thank You for that hedge of protection I feel that You have placed about me. Many dangers I have not experienced because of Your constant protection. O Lord, I am thankful for all Your showers of blessings. O Lord, please continue to take care of me like You do. I realize that I need You always. Thank You for Thanksgiving Day, and thank You because every day is a thanksgiving day. In Jesus's name. Amen.

Wisdom and Understanding
November 28

*The proverbs of Solomon the son of
David, king of Israel:
To know wisdom and instruction, to perceive
the words of understanding, to receive the
instruction of wisdom, justice, judgment, and equity;
to give prudence to the simple, to the young
man/woman knowledge and discretion—a wise man
will hear and increase learning, and a man of understanding
will attain wise counsel, to understand a proverb and
an enigma, the words of the wise and their riddles.
The fear of the Lord is the beginning of knowledge,
but fools despise wisdom and instruction.
My son, hear the instruction of your father,
and do not forsake the law of your mother; for they
will be a graceful ornament on your head, and chains
about your neck. My son, if sinners entice you, do not consent.
If they say, "come with us, let us lie in wait to shed blood;
let us lurk secretly for the innocent without cause;
let us swallow them alive like Sheol, and whole, like those who
go down to the Pit; we shall find all kinds of precious
possessions, we shall fill our houses with spoil; cast in
your lot among us, let us all have one purse"—my son/daughter,
do not walk in the way with them, keep your foot from their
path; for their feet run to evil, and they make haste to shed
blood. Surely, in vain the net is spread in the sight
of any bird; but they lie in wait for their own blood,
they lurk secretly for their own lives. So are the ways of
everyone who is greedy for gain; it takes away the life of its owners.
Wisdom calls aloud outside; she raises her voice in the
open squares. She cries out in the chief concourses,
at the openings of the gates in the city
She speaks her words.
—Proverbs 1:1–21 NKJV*

Read the rest of Proverbs. It's good to attain wisdom, understanding, and knowledge and to use them for good. Proverbs is a wonderful book of the Bible. All the books are great, each has their own character, style, reason, and teachings. We have no reason not to have answers to questions in our lives. The Bible has all the answers to all the questions. Be a part of a church or a group that studies the word. Read, study, and learn. No excuses. To God be the glory. Amen.

Wisdom and Understanding
November 29

*Beware lest anyone cheat you through
philosophy and empty deceit, according to the
tradition of men, according to the basic principles
of the world, and not according to Christ. For in Him
dwells all the fullness of the Godhead bodily; and you are
complete in Him, who is the head of all principality and power.*
—*Colossians 2:8–10 NKJV*

*If then you were raised with Christ, seek those things
which are above, where Christ is, sitting at the right hand
of God. Set your mind on things above, not on things
on earth. For you died, and your life is hidden with
Christ in God. When Christ who is our life appears, then
you also will appear with Him in glory.*
—*Colossians 3:1–4 NKJV*

*Let the word of Christ dwell in you richly in all
wisdom, teaching and admonishing one another
in psalms and hymns and spiritual songs, singing with
grace in your hearts to the Lord. And whatever
you do in word or deed, do all in the name of
the Lord Jesus, giving thanks to God the Father
through Him.*
—*Colossians 3:16–17 NKJV*

*I will praise You, for I am fearfully and wonderfully
made; marvelous are Your works, and that my soul
knows very well. My frame was not hidden from You,
when I was made in secret, and skillfully wrought in the
lowest parts of the earth, Your eyes saw my substance,
being yet unformed. And in Your book they all were
written, the days fashioned for me, when as yet there
were none of them. How precious also are Your*

thoughts to me, O God! How great is the sum of them!
—Psalm 139:14–17 NKJV

Amen.

Wisdom and Understanding
November 30

Things That Make You Go *Hhhhmmmmm*

*A soft answer turns away wrath, but a
harsh word stirs up anger.*

*The tongue of the wise uses knowledge rightly,
but the mouth of fools pours forth foolishness.*

*The eyes of the Lord are in every place,
keeping watch on the evil and the good.*

*A wholesome tongue is a tree of life, but
perverseness in it breaks the spirit.*

*A fool despises his father's instruction, but he who
receives correction is prudent.*

*In the house of the righteous there is much treasure,
but in the revenue of the wicked is trouble.*

*The lips of the wise disperse knowledge,
but the heart of the fool does not do so.*

*The sacrifice of the wicked is an abomination
to the Lord, but the prayer of the upright is His delight*

*The way of the wicked is an abomination to the Lord,
but He loves him who follows righteousness.*

*Harsh discipline is for him who forsakes the way,
and he who hates correction will die.*

*Hell and destruction are before the Lord;
so how much more the hearts of the sons of men.*

The scoffer does not love one who corrects him,
nor will he go to the wise.

A merry heart makes a cheerful countenance,
but by sorrow of the heart the spirit is broken.

The heart of him who has understanding seeks
knowledge, but the mouth of fools feeds on foolishness.

All the days of the afflicted are evil, but he who
is of a merry heart has a continual feast.

Better is a little with the fear of the Lord,
than great treasure with trouble.
—Proverbs 15:1–16 NKJV

The words of the Bible, the Word of God. Pray a prayer like Solomon did, a prayer for wisdom and understanding. Amen.

Some people are so busy with their tricks, plots, and plans for wickedness and wrongdoing against other children of God that they miss their own lives. They miss opportunities to grow and gain good fruit in their own existence. Those people enjoy their ill-gained things today, stealing from friends and family, using and abusing the elderly, etc. They lick their fingers and salivate while laughing, and they think they are conquerors in this sometimes hard and difficult life. They cheat their way to money and opportunity, and they fail because no one can prove their ill gains that they are as good as the honest person, but somebody knows and you know. As time passes and age is upon those wicked pretending to be upright people, you begin to see their lack of joy. A permanent frown appears on their forehead. They are constantly unhappy. Sometimes they have a lot of material gain like the rest of us, but even that gives them no satisfaction. Their children sometimes become their sorrow. they were spoiled and not thought right from wrong as their parents were stealing, lying, cheating, sly and slick that one opportunity to do right is gone. Those parents were busy trying to destroy other people's lives, living selfishly, seeing and knowing that others in their family, in their circle, needed help, and so they pretended they did not know, refusing to lend a hand. What then is your gain when your later days become your worse days? Whatsoever we sow, that is what we must reap.

Wisdom and Understanding
December 1

*O Lord, our Lord, how excellent is Your
name in all the earth, Who have set the glory
above the heavens! Out of the mouth of babes and
nursing infants You have ordained strength, because
of Your enemies, that you may silence the enemy
and the avenger. When I consider Your heavens,
the work of Your fingers, the moon and the stars, which
You have ordained, what is man that you are mindful of him,
for You have made him a little lower than the angels,
and You have crowned him with glory and honor. You have
made him to have dominion over the works of Your hands;
You have put all things under his feet, all sheep and oxen—
even the beasts of the field, the birds of the air, and the
fish of the sea that pass through the paths of the seas.
O Lord, our Lord, how excellent is Your
name in all the earth!
—Psalm 8 NKJV*

*Do not keep silent, O God! Do not hold Your
peace, and do not be still, O God!
For behold, Your enemies make a turmult;
and those who hate You have lifted up their head.
They have taken crafty counsel against Your people,
and consulted together against Your sheltered ones.
—Psalm 83:1–3 NKJV*

*How lovely is Your tabernacle, O Lord of hosts!
My soul longs, yes, even faints for the courts
of the Lord; my heart and my flesh cry out for the
living God. even the sparrow has found a home,
and the swallow a nest for herself, where she may
lay her young—even Your altars, O Lord of hosts
my King and my God. Blessed are those who
dwell in Your house; they will still be praising You.*

Blessed is the man/woman whose strength is in You,
whose heart is set on pilgrimage.
—Psalm 84:1–5 NKJV

Lord, we thank You for a word from the scriptures today. We thank You for always making a way in our lives by which we may rejoice in Your word, a psalm or a proverb or a word from Romans or Acts or some history from the books of the Old Testament. We thank You for Your word. In Jesus's name, we pray. Amen.

Wisdom and Understanding
December 2

Every word You give me is a miracle word-how could I help but obey?
Break open Your words; let the light shine out, let ordinary
People see the meaning. Mouth open and panting, I wanted Your
commands
More than anything.
Turn my way, look kindly on me, as you always do to those who
personally love you.
Steady my steps with Your Word of promise so nothing malign
Gets the better of me. Rescue me from the grip of
bad men and women
So I can live life Your way. Smile on me, Your servant; teach me the
Right way to live. I cry rivers of tears because nobody's
living by your Book!
—Psalms 119:129–136 The Message//Remix Version

Be good to Your servant, God; be as good as your Word.
Train me in good common sense; I'm thoroughly committed
To living Your way. Before I learned to answer You, I wandered all over
The place, but now I'm in step with your Word. You are
good, and the source of
Good; train me in Your goodness. The godless spread lies about me, but
I focus my attention on what You are saying; they're bland
as a bucket of lard,
While I dance to the tune of Your revelation. My troubles
turned out all for
The best-they forced me to learn from your textbook. Truth from Your
Mouth means more to me than striking it rich in a gold mine.
With Your very own hands You formed me; now breathe
Your wisdom over me
So I can understand You. When they see me waiting,
expecting Your Word,
Those who fear You will take heart and be glad.
I can see now, GOD, that Your
Decisions are right; your testing has taught me

what's true and right. Oh, love
Me-and right now!-hold me tight! Just the way you promised.
Now comfort me
So I can live, really live; Your revelation is the tune I dance to.
Let the fast—talking
Tricksters be exposed as frauds; they tried to sell me a
bill of goods, but I
Kept my mind fixed on Your counsel. Let those who fear
You turn to me for evidence
Of Your wise guidance. And let me live whole and holy, soul and body,
So I can always walk with my head held high.
—Psalms 119:65–80 The Message/Remix Version

Lord, I pray that more people would read the instructions You have provided for Your human beings to live by. It's simple; there are rules and regulations to live by for all humans. If we all assigned even five minutes a day to read a portion of the Bible, we would feed our Spirit those lessons for better living, and we would be compelled to follow those righteous guides. No, we must not lie, steal, kill, or make mischief against one another. No, we must not allow evil thoughts and spirits to penetrate our being and cause us to envy, hate, and malign one another. No, we must not do subtle wrongs against one another, thinking that if we are not exposed, we did not do wrong. God sees and knows everything and will repay us when we are old and feeble or when we least expect it. Father, please bless our spirits with love, joy, and peace that we may open our eyes and see the need of others and help them. Thank You, Holy Father, Amen.

Wisdom and Understanding
December 3

*Oh, that You would rend the heavens!
That You would come down! That the mountains
might shake at Your presence—as fire burns
brushwood, as fire causes water to boil—to make
Your name known to Your adversaries, that the nations
may tremble at Your presence! When You did awesome
things for which we did not look, You came down,
the mountains shook at Your presence. For since the
beginning of the world men have not heard nor perceived
by the ear, nor has the eye seen any God besides You,
who acts for the one who waits for Him. You meet him who
rejoices and does righteousness, who remembers You in Your
ways. You are indeed angry, for we have sinned—in these
ways we continue; and we need to be saved. But we are all
like an unclean thing, and all our righteousness are like
filthy rags; we all fade as a leaf, and our iniquities, like the
wind, have taken us away. And there is no one who calls on
Your name, who stirs himself up to take hold of You;
for you have hidden your face from us, and have consumed
us because of our iniquities.
But now, O Lord, You are our Father; we are the clay,
and You our potter; and all we are the work of Your hand.
Do not be furious, O Lord, nor remember iniquity
forever; indeed, please look—we all are Your people!
—Isaiah 64:1–9 NKJV*

*Restore us, O God of hosts; cause Your face
to shine, and we shall be saved!
—Psalm 80:7 NKJV*

Say a prayer for the children of the world today, for those little people who are vulnerable to danger and are at the mercy of careless parents and adults. Say a prayer for the people who are suffering in the world. Amen.

Wisdom and Understanding
December 4

*A soft answer turns away wrath, but
a harsh word stirs up anger.*

*The tongue of the wise uses knowledge rightly,
but the mouth of fools pours forth foolishness.*

*The eyes of the Lord are in every place,
keeping watch on the evil and the good.*

*A wholesome tongue is a tree of life,
but perverseness in it breaks the spirit.*

*A fool despises his father's instruction,
but he who receives correction is prudent.*

*In the house of the righteous there is much treasure,
but in the revenue of the wicked is trouble.*
—Proverbs 15:1–6 NKJV

*I will bless the Lord at all times; His praise shall
continually be in my mouth. My soul shall make
its boast in the Lord: The humble shall hear of it and
be glad. Oh, magnify the Lord with me, and let
us exalt His name together. I sought the Lord,
and He heard me, and delivered me from all my fears.*
—Psalm 34:1–4 NKJV

God is mighty and powerful over every power on earth. He will protect those who call on Him. I thank the Lord for His protection from dangers, seen and unseen. I thank the Lord for making a way when things seem like they will not work out right. God is always able to give us the ability to do the things we need to do in His name and for His honor and glory. God makes us look good as we remain in His will. Thank You, Lord, in Jesus's name. Amen.

Wisdom and Understanding
December 5

See then that you walk circumspectly, not as
fools but as wise, redeeming the time, because
the days are evil. Therefore do not be unwise, but
understand what the will of the Lord is. And do not
be drunk with wine, in which is dissipation; but be filled
with the Holy Spirit, speaking to one another in
psalms and hymns and spiritual songs, singing
and making melody in your heart to the Lord.
—Ephesians 5:15-1 NKJV

Unto You I lift up my eyes, Oh You who dwell in
the heavens. Behold, as the eyes of servants look
to the hand of their masters, as the eyes of a maid to the
hand of her mistress, so our eyes look to the Lord
our God, until He has mercy on us.
Have mercy on us, O Lord, have mercy on us!
For we are exceedingly filled with contempt.
Our soul is exceedingly filled with the scorn of those who
are at ease, with the contempt of the proud.
—Psalm 123 NKJV

Lord, we thank You for Your mercy and grace. We thank You for the
rain and the sunshine. We thank You for food, shelter, and clothing.
We thank You for cold weather and summer. We thank You for the sun
and the moon. We thank You for Your Son Jesus Christ Who died for
our sin, and You raised Him up again for our joy. Thank You, Father,
in Jesus's name. Amen.

Wisdom and Understanding
December 6

*The first thing I want you to do is pray.
Pray every way you know how; for everyone you
know. Pray especially for rulers and their governments
to rule well so we can be quietly about our business of
living simply, in humble contemplation. This is the way our
Savior God wants us to live. He wants not only us but
everyone saved, you know, everyone to get to know the
truth we've learned; that there's one God and only one, and
one Priest—Mediator between God and us—Jesus, who offered
Himself in exchange for everyone held captive by sin,
to set them all free. Eventually the news is going to get out.
This and this only has been my appointed work; getting this
news to those who have never heard of God, and
explaining how it works by simple faith and plain truth.
Since prayer is at the bottom of all this, what I want mostly is
for men to pray—not shaking angry fists at enemies but
raising holy hands to God. And I want women to get in there
with the men in humility before God, not primping before a mirror
or chasing the latest fashions but doing something beautiful for God
and becoming beautiful doing it. I don't let women take over and tell
the men what to do. They should study to be quiet
and obedient along
with everyone else. Adam was made first, then Eve; woman
was deceived first—our pioneer in sin! —with Adam
right on her heels.
On the other hand, her childbearing brought about
salvation, reversing Eve. But this salvation only comes to those
who continue in faith, love, and holiness, gathering it all
into maturity. You can depend on this
—1 Timothy 2:1–15 The Message Remix Version*

Well, Paul has his rules. Paul was allowed to write, even by the Holy Spirit, his understanding of how things should be. In that day and age, it was probably the norm. Today we have to hear the word and apply it with wisdom and understanding as the need arises. Thank God that today, even as He did in those days, women can preach and teach and admonish too. We pray for guidance and discernment as to when to speak and when to be quiet so we may hear more and learn more before we speak. We pray this in Jesus's name. Amen.

Parents ought to be aware every single day that they hold in their hands, in their power, the ability and responsibility to build and create a beautiful and wonderful world through their children or a horrible, insecure, and damaged future adult. Parents ought to understand that the early years of their child's future is in all the decisions made while that person that came through them is a child in their care. We have to do the hard work to get the good results with the children. The church, the temple can be a good place to help raise your children. One ought not to do it alone. A congregation with a good reputation will support you as a family and as a single parent. The community of believers will serve as the village that helps and supports, counsels and encourages you and your children. Engage the children in the choir, summer programs, classes that teach morals and build character. Children learn to give to the needy. They learn to sit still and listen to counsel and instruction, and so much more is there in the temple that will build and help shape you and your child as you worship together with your extended congregational family. Don't do it alone. Thank God for free help. As you give, you will also receive.

Wisdom and Understanding
December 7

*We then, as workers together with Him also
plead with you not to receive the grace of
God in vain. For He says: "In an acceptable time
I have heard you, and in the day of salvation I have
helped you." Behold, now is the accepted time; behold,
now is the day of salvation. We give no offense in anything,
that our ministry may not be blamed. But in all things we
commend ourselves as ministers of God: in much
patience, in tribulations, in needs, in distresses, in stripes, in
imprisonments, in tumults, in labors, in sleeplessness,
in fastings; by purity, by knowledge, by longsuffering,
by kindness, by the Holy Spirit, by sincere love
by the word of truth, by the power of God, by the armor
of righteousness on the right hand and on the left, by honor
and dishonor, by evil report and good report; as deceivers,
and yet true; as unknown and yet well known; as dying,
and behold we live; as chastened, and yet not killed;
as sorrowful, yet always rejoicing; as poor, yet making many
rich; as having nothing, and yet possessing all things.
—2 Corinthians 6:1-10 NKJV*

*Lord, You have been our dwelling place in all
generations. Before the mountains were brought
forth, or ever You had formed the earth and the world,
even from everlasting to everlasting, You are God.
—Psalm 90:1-2 NKJV*

Blessed be the name of our Lord Jesus Christ, our protector, and our sword and shield; He who goes before us when we have to face the world and its madness; He who goes before us whenever we have to face trouble or uncertainty; You who speak through us whenever we have to make a difference or a change in this world for those who cannot speak and stand up for themselves. O Lord God Almighty, we praise You, we love You, we adore You, we need You. We thank You. Never leave us. In the name of Your Son, we pray. Amen.

Whatever you want, you can have, you can achieve. Yes, it will take hard work, dedication, discipline, and time, but you can have it. Don't expect to have it when time passes and you have not worked hard for it and you have not lived a disciplined life. If you chose to be a trickster, a liar, a con artist, a thief, a hater, a person who lived your life avenging every petty disagreement you had with others, then don't wonder why your life at a mature age did not turn out how you hoped it would when you were younger. It was your choice. Your choice results are your choice results. While you are young, choose wisdom and understanding. Look for good teachings and learn the lessons of life that will help your future to be bright. You can start with the Holy Bible. It has amazing teachings, instructions, parables, and lots of stories of our ancestors and how they lived and thought. There are many other good books to read also and learn great lessons of life from. Do the work. Do the hard work and get the great results later in your life. The Bible says, "They that go down to the sea in ships, that do business in great waters: These see the works of the Lord and His wonders in the deep." You must take a chance. You must be brave and not allow fear to be a part of your life's journey. You must go further than what you can see. You must use your "third eye," your "sixth sense." You must live through your spirit self also, not just your physical self. You must study and read and learn and teach and grow and challenge yourself to be better and greater every day. You must discipline yourself beyond the place of comfort. You have to work hard and play less while you are young. You can play more after you have achieved much and when you are older and wiser with much understanding. You have to learn to shut up and listen more. You have to seek good counselors, elders, sensible aunts and uncles, somebody's wise grandparents. You have to choose a few good friends to converse with, people who are reading and learning and growing as you are. After living a young conscientious, good, and productive life, now that you are older, you will see the benefits. Now you can teach and counsel others. Now it's your turn to talk and share and have fun and wisely spend your earned money and have a good time. Life is short. We realize that after maybe fifty years of age or so. After life is death, it's inevitable, so why not live a life of service to others? Service to others is high on God's requirement for blessings, grace, and mercy to be showered on us from Him. I want those unmerited blessings, grace and mercy. We can never earn enough points to match God's blessings, so let's do all we can, and He promises to shower us with more. Read about His promises in the Bible, the Word of God.

Wisdom and Understanding
December 8

The Lord God Speaks to Us

*"Yes, I'm on my way to visit you with judgment. I'll present
compelling evidence against sorcerers, adulterers, liars,
those who exploit workers, those who take advantage
of widows and orphans, those who are inhospitable to
the homeless—anyone and everyone who doesn't honor me,"
A message from God-of-the-Angel-Armies.
"I am God—yes, I AM. I haven't changed. And because
I haven't changed, you, the descendants of Jacob,
haven't been destroyed. You have a long history of ignoring
my commands. You haven't done a thing I've told you.
Return to me so I can return to you," says God-of-the-Angel-Armies.
"You ask, 'But how do we return?' "Begin by being honest.
Do honest people rob God? But you rob me day after day.
"You ask, 'How have we robbed you?' "The tithe and the
offering—that's how! And now you're under a curse—the
whole lot of you—because you're robbing me. Bring your full
tithe to the Temple treasure so there will be ample
provisions in my Temple. Test me in this and see if I
don't open up heaven itself to you and pour out blessings
beyond your wildest dreams. For my part, I will defend you
against marauders, protect your wheat fields and vegetable
gardens against plunderers." The Message of
God-of-the-Angel-Armies.
"You'll be voted 'Happiest Nation.' You'll experience what
it's like to be a country of grace."
God-of-the-Angel-Armies says do.*
—Malachi 3:5–11 The Message/Remix Version

*Your mercy, O Lord, is in the heavens;
Your faithfulness reaches to the clouds. Your righteousness
is like the great mountains; Your judgments are a great deep;
O Lord, You preserve man and beast. How precious is*

Your loving kindness, O God! Therefore the children
of men put their trust under the shadow of Your wings.
—Psalm 36:5–7 NKJV

O Lord, give us strength to trust You, to rely solely on Your word, to open our spirit's eyes and touch the hem of Your garment and walk in faith. We want to trust You more and obey Your word. In Jesus's name, we pray. Amen.

Wisdom and Understanding
December 9

Have you not known?
Have you not heard?
Has it not been told you from the beginning?
Have you not understood from the foundations
of the earth? It is He who sits above the circle
of the earth, and its inhabitants are like
grasshoppers, who stretches out the heavens
like a curtain, and spreads them out like a
tent to dwell in. He brings the princes to nothing;
He makes the judges of the earth useless.
Scarcely shall they be planted, scarcely shall they
be sown, scarcely shall their stock take root
in the earth, when He will also blow on them,
and they will wither, and the whirlwind will take
them away like stubble.
"To whom then will you liken Me, or to
whom shall I be equal?" Says the Holy One.
Lift up your eyes on high, and see who
has created these things, Who brings out
their host by number; He calls them all by name,
by the greatness of His might and the strength of
His power; not one is missing.
—Isaiah 40:21–26 NKJV

Have you not known? Have you not heard?
The everlasting God, The Lord, The Creator of the
ends of the earth, neither faints nor is weary. His
understanding is unsearchable. He gives power
to the weak, and to those who have no might He
increases strength. Even the youths shall faint
and be weary, and the young men shall utterly fall,
but those who wait on the Lord shall renew
their strength; they shall mount up with wings like
eagles, they shall run and not be weary, they

shall walk and not faint.
—Isaiah 40:28–31 NKJV

Praise be to our Great God, forever and ever. Pray for your neighbors, your enemies, and your friends today.

Wisdom and Understanding
December 10

The Holy Spirit Is Always with Us

*"These things I have spoken to you, that you
should not be made to stumble. "They will put
you out of the synagogue; yes, the time is coming
that whoever kills you will think that he offers God
service. "And these things they will do to you
because they have not known the Father nor Me.
"But these things I have told you, that when
the time comes, you may remember that I told you
of them. And these things I did not say to you at the
beginning, because I was with you. "But now I go away
to Him Who sent me, and none of you asks me, "Where
are You going? "But because I have said these things
to you, sorrow has filled your heart. "Nevertheless I tell
you the truth, it is to your advantage that I go away;
for if I do not go away, the Helper will not come to
you; but if I depart, I will send Him to you.
"And when He has come, He will convict the world
of sin, and of righteousness, and of judgment:
"Of sin, because they do not believe in Me;
"Of righteousness, because I go to My Father and you
see Me no more;
"Of judgment, because the ruler of this world is
judged. "I still have many things to say to you,
but you cannot bear them now. However, when He, the
Spirit of truth, has come, He will guide you unto
all truth; for He will not speak on His own
authority, but whatever He hears He will speak; and
He will tell you things to come.
—John 16:1–13 NKJV*

The Holy Spirit, Lord, we thank You for sending the Holy Spirit to abide
with us always. Help us to remember that we are never alone because

You have sent Your Spirit, Your Holy Spirit, to keep us company, to guide and protect us. I acknowledge the presence of the Holy Spirit. Thank You, Father, in Jesus's name. Amen.

Wisdom and Understanding
December 11

Praise Him, Praise Him

Make a joyful shout to God, all the earth!
Sing out the honor of His name; make His praise
glorious. Say to God, "How awesome are Your works!
Through the greatness of your power Your enemies shall
submit themselves to You. All the earth shall worship You and
sing praises to You; they shall sing praises to Your name."
Come and see the works of God; He is awesome in His
doing toward the sons of men. He turned the sea into dry land;
They went through the river on foot. There we will rejoice in Him.
He rules by His power forever; His eyes observe the nations; do not
let the rebellious exalt themselves. Oh, bless our God, you peoples!
And make the voice of His praise to be heard, who keeps our
soul among the living, and does not allow our feet to be moved.
—Psalm 66:1–9 NKJV

The Lord lives! Blessed be my Rock!
Let the God of my salvation be exalted. It is God who
avenges me, and subdues the peoples under me; He delivers
me from my enemies. You also lift me up above those who
rise against me; You have delivered me from the violent man/woman.
Therefore I will give thanks to You, O lord, among the
Gentiles, and sing praises to Your name. Great deliverance
He gives to his king, and shows mercy to His anointed,
to David and His descendants forever.
—Psalm 18:46–50 NKJV

Lord, as You covered King David in those days, we know You cover Your servants today. We praise You and adore You. We know we fall under the same protection You gave our ancestors in days gone by, many of them have prayed for us and have guided us in Your laws and statutes, teaching us how to live a God-guided life. We thank You for them right now, and we pray that we will do the same for generations to come. In the precious name of Jesus, we pray. Amen.

Wisdom and Understanding
December 12

Praise Him, Praise Him

The Lord is my light and my salvation;
Whom shall I fear? The Lord is the strength of my life;
of whom shall I be afraid? When the wicked, even mine
enemies and my foes, came upon me to eat up my flesh, they
stumbled and fell. Though an host should encamp
against me, my heart shall not fear; though war may rise against
me, in this I will be confident. One thing I have desired
of the Lord, that will I seek; that I may dwell in the house of
the Lord all the days of my life, to behold the beauty of the Lord,
and to inquire in His temple.
—Psalm 27:1–4 KJV

Great is the Lord, and greatly to be praised
In the city of our God, in His holy mountain.
Beautiful in elevation, the joy of the whole earth,
is Mount Zion on the sides of the north, the city of the
great King. God is in her palaces; He is known as her refuge.
For behold, the kings assembled, they passed by together.
They saw it and so they marveled; they were troubled,
they hastened away. fear took hold of them there,
and pain, as of a woman in birth pangs, as when You
break the ships of Tarshish with an east wind. As we have heard,
so we have seen in the city of the Lord of hosts, in
the city of our God: God will establish it forever. Selah
We have thought, O God, on Your loving kindness, in the midst
of Your temple. According to Your name, O God, so is Your
praise to the ends of the earth; Your right hand is full of
righteousness. Let Mount Zion rejoice, let the daughters of
Judah be glad, because of Your judgments. Walk about Zion,
and go all around her. Count her towers; mark well her palaces;
that you may tell it to the generation following.
For this is God,

Our God forever and ever.
He will be our guide even to death.
—Psalm 48 NKJV

Lord, Your Bible is amazing. It makes me want to research in the Internet Mount Zion and its importance in those days; the daughters of Judah, who they were, their names, and all about Zion. Thank You for seeing it fit to share great history about our ancestors that we may grow by and teach others. Amen.

Wisdom and Understanding
December 13

The trees of the Lord are full of sap, the cedars of Lebanon
which He planted, where the birds make their nests; the stork has
her home in the fir trees. The high hills are for the wild goats;
The cliffs are a refuge for the rock badgers. He appointed
the moon for seasons; the sun knows its going down. You
make darkness, and it is night, in which all the beasts of the
forest creep about. The young lions roar after their prey, and
seek their food from God. When the sun rises, they gather together
and lie down in their dens. Man goes out to his work and to his
labor until the evening. O Lord, how manifold are your works!
In wisdom You have made them all.
The earth is full of Your possessions—this great and wide sea,
in which are innumerable teeming things, living things both small
and great. There the ships sail about; there is that Leviathan which
You have made to play there.
These all wait for You, that You may give them their food in
due season. What you give them they gather in; You open your hand,
they are filled with good. you hide Your face, they are troubled;
You take away their breath, they die and return to their dust.
You send forth Your Spirit, they are created;
and you renew the face of the earth.
May the glory of the lord endure forever;
may the Lord rejoice in His works.
He looks on the earth, and it trembles; he touches the hills,
and they smoke. I will sing to the Lord as long as I live; I will sing
praise to my God while I have my being. May my meditation be sweet
to Him I will be glad in the LORD. May sinners be consumed from the
earth,
and the wicked be no more.
—Psalm 104:16–35 NKJV

What a mighty God we serve. He created the earth and all its inhabitants with great power and beauty. He still does great things. We just have to avail ourselves because He does many of His miracles and wondrous acts through us. He loves us so. Lord, show me how to make myself available to receive Your Spirit as it is Your will, in Jesus's name, Amen.

Wisdom and Understanding
December 14

"For behold, I create new heavens and a new earth;
and the former shall not be remembered of come to mind.
But be glad and rejoice forever in what I create;
For behold, I create Jerusalem as a rejoicing, and her
people a joy. I will rejoice in Jerusalem, and joy in My people.
The voice of weeping shall no longer be heard in her,
nor the voice of crying. "No more shall an infant from there
live but a few days, nor an old man who has not fulfilled his days;
for the child shall die one hundred years old. But the sinner being
one hundred years old shall be accursed. They shall build houses
and inhabit them; they shall plant vineyards and eat their fruit.
They shall not build and another inhabit; they shall not plant and
another eat; for as the days of a tree, so shall be the days of My people,
and My elect shall long enjoy the work of their hands.
They shall not labor in vain, nor bring forth children for trouble; for
they shall be the descendants of the blessed of the LORD, and their
offspring with them. "It shall come to pass that before they call, I will
answer; and while they are still speaking, I will hear.
The wolf and the lamb shall feed together, the lion shall eat straw
like the ox, and dust shall be the serpent's food.
They shall not hurt nor destroy in all My holy mountain,"
Says the Lord.
—Isaiah 65:17–25 NKJV

O God, my heart is steadfast; I will sing and give praise,
even with my glory. Awake, lute and harp!
I will awaken the dawn. I will praise You, o Lord,
among the peoples, and I will sing praises to You among
the nations. For Your mercy is great above the heavens,
and Your truth reaches to the clouds. Be exalted, O God,
above the heavens, and Your glory above all the earth;
that Your beloved may be delivered, save with Your right hand
and hear me.
—Psalm 108:1–6 NKJV

Our God is large, and He is real, and He is able do to great and beautiful and impossible things in our lives. Let us trust Him and believe that, indeed, God will do a new thing, a wonderful thing, and a thing that has never been done and that He will do it through His people and just because He can and He wants to. Blessed be the name of the Lord God, our God and our Maker.

Wisdom and Understanding
December 15

Who are Israelites, to whom pertain the adoption,
the glory, the covenants, the giving of the law,
the service of God, and the promises; of whom are
the fathers and from whom, according to the flesh,
Christ came, who is over all, the eternally blessed God. Amen.
But it is not that the word of God has taken no effect. for
they are not all Israel who are of Israel, nor are they all
children because they are the seed of Abraham; but, "In
Isaac your seed shall be called." That is, those who are the
children of the flesh, these are not the children of God;
but the children of the promise are counted as the seed.
For this is the word of promise: "At this time I will come and
Sarah shall have a son." And not only this, but when Rebecca
also had conceived by one man, even by our father Isaac
(for the children not yet being born, nor having done any good or
evil, that the purpose of God according to election might
stand, not of works but of Him who calls), it was said
to her, "The older shall serve the younger." As it is written,
"Jacob I have loved, but Esau I have hated."
What shall we say then? Is there unrighteousness with God?
Certainly not! For He says to Moses, "I will have mercy
on whomever I will have mercy, and I will have compassion
on whomever I will have compassion." So then it is not of him
who wills, nor of him who runs, but of God who shows mercy.
—Romans 9:4–16 NKJV

I was glad when they said to me, "let us go into the
house of the Lord." Our feet have been standing within
your gates, O Jerusalem! Jerusalem is built as a city that
is compact together, where the tribes go up, the tribes of the Lord,
to the testimony of Israel, to give thanks to the name of the Lord.
—Psalms 122:1–4 NKJV

I am so glad I am a member of the body of Christ. I am so glad that I know Jesus Christ, my Savior. Do you know your Maker, your Savior, your God? Father God, we thank You for parents that teach their children about You and about Your love for us. Help to remember that You can bring us peace just by our receiving Your sacrifice for us, Your Son Jesus, and all we have to do is ask. Thank you, Lord, in Jesus's name. Amen.

Wisdom and Understanding
December 16

*And He said to me, "Son of man, stand on your
feet, and I will speak to you." Then the Spirit
entered me when He spoke to me, and set me on my feet;
and I heard Him who spoke to me. And he said to me: "Son
of man, I am sending you to the children of Israel, to a rebellious
nation that has rebelled against Me; they and their fathers have
transgressed against Me to this very day. "For they are impudent and
stubborn children. I am sending you to them, and you shall say
to them, "Thus says the Lord god." "As for them, whether they hear
or whether they refuse—for they are a rebellious house—yet they will
know that a prophet has been among them. "And you, son of man, do
not be afraid of them nor be afraid of their words, though briers and
thorns are with you and you dwell among scorpions; do not be
afraid of their words or dismayed by their looks, though they are a
rebellious house. "You shall speak My words to them, whether they
hear or whether they refuse, for the are rebellious. "But you, son of
man, hear what I say to you. Do not be rebellious like that rebellious
house; open your mouth and eat what I give you." Now when I
looked, there was a hand stretched out to me; and behold, a scroll of
a book was in it. Then He spread it before me; and there was writing
on the inside and on the outside, and written on it were lamentations
and mourning and woe.
—Ezekiel 2 NKJV*

*Moreover he said to me, "Son of man, eat what you find; eat this
scroll, and go, speak to the house of Israel." So I opened my mouth,
and He caused me to eat that scroll. And He said to me, "Son of man,
feed your belly, and fill your stomach with this scroll that I give you."
So I ate, and it was in my mouth like honey in sweetness.
—Ezekiel 3:1–3 NKJV*

The Bible is full of mysterious, amazing, and intriguing stories and
writings. Read the Bible, read those books that are rarely visited. It
might lead you to write your own inspiring thoughts and ideas to share

with the world. Lord, thank You for Your word, the Bible that You share with us. Great history, great teachings, great food for thought, great wisdom. Thank you, Father, Amen.

Wisdom and Understanding
December 17

Prayer and Supplication

O Lord, do not rebuke me in Your anger,
nor chasten me in Your hot displeasure. Have mercy
on me, O Lord, for I am weak; O lord, heal me, for my
bones are troubled. My soul also is greatly troubled; but You,
O Lord—how long? return, O Lord, deliver me! Oh, save
me for Your mercies' sake! For in death there is no remembrance
of You; in the grave who will give You thanks? I am weary with
my groaning; all night I make my bed swim; I drench my couch
with my tears. My eye wastes away because of grief; it grows old
because of all my enemies. Depart from me, all you workers
of iniquity; for the Lord has heard the voice of my weeping. The Lord
has heard my supplication; the Lord will receive my prayer.
Let all my enemies be ashamed and greatly troubled;
let them turn back
and be ashamed suddenly.
—Psalm 6 NKJV

In the Lord I put my trust; how can you say to my soul,
"Flee as a bird to your mountain"? For look! The wicked
bend their bow, they make ready their arrow on the string,
that they may shoot secretly at the upright in heart. If the
foundations are destroyed, what can the righteous do? The Lord
is in His holy temple, the Lord's throne is in heaven; His eyes behold,
His eyelids test the sons of men. The Lord tests the righteous,
but the wicked and the one who loves violence His soul hates.
Upon the wicked He will rain coals; fire and brimstone and a burning
wind shall be the portion of their cup. For the Lord is righteous,
He loves righteousness; His countenance beholds the upright.
—Psalm 11 NKJV

Read a psalm before you close your eyes to sleep. Father, we thank You for Your protection daily, from dangers seen and unseen. We thank You because we need You. What shall we do without Your loving protection and guide? Thank You, in Jesus's name. Amen.

Wisdom and Understanding
December 18

Praise Him, Praise Him

Praise the Lord! praise the Lord from the heavens;
Praise Him in the heights!
Praise Him, all His angels;
Praise Him, all His hosts!
Praise Him, sun and moon;
Praise Him, all you stars of light!
Praise Him, you heavens of heavens.
And you waters above the heavens!
Let them praise the name of the Lord, for He commanded and
they were created. He also established them forever and ever;
He made a decree which shall not pass away. Praise the Lord
from the earth, you great sea creatures and all the depths; fire and
hail, snow and clouds; stormy wind, fulfilling His word; mountains
and all hills; fruitful trees and all cedars; beasts and all cattle; creeping
things and flying fowl; kings of the earth and all peoples; princes
and all judges of the earth; both young men and maidens;
old men and children. Let them praise the name of the Lord,
for His name alone is exalted; His glory is above the earth and
heaven. And He has exalted the horn of His people, the praise
of all His saints—of the children of Israel, a people near to Him.
Praise the Lord!
—Psalm 148 NKJV

For those who don't know, there is healing in praising the Lord. You wonder why some people seem lose it and cry and jump and pace in church services, etc. There is healing in praising God, not to mention great release of stress and grievous feelings. Those who hide their passion are not usually able to release stress and move on with a clean slate. Try it, let go, and let God. Let go of all that facade and all the hiding of your emotions. Destress and praise the Lord. Huh . . . Try it. Go to a good old Baptist church or whatever God-worshipping temple and praise the Lord.

Wisdom and Understanding
December 19

*Cast your bread upon the waters, for you will
find it after many days, give a serving to seven,
and also to eight, for you do not know what evil
will be on the earth. If the clouds are full of rain,
they empty themselves upon the earth; and if a tree falls
to the south or the north, in the place where the tree falls,
there it shall lie. he who observes the wind will not sow,
and he who regards the clouds will not reap. As you do
not know what is the way of the wind, (or spirit), or how the
bones grow in the womb of her who is with child, so you
do not know the works of God who makes everything. In the
morning sow your seed, and in the evening do not withhold your
hand; for you do not know which will prosper, either this or that,
or whether both alike will be good. Truly the light is sweet, and it is
pleasant for the eyes to behold the sun; but if a man/woman lives
many years and rejoices in them all, yet let him/her remember
the days of darkness, for they will be many. All that is coming is
vanity. Rejoice, O young man/woman, in your youth,
and let your heart cheer you in the days of your youth;
Walk in the ways of your heart, and in the sight of your eyes;
but know that for all these God will bring you into judgment.
Therefore remove sorrow from your heart, and put away evil
from your flesh, for childhood and youth are vanity.*
—Ecclesiastes 11 NKJV

*May the Lord answer you in the day of trouble; may the name of
the God of Jacob defend you; may He send you help from the
sanctuary, and strengthen you out of Zion; may He remember all
your offerings, and accept your burnt sacrifice. May He grant you
according to your heart's desire, and fulfill all your purpose.*
—Psalm 20:1–4 NKJV

Wisdom and Understanding
December 20

The Lord Rules

Now this is the main point of the things we are saying:
We have such a High priest, who is seated at the right
hand of the throne of the Majesty in the heavens, a Minister
of the sanctuary and of the true tabernacle which the Lord
erected, and not man. For every high priest is appointed to
offer both gifts and sacrifices. Therefore it is necessary that this
One also have something to offer. For if He were on earth, he would
not be a priest, since there are priests who offer the gifts according
to the law; who serve the copy and shadow of the heavenly things,
as Moses was divinely instructed when he was about to make the
tabernacle. For he said, "See that you make all things
according to the pattern shown you on the mountain."
But now He has obtained a more excellent ministry, inasmuch as
He is also Mediator of a better covenant, which was established
on better promises. For if that first covenant had been faultless, then
no place would have been sought for a second. Because finding
fault with them, He says: "Behold, the days are coming, says the Lord,
when I will make a new covenant with the house of Israel and with
the house of Judah—
"not according to the covenant that I made with their fathers in
the day when I took them by the hand to lead them out of the
land of Egypt; because the did not continue in My covenant, and I
disregarded them, says the Lord.
"For this is the covenant that I will make with the house of Israels
after those days, says the Lord: I will put my laws in their mind and
write them on their hearts; and I will Be their God, and they shall
be My people. "None of them shall teach his neighbor, and none
his brother, saying, 'Know the Lord.' for all shall know Me, from
the least of them to the greatest of them. "For I will be merciful to
their unrighteousness, and their sins and their lawless deeds I will
remember no more." In that He says, "A new covenant," He has made
the first obsolete. Now what is becoming obsolete and growing old
is ready to vanish away.

—Hebrews 8 NKJV
Blessed be the Lord God, the God of Israel, Who only
does wondrous things! And blessed be His glorious name
forever! And let the whole earth be filled with His
glory. Amen and Amen.
The prayers of David the son of Jesse are ended.
—Psalm 72:18–20 NKJV

The Lord rules, He ruled, and He will rule. Blessed be the name of our Lord God. Amen.

Wisdom and Understanding
December 21

*"Take heed that you do not do your
charitable deeds before men, to be seen by them.
Otherwise you have no reward from your Father in
heaven. "Therefore, when you do a charitable deed, do
not sound a trumpet before you as the as the hypocrites do
in the synagogues and in the streets, that they may have glory
from men. Assuredly, I say to you, they have their reward.
"But when you do a charitable deed, do not let your left hand know
what your right hand is doing, "that your charitable deed may
be in secret; and your Father who sees in secret will Himself
reward you openly. "And when you pray, you shall not be like
the hypocrites. For they love to pray standing in the synagogues and
on the corners of the streets, that they may be seen by men.
Assuredly,
I say to you, they have their reward. "But you, when you pray, go into
your room, and when you have shut your door, pray to your Father
who is in the secret place; and your father who sees in
secret will reward you openly. "And when you pray, do
not use vain repetitions as the heathen do. For they think that
they will be heard for their many words. "Therefore do not be
like them. For your Father knows the things you have need of
before you ask Him. "In this manner, therefore, pray:
Our Father in heaven, Hallowed be Your name.
Your kingdom come. Your will be done on earth
as it is in heaven. Give us this day our daily bread.
And forgive us our debts, as we forgive our debtors.
And do not lead us into temptation, but deliver us
from the evil one. For Yours is the kingdom and the
power and the glory forever. Amen.
—Matthew 6:1–13 NKJV*

Lord, help me to do good things for others. Help me to do good and
not to do it expecting a reward. Help me to just do it knowing that You
always bless those who do good deeds. Help me to learn to be a giving
person, an unselfish person, and a kind person, in Jesus's name. Amen.

If you are friend, a genuine friend, and a friendly person, then you must know that friends are treasures, true and rare treasures. One can save time, money, energy, and worry when you have a friend to call on. Valued information, valued time, and unique moments are shared with a friend who can listen to you and can encourage you. Experience shared with a friend can save you trouble, agony, distress, and worry that will lead to a healthier heart, mind, spirit, and soul. Be a friend and be friendly. Don't be a user, do not be an abuser, that's not being a friend, and friends will soon leave you. Slickness and trickery will soon be exposed. Be nice, be humble, and wait for your blessings. Give freely and you will receive unexpected blessings.

Wisdom and Understanding
December 22

*"Behold My Servant whom I uphold, My Elect One in whom
My soul delights!
I have put My Spirit upon Him; He will
bring forth justice to the Gentiles. He will not cry
out, nor raise His voice, nor cause His voice to be
heard in the street. A bruised reed he will not break,
and smoking flax He will not quench; He will bring
forth justice for truth. he will not fail nor be discouraged,
till He has established justice in the earth; and the
coastlands shall wait for His law." Thus says God the
Lord, Who created the heavens and stretched them out,
Who spread forth the earth and that which comes from it,
Who gives breath to the people on it, and spirit to those
who walk on it: "I, the Lord, have called You in
righteousness, and will hold Your hand; I will keep
You and give You as a covenant to the people, as a light
to the Gentiles, to open blind eyes, to bring out prisoners
from the prison, those who sit in darkness from the prison house.
I am the Lord, that is My name; and My glory I will not give
to another, nor My praise to carved images. Behold,
the former things have come to pass, and new things I declare;
before they spring forth I tell you of them."
Sing to the Lord a new song, and His praise from the ends of the
earth,
you who go down to the sea, and all that is in it, you
coastlands and you inhabitants of them!
—Isaiah 42:1–10 NKJV*

*God be merciful to us and bless us,
and cause His face to shine upon us,
That Your way may be known on earth,
Your salvation among all nations. Let the
peoples praise You, O God; let all the peoples
praise You. Oh, let the nations be glad and sing*

for joy! For You shall judge the people righteously,
and govern the nations on earth.
—Psalm 67:1–4 NKJV

There is only one God, one true God; my God, your God, our God; the same One yesterday, today, and tomorrow. Blessed be the Lord our God. Amen.

Wisdom and Understanding
December 23

Bless the Lord, O My Soul

Oh, that You would rend the heavens!
That You would come down! That the mountains
might shake at Your presence—as fire burns
brushwood, as fire causes water to boil—to make
Your name known to Your adversaries, that the nations
may tremble at Your presence! When You did awesome
things for which we did not look, You came down,
the mountains shook at Your presence. For since the
beginning of the world men have not heard nor perceived
by the ear, nor has the eye seen any God besides You,
who acts for the one who waits for Him. You meet him who
rejoices and does righteousness, who remembers You in Your
ways. You are indeed angry, for we have sinned—in these
ways we continue; and we need to be saved. But we are all
like an unclean thing, and all our righteousness are like
filthy rags; we all fade as a leaf, and our iniquities, like the
wind, have taken us away. And there is no one who calls on
Your name, who stirs himself up to take hold of You;
for you have hidden your face from us, and have consumed
us because of our iniquities.
But now, O Lord, You are our Father; we are the clay,
and You our potter; and all we are the work of Your hand.
Do not be furious, O Lord, nor remember iniquity
forever; indeed, please look—we all are Your people!
—Isaiah 64:1-9 NKJV

Restore us, O God of hosts; cause Your face
to shine, and we shall be saved!
—Psalm 80:7 NKJV

Wisdom and Understanding
December 24

Praise Him, Praise Him

Let God arise, Let His enemies be scattered;
Let those also who hate Him flee before Him.
As smoke is driven away; so drive them away;
as wax melts before the fire, so let the wicked perish at the
presence of God. But let the righteous be glad; let them
rejoice before God; Yes, let them rejoice exceedingly. Sing
to God, sing praises to his name; Extol him who rides on the
clouds, by His name YAH, and rejoice before Him. A father
of the fatherless, a defender of widows, is God in His holy
habitation. God sets the solitary in families; He brings out
those who are bound into prosperity; but the rebellious dwell in
a dry land. O God, when You went out before Your people,
when You marched through the wilderness, the earth shook; the
heavens also dropped rain at the presence of God; Sinai
itself was moved at the presence of God, the God of Israel.
You, O God, sent a plentiful rain, whereby You confirmed Your
inheritance, when it was weary. Your congregation dwelt in it; You,
O God, provided from Your goodness for the poor. The Lord
gave the word; great was the company of those who proclaimed it:
—Psalm 68:1-10 NKJV

Make a joyful shout to God, all the earth! Sing out
the honor of His name; make His praise glorious. Say to God,
"How awesome are Your works! Through the greatness of Your
power Your enemies shall submit themselves to You.
All the earth shall worship You and sing praises to You;
They shall sing praises to your name."
—Psalm 66:1-4 NKJV

Father, we thank You for the privilege to praise You. There is none like You, none that will give us peace and joy and hope to carry on. Thank You, Lord, in Jesus's name. Amen.

Wisdom and Understanding
December 25

*"And behold, you will conceive in your womb
and bring forth a Son, and shall call His name JESUS.
"He will be great, and will be called the Son of the
Highest; and the Lord God will give Him the throne
of His father David. "And he will reign over the house of
Jacob forever, and of His kingdom there will be no end."
Then Mary said to the angel, "How can this be, since I
do not know a man? And the angel answered and said to
her, "The Holy spirit will come upon you, and the power of the
Highest will overshadow you; therefore, also, that Holy
One who is to be born will be called the son of God.
—Luke 1:31–34 NKJV*

*Blessed is the Lord God of Israel, for He has visited
and redeemed His people, and has raised up a horn of
salvation for us in the house of His servant David, as
He spoke by the mouth of His holy prophets, who have
been since the world began, that we should be saved from
our enemies and from the hand of all who hate us, to perform
the mercy promised to our fathers and to remember His holy
covenant, the oath which He swore to our father Abraham:
To grant us that we, being delivered from the hand of our enemies,
might serve Him without fear; in holiness and righteousness
before Him all the days of our life.
—Luke 1:68–75 NKJV*

Father, we celebrate the birth of Your Son Jesus in this season. O Lord, the whole nation and much of the world celebrate Your greatness and Your uniqueness and Your sovereignty as we celebrate Christmas, the lights and the carols and the gift-giving and the families and friends coming together. O Lord, even when we seem to forget the real reason for the season, the celebration still happens all around the world. Lord, I pray that every single human being today and tomorrow will learn the real reason for Christmas and will accept Your Son Who was born and died and rose again for all of us. What kind of awesome love is that. Thank You, Father, for loving us so. In Jesus's name, we pray. Amen.

Wisdom and Understanding
December 26

*Dead flies putrefy the perfumer's ointment,
and cause it to give off a foul odor; so does a little
folly to one respected for wisdom and honor. A wise
man's heart is at his right hand, but a fool's heart at his left.
Even when a fool walks along the way, he lacks wisdom,
and he shows everyone that he is a fool.
If the spirit of the ruler rises against you, do not leave your post;
for conciliation pacifies great offenses. There is an evil I have seen
under the sun, as an error proceeding from the ruler; folly is set in
great dignity, while the rich sit in a lowly place. I have seen
servants on horses, while princes walk on the ground like servants.
He who digs a pit will fall into it, and whoever breaks through a wall
will be bitten by a serpent. He who quarries stones may be hurt by
them, and he who splits wood may be endangered by it. If the ax
is dull, and one does not sharpen the edge, then he must use more
strength; but wisdom brings success. A serpent may bite when it is
not charmed; the babbler is no different. The words of a wise man's
mouth are gracious, but the lips of a fool shall swallow him up; the
words of his mouth begin with foolishness, and the end of his talk
is raving madness. a fool also multiplies words. No man knows what is to
be; who can tell him what will be after him? The labor of fools
wearies them, for they do not even know how to go to the city! Woe
to you, O land, when your king is a child, and your princes feast in
the morning! Blessed are you, O land, when your king is the son of
nobles, and your princes feast at the proper time—for strength and
not for drunkenness! Because of laziness the building decays, and
through idleness of hands the house leaks. A feast is made for
laughter, and wine makes merry; but money answers everything. Do
not curse the king, even in your thought; do not curse the rich,
even in your bedroom; for a bird of the air may carry your voice,
and a bird in flight may tell the matter.
—Ecclesiastes 10 NKJV*

If this scripture is somewhat strange or not easy to understand, then read the chapters before and after and ask God for understanding as you continue to read the Bible and to study and research its meaning. Read the Bible. Yeah! Try one chapter before bedtime. Amen.

Wisdom and Understanding
December 27

*Remember now your Creator in the days of your youth,
before the difficult days come, and the years draw near when
you say, "I have no pleasure in them": While the sun and the
light, the moon and the stars are not darkened, and the clouds
do not return after the rain; in the day when the keepers of the house
tremble, and the strong men bow down; when the grinders cease
because they are few, and those that look through the windows
grow dim; when the doors are shut in the streets, and the sound of
grinding is low; when one rises up at the sound of a bird, and all the
daughters of music are brought low. Also they are afraid of height,
and of terror in the way; when the almond tree blossoms, the
grasshopper is a burden, and desire fails. For man goes to his eternal
home, and the mourners go about the streets. Remember your
Creator before the silver cord is loosed, or the golden bowl is broken,
or the pitcher is shattered at the fountain, or the wheel broken at the
well. Then the dust will return to the earth as it was, and the spirit
will return to God who gave it. "Vanity of vanities," says the Preacher,
"All is vanity." and moreover, because the preacher was wise, he still
taught the people knowledge; yes, he pondered and sought out and
set in order many proverbs. The Preacher sought to find acceptable
words; and what was written was upright—words of truth. The
words of the wise are like goads, and the words of scholars are like
well-driven nails, given by one Shepherd. And further, my son, be
admonished by these, of making many books there is no end, and
much study is wearisome to the flesh. Let us hear the conclusion of
the whole matter: Fear God and keep His commandments,
for this is man's all. For God will bring every work
into judgment, including every secret thing, whether good or evil.
—Ecclesiastes 12 NKJV
O Lord, You are the portion of my inheritance
and my cup; You maintain my lot. The lines have fallen to me
in pleasant places; yes, I have a good inheritance. I will
bless the Lord who has given me counsel; my heart also instructs
me in the night seasons. I have set the Lord always before me;*

because He is at my right hand, I shall not be moved.
—Psalm 16:5–8 NKJV

God, Almighty Father, we thank You for Your precious and pleasant Spirit guiding us daily to help our spirit enjoy this physical experience here on earth. We praise You, and we bless Your name. You are an awesome God. In Jesus's name. Amen.

Wisdom and Understanding
December 28

*The words of King Lemuel, the utterance which
his mother taught him: What, my son? And what,
son of my womb? And what, son of my vows?
Do not give your strength to women, nor your ways
to that which destroys kings, it is not for kings, O Lemuel,
it is not for kings to drink wine, nor for princes
intoxicating drink; lest they drink and forget the law,
and pervert the justice of all the afflicted. Give strong drink
to him who is perishing, and wine to those who are bitter
of heart. Let him drink and forget his poverty, and remember his
misery no more. Open your mouth for the speechless, in the cause
of all who are appointed to die. Open your mouth, judge righteously,
and plead the cause of the poor and needy. Who can find a
virtuous wife? For her worth is far above rubies. The heart
of her husband safely trusts her; so he will have no lack of gain.
—Proverbs 31:1–11 NKJV*

*Praise the Lord, O Jerusalem! Praise your God, O Zion!
For He has strengthened the bars of your gates; He has
blessed your children within you. He makes peace in
your borders, and fills you with the finest wheat. He sends
out His command to the earth; his word runs very swiftly.
He gives snow like wool; He scatters the frost like ashes;
He casts out His hail like morsels; who can stand
before His cold? He sends out His word and melts them;
He causes His wind to blow, and the waters flow. He
declares His word to Jacob, His statutes and His judgments unto
Israel. He has not dealt thus with any nation; and as for His
judgments, they have not known them.
Praise the Lord.
—Psalm 147:12–20 NKJV*

What does all this mean? Am I included in all of God's promises and blessings? Study to know. Read the Bible, the Word of God. Thank God for His word to us through the Bible. Amen.

Wisdom and Understanding
December 29

And Hannah Prayed and Said:

*"My heart rejoices in the Lord; my horn
is exalted in the Lord. I smile at my enemies,
because I rejoice in Your salvation. "No one is
holy like the Lord, for there is none besides You,
nor is there any rock like our God. "Talk no more so very
proudly; let no arrogance come from your mouth, for the
Lord is the God of knowledge; and by Him actions are
weighed. "The bows of the mighty men are broken,
and those who stumbled are girded with strength. Those who
were full have hired themselves out for bread, and the hungry have
ceased to hunger. Even the barren has borne seven, and she who has
many children has become feeble. "The Lord kills and makes alive;
He brings down to the grave and brings up. The Lord makes poor and
makes rich; He brings low and lifts up. He raises the poor from the dust
and lifts the beggar from the ash heap,
to set them among princes
and make them inherit the throne of glory.
"For the pillars of the earth
are the Lord's, and He has set the world upon them. He will guard
the feet of His saints, but the wicked shall be silent in darkness.
"For by strength no man shall prevail. The adversaries of the Lord
shall be broken in pieces; from heaven He will thunder against
them. The Lord will judge the ends of the earth. "He will give
strength to His king, and exalt the horn of His anointed.
—1 Samuel 2:1–10 NKJV
Let the peoples praise You, O God; let all the
peoples praise You. Then the earth shall yield her
increase; God, our own God, shall bless us. God
shall bless us, and all the ends of the earth shall fear Him.
—Psalm 67:5–7 NKJV*

As we approach the end of this year and prepare to welcome a brand
new year, thankfulness comes to mind. Gratefulness is in my spirit,

hopefulness is all around, and expectation is floating in the air. May God protect us, His people, from worldwide harm, from the evil countries can wreak on one another. May God speak to the hearts and minds of our leaders in all the world, in every single country, in every single city, all around. May He whisper in their hearts great sounds of love and peace and harmony and goodness toward their people and their neighbors in the whole world. May peace abide in the world and, therefore, in all our neighborhoods also. In Jesus's name. Amen.

Wisdom and Understanding
December 30

Praise Him, Praise Him

I will sing of mercy and justice; to You,
O Lord, I will sing praises. I will behave
wisely in a perfect way. Oh, when will You
come to me? I will walk within my house with
a perfect heart. I will set nothing wicked before
my eyes; I hate the work of those who fall away;
It shall not cling to me. A perverse heart shall
depart from me; I will not know wickedness.
Whoever secretly slanders his neighbor, Him
I will destroy; the one who has a haughty look
and a proud heart, Him I will not endure. My eyes
shall be on the faithful of the land, that they may dwell
with me; he who walks in a perfect way, he shall
serve me. He who works deceit shall not dwell
within my house; he who tells lies shall
not continue in my presence. Early I will destroy all
the wicked of the land, that I may cut off all the
evildoers from the city of the Lord.
—Psalm 101 NKJV

Bless the Lord, O my soul! O Lord my God,
You are very great; You are clothed with honor
and majesty, Who cover Yourself with light as
with a garment, Who stretch out the heavens like a curtain.
—Psalm 104:1–2 NKJV

He sends the springs into the valleys; they flow among
the hills. They give drink to every beast of the field;
The wild donkeys quench their thirst. By them the birds
of the heavens have their home; they sing among the branches.
He waters the hills from His upper chambers; the earth is
satisfied with the fruit of Your works.
—Psalm 104:10–13 NKJV

Oh, mighty God, You are great in all the earth. Your creation is wonderful and cannot be duplicated, not even by Your creation, man. Blessed is Your holy name forever. Amen.

Although it's just time, continuous time, when it's the last day of the year and tomorrow is the beginning of a new year, the finality of the past period can be so powerful in our spirit, in our being, that sometimes it causes joy or sadness or hope or despair or all those feelings jumbled up together to cause some confusion in our mind, making us wonder what the new beginning will bring. Will this year be a better year for me than the past year? Will it bring good things as the past year, or will it bring sorrow and death and financial woes? We don't know. Trusting in God helps me a whole lot to bring peace to those concerns. Continuing to do my best at everything, showing love to my neighbors, friends, family, and strangers, I find peace in expecting better and trusting God that as I do the little that is charged to me that He, God, will do the great big things in my life that I cannot do. We should walk into the new year with great expectation, hope, praises to the great Spirit, the Almighty One in your life, the Almighty Spirit that's able to create abundance, joy, and peace in your life for the new year and beyond.

Wisdom and Understanding
December 31

Finally, my brethren, be strong
in the Lord and in the power of His might.
Put on the whole armor of God, that
you may be able to stand against the wiles
of the devil. For we do not wrestle against
flesh and blood, but against principalities,
against powers, against the rulers of the darkness
of this age, against spiritual hosts of wickedness
in the heavenly places. Therefore take up
the whole armor of God, that you maybe able
to withstand in the evil day, and having
done all, to stand. Stand therefore,
having girded your waist with truth, having put on
the breastplate of righteousness, and having shod
your feet with the preparation of the gospel of peace;
Above all, taking the shield of faith with which you
will be able to quench all the fiery darts of the
wicked one. And take the helmet of salvation,
and the sword of the Spirit, which is the word
of God; Praying always with all prayer an supplication
in the Spirit, being watchful to this end with all
perseverance and supplication for all the saints.
—Ephesians 6:10–18 NKJV

Imitate me, just as I also imitate Christ.
Now I praise you, brethren, that you remember
me in all things and keep the traditions just as I delivered
them to you. But I want you to know that the head of
every man is Christ, the head of woman is man, and the head
of Christ is God.
—1 Corinthians 11:1–3 NKJV

Father God, as we come to the end of another year that You have granted us, we thank You for all the ups and for all the downs. We thank You for all the bad and uncomfortable times and events because they have made us stronger and wiser. Most of all, Lord, we thank You for bringing us through those awful times and bringing us into Your light, into a better time, and into a better situation. We thank You For all the happy experiences, all the joyous moments. We are glad that we are Your people and that You are our God. Please continue to bless us and keep us and guide us along the right path. As we walk into this new year, help us to love one another more, help us to be more patient with one another, and help us to love You more. Only You can give us a great new year. In Jesus's name, we pray. Amen.